PRAYING THROUGH IT

VOLUME II

WILLIAM MURPHY, III

365 DAYS WORTH OF PRAYERS, THAT MAKE PRAYING EASY.

Bible references from the New American Standard Bible

ISBN-13: 978-1-7356112-1-1

Available from Amazon.com and other retail outlets
Available on Kindle and other devices

Written by: William H. Murphy III
Cover Design by: TBT Media and Nations28, LLC
Interior by: Nations28, LLC

DEDICATION

Praying Through it, Volume II is dedicated to my mom, Dr. Carolynne Michele Phillips, who made her transition on November 3, 2016. Thank you for keeping me in church. Thank you for keeping me close to my spiritual inheritance. Thank you for allowing my father's the opportunity to love me, and to train me, and to prepare me, for the call of God on my life. thank you for teaching me how to believe God, in spite of how things look, and in spite of how I feel physically, emotionally, and even spiritually. thank you, mom, for teaching me how to live by faith. thank you for loving me unconditionally, and for making sure that I knew, my mistakes, and my sins, did not disqualify me, from fulfilling my purpose and destiny.

I dedicate this second volume to you Mother, and I pray that God will give me Grace to continue to expand your legacy of loving others, and caring for others, and encouraging others, until they see their purposed fulfilled. I pray that when they see my name, or hear my voice, that you will yet be proud, and tell the angels, ". that's my son!"

I Love YOU, and I'm going to keep Praying Through It, until I see you again!

To the ministers and elders of The dReam Center Church of Atlanta, I honor your dedication and thank you for making the commitment to do ministry with me. To my wife, kids, and entire family, thank you for your consistent and unconditional love and support.

FOREWORD
By Bishop William Murphy, Jr.

The legacy In the New Testament writings of Matthew, Mark Luke and John, Jesus gives us both a model as well as a pattern for prayer. It is through this model that we have been released with power and to a new place in prayer and intercession.

I believe that as you not only read these prayers, that you literally *Pray Through It*. These prayers that have been given to us by my son, Bishop William Murphy, III, and I declare that the same anointing that was released by Jesus in those New Testament writings will overtake you even today!

Even as you participate and engage in the reading of these prayers, I believe that the spirit of prayer and Intercession will be released upon you to carry this anointing for spiritual breakthroughs for you and your family. I declare that a generational blessing is being released upon you from four generations of Murphy prayer warriors.

As you read and pray, I pray that the words that you speak from this devotional, will manifest from the spirit realm into the realm of the natural. We shall have whatsoever we say, so do not look at these prayers as merely words but look at them and receive them as the manifestation of what is to come as you release them into your own personal atmosphere!

Bishop William H. Murphy, Jr., Senior Pastor
New Mt. Moriah Int'l Church
Bishop of Prayer, Full Gospel Baptist Church Fellowship

INTRODUCTION

A few years ago, I wrote a song called "All Day". the chorus went like this, "all day, I've been walking around, I've been talking with You. all day, I'm determined to spend more time with You. all day, I've been walking around, with You in my soul. all day, my time with You is gonna make me whole." this song was the result of me trying to find my own personal private space with God and trying to find balance between what I felt calling me, and what I'd seen modeled in church. I quickly began to discover, that my prayer "closet", was not a place in my house, but rather a place in my heart. and so, I began having this day long dialogue with God, and these conversations that would begin in the morning, and continue throughout my day.

So "praying through it", is the physical manifestation of years' worth of conversations, and learning how to develop my personal space, and relationship with God, via prayer. this book of prayers, this documenting of daily, divine dialogue, chronicles my personal journey of faith, and failure, and it demonstrates how you get through the difficulties of life, without losing your relationship with God, without losing your faith in God, and without losing your mind.

God told me He would, "use this book, to impart the language of prayer" to a generation that's had a difficult time talking to God." So, I pray for you and with you, as you take this year long, one day at a time, one prayer at a time, journey with me, and the thousands, who are a part of our #1000peoplepraying family.

I pray that you would discover, develop, and embrace your own personal space with God. I pray that you would come to know that *Praying Through It*, is how you get through it! and I set my faith in agreement with yours, that as you use these prayers, to trigger day long dialogue with The Father, that you will find yourself walking around, talking to God, all day. I pray that praying becomes easy for you, and that it becomes this unshakable habit of yours, in Jesus' name!

On your mark, get ready, get set...GO!

+William Murphy

JANUARY

JANUARY 1

Chronicles 28:19 (NASB): All this," said David, "the Lord made me understand in writing by His hand upon me, all the [g]details of this pattern.

THIS IS MY YEAR

This is going to be one of the best years of my life...spiritually, emotionally, physically, AND financially. So, I call every area of my life into divine order. Holy Spirit have your way in my life, and set me free from every trick, scheme, and attack that the enemy sent to keep me, to keep me distracted. I plead the blood over my mind, my will, and my emotions. I call them subject to the word of God and to God's plan for my life. Depression, go! Fatigue, go, in the name of Jesus! I release my faith for complete restoration of my body and my strength, in Jesus' name! By the time, this year is over, I will be off all prescription meds and my health will be completely restored.

Father I thank You that as I set my spiritual life, my emotions, and my body in line with Your will, that my finances will HAVE to follow suit! I will not be full of the Spirit and at the same time have lack in my life. This is my season to prosper and be in good health! This is the season that my soul prospers, and all things are made whole, in Jesus' name! I decree and declare, this is going to be one of the best years of my life, SPIRITUALLY, EMOTIONALLY, PHYSICALLY and FINANCIALLY! It's in the mighty name of Jesus I pray, Amen!

JANUARY 2

Deuteronomy 14:26 (NASB): ....and there you shall eat in the presence of the LORD *your God and rejoice, you and your household.*

WE GOT THEM KEYS

We got them keys! So, closed doors don't deter us, and they do not discourage us! My prayer is, that we don't waste any more time trying to open doors that are not for us.

I pray for clarity regarding what is ours and what belongs to us. I pray that we do not covet or crave what belongs to someone else. Holy Spirit. show us what you have given to us and show us the doors that are for us. Guide our hearts and our thoughts. Guide our steps. It's in Jesus' name Amen.

JANUARY 3

Proverbs 18:12 (NASB): The tongue has the power of life and death and those who love it will eat its fruit.

CLEANSE MY TEMPLE

Father I pray that Jesus will return to my physical temple today and that He will set things in proper order. I pray that He will once again, give me the desires of my heart and that He will cause me only to desire, what He desires for me to have. I pray that my flesh won't have me out of your will. That even though I may still desire what my flesh wants, it won't control me or render me helpless to its call. I say yes to what you're doing in my life. I recommit to laying all my affections, devotions, and desires at your feet.

Holy Spirit cleanse my temple, wash my brain, and purify my soul. Sever every soul tie that keeps me in yesterday. Cut everything that causes me to live outside of your will. Father grant me grace to overcome every temptation and to lay aside every sin that so easily besets me. I decree and declare, that what I tripped over last year, I'm going to leap over this year! That what caused me to stumble, to live in fear, in guilt and to be bound by shame; will no longer have power. I decree and declare that the chains are broken. I am free, in the name of Jesus! From today forward, I'll be able to discern and to see. That from today forward, my walk is right, and my heart is pure. In Jesus' name I pray, Amen!

JANUARY 4

Philippians 1:6 (NASB): being confident of this, that He who began a good work in you will carry it on to completion until the day of Christ Jesus

LORD, HELP ME TO SEE

Lord help me to see and don't let me go another day in the dark and in the blind. Show me what I need to see and what I need to do. Don't let the trials of life blind me ever again. I'm praying for vision as well. I pray for the grace to see beyond today and to look into the future; so, I don't do anything that'll cause me to be out of your will.

I pray for foresight, for a prophetic eye and the ability to see what's coming before it actually comes. Lord help me to see beyond the present, beyond the past and then grace me to walk fearlessly into what you've prepared. Lord help me to see, so that what I tripped over last year, I can leap over this year! Open my eyes, so that I can see every stumbling block, every roadblock and cause me to see my way of escape! It's in Jesus' name I pray, Amen!

JANUARY 5

Proverbs 14:29 (NASB): Whoever is patient has great understanding, but one who is quick-tempered displays folly

HELP ME TO WALK RIGHT

Father I need your help! My mind, my body and my soul are yours. Yet, I still feel myself struggling with my flesh. So today I stretch my hands to you because you really are the only help, I know. Help me to walk and live right. Help me to master my flesh and call every one of my desires, subject to your Spirit.

Holy Spirit, I yield to you and I'm praying that you will help me to get my walk together. Don't let me live another day outside of your will. Don't let me waste another second of my life, pursuing something that takes me outside of your will. Help me to walk right and grant me the grace to leap over what I've always tripped over. Change me! Cleanse me! Cover me! Help me to walk upright before you. My soul says yes again, and I pray for the constraining power of the Holy Ghost to take full control of my life. In Jesus' name I pray, Amen!

JANUARY 6

Psalms 4:4-5 (NASB): In your anger do not sin; when you are on your beds, search your hearts and be silent. "Selah". Offer right sacrifices and trust in the Lord.

DRAIN THE SWAMP

Father I confess that I have no idea what I'm doing. I need you. If you don't help me, my flesh is going to mess up what you've planned and completely ruin my future. Father, I stretch my hands to thee, because you really are the only real help that I know. I lay my life, my desires, and my dReams at your feet. I pray for grace to drain the swamp! This water I've been standing in is toxic and it poses a direct threat to what you've planned for my life.

So today, by faith, I pull the plug and I let go of everything that you've not said yes to. I take my hands off and I refuse to hold on to anything or anybody that you no longer approve of. Help me Holy Spirit to win the battle with my flesh because it's strong and it's controlled my life for so long. In fact, true freedom has begun to look like somebody else's portion. Walking and living in the spirit and in your will has been such a struggle for me. But I know that today, it is for me and it is on me to walk in the spirit, to live in the spirit and to please you with my life. So today, I take the necessary steps to drain the swamp and I submit myself to the tool of sacrifice, via fasting and prayer. My soul says yes to your will and yes to your way. In Jesus' name, Amen!

JANUARY 7

Psalms 63:1 (NASB): O God, you are my god, earnestly I seek you; my soul thirsts for you in a dry and weary land where there is no water.

FIGHT FOR THE FUTURE

I've finally made up my mind to forget those things which are behind me and I've determined within my soul, that I'm going to reach for what is ahead. I can't do anything about what's behind me other than leave it there. So, I choose to fight for my future and not over my past! I choose to keep my focus forward and not to ignore the past, but to make the past a steppingstone. There's too much in front of me, to be glued to what's behind me. So, I choose to fight for my future.

Holy Spirit help me to be present, mentally, and spiritually. Help me to stay in the moment and yet see into the future. I pray for foresight and for insight, so I don't get stuck fighting over things that don't matter anymore and those things that don't have any relevance in my future. I'm not wasting another minute of my life, rehashing the past. I'm not wasting another day living in fear because of what didn't happen, what I did or did not do! My fight is for my future and for what God has in-store for me. I'm fasting for my future. I'm praying for his will. I'm positioning myself for something big, for something greater, for something huge, for something that cements my significance because it's not all about me. Holy Spirit help me to stay submitted to the process and your desires for my life. In Jesus' name we pray, Amen!

JANUARY 8

II Corinthians 2:14 (NASB): Thanks be to God, who always leads us in triumphal procession in Christ and through us spreads everywhere the fragrance of the knowledge of him.

I'VE GOT A PROMISE

Life's pressures are real and there's no way of escaping them, but we do have a choice. In First Corinthians chapter 16, verse 9, Paul says this, "for a wide door for effective service has opened to me, and there are many adversaries." I'm feeling the same way, as I'm sure you are too. So, my prayer today is that we stay focused on the right thing. I pray that we overcome the temptation to make the adversity the focus and that we choose to focus on the wide door.

I pray against the spirit of anxiety and fear. I pray that we'll find the faith to set our affections on what God has promised. Yes, we're in a fight, but the battle is the Lord's, not ours! His name is on the line, not ours. His character is at question, not ours. All we must do is obey His commands and do what He has instructed us to do. All things will have to work together for our good. I pray for the strength of will to make the hard decisions. I pray for the mental fortitude to stick to what we've committed to do. I pray that the promise will become our focus and not the pressure. I pray that we will position ourselves to leap and let everything against us, push us. I pray that the pressure pushes us, that the opposition will become the thing that guarantees the victory! In Jesus' name we pray, Amen!

JANUARY 9

Proverbs 13:20 (NASB): He who walks with the wise grows wise, but a companion of fools suffers harm.

A FRESH START

I pray that we all take time to breathe and that we realize that the air is fresh again. What happened is over. What they did, no longer matters. We are ready to move on to something fresh and new. I pray for the strength to want to start over, for the faith to pursue something new. I pray for the chains of yesterday to break. And that all of us would experience a divinely orchestrated fresh start. All things are new! All things are ready! And this is our time to move forward, in Jesus' name.

So, we embrace our season of do overs. We will not be frustrated by the blessing of getting to try again. We have the grace to start over. We have the grace to do it all over again. And we have been given the grace to WIN! So, we lift up our heads, our hearts, and our voices, decreeing and declaring, "This is the day that the Lord has made, and we will rejoice and be glad in it." It's in Jesus' mighty name I pray, Amen, Amen, and Amen!

JANUARY 10

Proverbs 4:25-27 (NASB): Let your eyes look straight ahead; fix your gaze directly before you.

STAY THE COURSE

Listen, if this were easy, everybody would be doing it! So, calm down, get out of your feelings, recommit yourself to God and to the process. It's not too late and you are not going to miss your moment. There's still time. So, let's pray. Father, we need patience. We need your help, so today we turn our hearts to you again. We stretch our hands to you Father and we unashamedly ask that you lift us up where we belong. We're frustrated, but we're going to do everything we can do to hold on to our faith. We're hard pressed on every side, but we still trust that you'll never put more on us, than we can bear. Father we trust you, so we choose to walk by faith.

Our hope is in you, so we say to ourselves today, "I'm going to stay the course." We commit to you, to obey you, one choice and one decision at a time. We commit to ourselves, to do better by ourselves, so we pray for laser focus. But Father, please don't let us be narrow minded. And at the same time, don't allow us to see so much that we become distracted. Father show us what you know you can trust us with and hold back everything else until we're mentally and spiritually able to handle what we see. Help us to stay the course. Help us to stay on task and don't allow the pressures of life to detour us. We trust you. We love you. And we're going to follow hard after you today. It's in Jesus' name we pray, Amen.

JANUARY 11

Proverbs 23:7 (NASB): "...As a man thinks, so is he!"

GRACE TO LEAP

I'm praying that the grace to let everything that works against you would push you and cause you to prevail strongly on your life. I pray for wisdom and for insight, so that you don't start tripping because of the many adversaries. God has opened a wide door for us. My prayer is that we don't get so distracted by the adversity that we miss the opportunity. This is our season again, so Father help us to remain focused, confident, and never losing sight of what we're fighting for.

We have the grace to leap, so we call our hearts, our minds, and our emotions subject to God's word. No more panic attacks. No more uncontrolled episodes of anxiety and fear. We pull down every stronghold and every thought, that would cause us to get in fear and to walk in unbelief. Holy Spirit help us to see beyond the present and give us another sneak peek into our future. Cause us to see that what's in front of us is better than everything behind us. Remind us, that your thoughts towards us are good and that settles it. Remind us, that our latter will be greater than our former and help us to focus forward. Don't let us waste another day tripping over what was. Father help us to forgive and forget. My prayer is that we don't waste another day tripping over something, that you're going to use to make us better. Glorify yourself in my come up and let your name be praised. It's in Jesus' name we pray, Amen!

JANUARY 12

Psalms 51:10 (NASB): Create in me a pure heart, O God, and renew a steadfast spirit within me.

GRACE TO FORGIVE

In Luke chapter 17, verse 1, Jesus says to His disciples, "It is impossible that no offenses should come." So then, we must stop allowing the devil to use the spirit of offense, as a means of holding us back and keeping us trapped in the past. I pray that we finally see what anger, fear, guilt and unforgiveness has done to us. How they've negatively affected our lives and infected our future. I pray for wisdom and strength to release everything and everybody that's kept our focus on yesterday. And on what happened, what they did or did not do.

I pray that the grace to forgive would overtake us. That holding on to how we felt and to the pain that we've grown accustomed to would become intolerable to us. I pray for a breakthrough in the spirit. That the power of God would break every anger chain, revenge chain, and blame chain that keeps us looking back instead of looking ahead. We have the grace to forgive. We have been divinely enabled to change the way we've felt and the way we've looked at our past and our story. We have grace to forget about it, to let it go and to go on with our lives. Grace to see the good in the bad, to grow and to keep it moving. We have the grace to overcome. We will never be stuck in the past ever again! It's in Jesus' name we pray, Amen!

JANUARY 13

Ephesians 4:31-32 (NASB): Get rid of all bitterness, rage, anger, brawling and slander, along with

CELEBRATE THE WINS

14 years ago, I did the craziest, dumbest thing that I could've ever done. I started a church, in Atlanta! I was scared to death. I knew that within myself, I was unqualified, unrighteous, and unable to lead a church. But I knew that I heard from God. So, like a crazy person, I for once in my life, obeyed His voice. This by far has been the smartest and bravest decision I've ever made. While the journey has been definitely challenging. It's been full of joy, love, grace, and mercy. I haven't been perfect, but the record reflects that I have been faithful.

My prayer today, is that the same grace will explode in your life. I pray for the courage to trust God even when you know you're crazy and afraid. I pray for the desire to please God with your faith. For the courage to trust His word over the words of the people who were always comfortable with you living a compromised life of fear. I pray for an explosion of faith to take place in your heart and mind again. That you will be so overwhelmed by His love and His grace that you will pause to celebrate the wins along the way. I pray for the wisdom, the freedom, and the peace of mind to actually acknowledge and enjoy the victories that take place during your journey. I pray that you are not so consumed with winning, that you fail to realize that you are to celebrate the wins. God knows you've talked enough about the losses. I heard the Lord say, "It's not arrogance and it's not a distraction. It's an outward expression of your faith and a necessary part of your process." Celebrate your faith and your father. Celebrate yourself and your savior. Celebrate your faith and your future. That's my prayer for us today, that we'll make reflection and celebration mainstays and a permanent part of our culture. It's in Jesus' name I pray. Amen!

JANUARY 14

Romans 7:21(NASB): ..when I would do good, evil is present with me

YOU HAVE ENOUGH

I'm praying that Holy Spirit would open the eyes of our heart. That we would stop discounting what we have. That we would stop looking at what's in our hand as if it's not enough. What we already have is enough. I'm praying that the same grace, that was upon the woman in Matthew chapter 15, would come upon us. Realizing that whatever falls to us and whatever God has already given us, is enough. Holy Spirit expose to us the truth about what we already have and show us how to trigger the grace for multiplication. Don't let the size or the amount of what we have, discourage us. But cause us to see that what we have is a seed that's got the potential to produce something that's going to elevate us spiritually, socially, and economically.

I pray for time to run its course concerning our seed and that we would begin to discern that a harvest is soon to come. Don't let the process break us down. Don't allow time to become our enemy, but let patience have her perfect work. I pray that this year would be the year that we are perfect, complete, and lack nothing. Open our eyes. Take the blinders off and cause us to see that we're right where you want us to be. Let us see what's in our hand for what it really is and don't let us grow weary in doing good. We are going to reap and have more than enough. We will be a blessing, soon. Thank you, for changing our minds about quitting. In Jesus' name, Amen!

JANUARY 15

John 13:34 (NASB): A new commandment I give unto you, that ye love one another; as I have loved you, that ye also love one another

SUDDENLIES

Today we're praying for things to happen for us suddenly! We've been praying and we've been in faith for the supernatural and we're declaring that today is the day. This is the day that the Lord has made, and He fashioned it in a way, where good things are going to start happening for us. We declare that doors are opening today. Major opportunities are being made available to the believers in Jesus' name.

We declare this, "The Season of the Suddenly," and we're in expectation for miracles, signs, and wonders in the name of Jesus! This is the season that our faith produces our expected end. And God responds to our sacrifice. Super is being released upon our natural and our lives are going to change for the better overnight. We're praying for things to happen suddenly and immediately. We're praying for divine intervention and supernatural turn arounds. In Jesus' name, Amen!

JANUARY 16

II Corinthians 4:16-17 (NASB): For our light and momentary troubles are achieving for us an eternal glory that far outweighs them all.

WINNING ON MY HEAD

I got winning on my head. My mind is changing. My thoughts are changing. I'm finally starting to see things differently and divinely. Losing isn't my focus anymore and the "what if's", Father I've left those in Your hands. I declare that this is my season to win and I boldly decree, "all I do, is win!" I got winning on my head and whatever happens to me today, I'm going to process it through the filter of victory. Whatever happens to me today, I'm going to look at it through the lens of a winner. I might be down, but I'm not out. I might be behind, but this is far from being over. I got winning on my head.

Although it may have been a long time since I've had a significant victory; I declare that this is my season to win. This is my season to come from behind. This is my time to overcome. It's my turn now and I'm about to mount one of the greatest comebacks of all times. So, I call my mind, my will, my emotions, and my feelings subject to the spirit of God! Because "All I Do Is Win!" And win! And win! And win again! Because I got winning on my head, in Jesus' name, Amen!

JANUARY 17

Jeremiah 29:11(NASB): For I know the plans I have for you, "declares the Lord", plans to prosper you and not to harm you, plans to give you hope and a future.

EVERYTHING WILL BE OK

I know things are not as you thought they would be especially not at this stage in your life. But you have to know that God is still in control! God is still on the throne. His word concerning your life is still true. So, let's pray for patience. Let's ask Holy Spirit to give us peace in our minds, in our hearts and let's believe for something big. That's my prayer, that Holy Spirit would help our unbelief and increase our capacity to believe even though things are super weird and seemingly uncertain.

God is in control and everything is going to be alright. It's going to be alright, so hold your head up! It's working for your good, so stop tripping. Trust in the Lord and lean not to your own understanding. It's going to be alright. All of it is. Every single issue. So, lift up your head. Dry your eyes. Get your faith up and expect a miracle, in Jesus' name, Amen!

JANUARY 18

Hebrews 4:13 (NASB): Nothing in all creation is hidden from God's sight. Everything is uncovered and laid bare before the eyes of him to whom we must give account.

PRAYING FOR THE POTUS

Romans chapter 13, verses 1 and 2, are truly clear on this, "Every person is to be in subjection to the governing authorities. For there is no authority except from God, and those which exist are established by God. 2 Therefore whoever resists authority has opposed the ordinance of God; and they who have opposed will receive condemnation upon themselves."

The Apostle Paul was speaking to the religious community, and to secular culture. Making it clear that whoever is in office or in authority is there by divine design and purpose. So, you might as well stop tripping and start praying! He is our President. Whether you like it or not, our president is the person that God's going to use to bless us and to accomplish His will in the earth. So, Father our souls say "yes", even though we're struggling to see your hand in this. We pray for our president, their family and for the administration that you will use to heal our land.

It's in Jesus' name, that we make our requests known and we ask that you constrain every politician and every person connected to this. Father don't let them do anything that will cause The United States of America to continue to stray from your will. Use the POTUS, every Republican and every Democrat to accomplish your will for your people. Make the Church great again, and help us to make you known again, in Jesus' name. Use this administration to turn the hearts of America back to you. But don't let their policies and plans, put us in a position where we have to play games or compromise our faith. Father we trust you and we set our hope in you. And we believe that this is still our season for grace and for favor. It's in Jesus' name we pray, Amen!

JANUARY 19

Psalms 139:14 (NASB): I praise you because I am fearfully and wonderfully made; your works are wonderful; I know that full well.

PUT YOUR NAME ON IT

You are not a victim. You are not helpless. You are not without hope and you are not without options. So today, we're going to change our approach. We're going to stop living in fear and speak up. I'm praying for grace to put your name on everything that you know belongs to you. I pray for revelation and for courage to name it and then to claim it. I pray for courage to speak up and for strength to do the work. I break the bondage of fear. I declare us free from the prison of guilt, failure, and shame. What God has for us, is for us. And nobody else can take it if we put our names on it.

So, Father show us what you've freely given to us. Equip us to take hold of it with our words and with our actions. Don't let the fear of losing, prevent us from winning. And don't let the past, prevent us from enjoying our future. We stake claim to every promise and every open door. We declare, "This is our season, for grace and for favor," and this is the season we do twice as much without working twice as hard. Holy Spirit we thank you for grace to work smarter and not harder. Thanks for giving us patience, authority, and the peace of mind to stop tripping. And cause us to start using the words of our mouth to change our circumstances. It's in Jesus' name we pray, Amen!

JANUARY 20

Ephesians 2:10 (NASB): For we are God's handiwork, created in Christ Jesus to do good works, which God created in advance for us to do.

HAVE A FRUITFUL DAY

The Bible says in Galatians chapter 5, verse 19, that "The works, or the deeds of the flesh are evident", so that's where our attention needs to be. Our choice is to focus on the opportunities we have and to let God deal with the adversity or the things that would prevent us from taking advantage of the opportunities. My prayer today is for discipline and divine intervention. Holy Spirit help our infirmities and help us to walk in the Spirit, so we do not fulfill the lusts of our flesh. Cause our choices to align with your will and let the fruit of the spirit become the things that govern our lives. We declare today to be a fruitful day that we walk in and demonstrate each fruit: love, joy, peace, patience, kindness, goodness, faithfulness, gentleness, and self-control in Jesus' name.

We take our focus away from the past and we forget those things which are behind us, on purpose. We choose to let go of every failure and everything that we've done to make life harder. We declare, "this is our season to produce fruit, spiritual fruit!" We are filled with the spirit. God lives in us, and today we will demonstrate the fruit of the spirit. We submit to the spirit of God in our personal and professional lives. Today we demonstrate self-control, and we show our flesh who is king. We glorify God in our body and in our spirit, in Jesus' name, Amen!

JANUARY 21

Ephesians 5:15-17 (NASB): Be very careful, then, how you live – not as unwise but as wise, (16) making the most of every opportunity, because the days are evil. Therefore, do not be foolish, but understand what the Lord's will is.

GOD'S RESTORING SIGHT

Second Corinthians chapter 5, verse 7 says, "We walk by faith, and not by sight", but what does that really mean, for us? Well I heard The Lord say, "I'm restoring your sight and your ability to see. I'm giving you back the grace to look beyond the past. Beyond where you are presently. And to govern your life by vision and by what's ahead of you, instead of by what's behind you." So that's my prayer today, that Holy Spirit would restore our ability to see. That we would no longer make plans for the future, based upon what's happened in the past. I pray for tunnel vision and that for a season, the peripheral stuff would no longer be a distraction. I pray for laser focus and that at the same time, we find grace to leave no stone unturned.

I pray that we are able to see things and people, for what and who they really are. That we don't misread or misjudge their place in our lives. I pray for insight concerning every connection and relationship. That Holy Spirit would dictate the restructuring and the replacement of everything and everybody, who represents who we used to be. I pray for grace to see, beyond the past and beyond the present.

I pray for insight and foresight. I pray that Holy Spirit would show us what to do to move closer to our dReams becoming our reality. Father don't let us fall victim to "the blind leading the blind" again. Cause us to see the games and incompetence before we waste our time dealing with people who love us and need us but can't help us.

Thank you for restoring our vision! Thank you for the grace to visualize, conceptualize and solidify the mental picture. Help us, so that fear and doubt, don't make us settle for something we didn't see with our spiritual eyes. It's in Jesus' name we pray!

JANUARY 22

James 1:12 (NASB): Blessed is the one who perseveres under trial because, having stood the test, that person will endure the crown of life that the Lord has promised to those who love him.

GOD WILL NOT LET YOU FALL

Jude 24 says, "Now to Him who is able to keep you from stumbling, and to make you stand in the presence of His glory blameless with great joy." That's the promise that God is not going to let us fall. So, Father, in the name of Jesus, I give You praise today for watching over Your word to perform it and for covering us with Your blood. Thank you, Lord, for walking with us daily, especially on the days when we weren't necessarily walking with You. Thank you for Your divine protection, grace, and mercy. Thank you for staying the hand of the enemy and for blocking every attack that would've killed us. Thank you, Lord, for keeping us alive and for blessing us to see another day.

Now I pray for a heart to please you every day. I pray for wisdom to avoid pitfalls and traps. I pray for grace to stand. Father I pray for mercy and grace to overcome every stumbling block and the sin that so easily besets us. Father help our infirmities and give us wisdom and the desire to maintain our balance. Help us to stop tripping over the same things we've been tripping over for years.

Father don't let us fall. Hold us down and at the same time, hold us up. Father don't let us fail or falter. And don't let the enemy take advantage of our weaknesses and vulnerabilities. Keep us

balanced and don't let us get out of control. Keep us focused, and don't let us get off track. Help us Holy Spirit, to keep our eyes on the prize, and forever stayed on You. This is our prayer today, in Jesus' name we pray, amen!

JANUARY 23

Lamentations 5:21(NASB): Restore us unto yourself, O Lord, that we may return; renew our days of old

JOY IS ON THE WAY

This joy I have, the world didn't give it and the world can't take it away, Selah. So, no matter what's happened and no matter what's happening, I cannot, and I will not lose my joy. I pray for the truth to prevail and for the truth to make us free! No more living in fear or torment, because of what might happen or because of what usually happens. There's an unusual grace on our lives and what took other people out, is going to take us to our next place in God. What the enemy meant for evil, God meant it for our good. And soon we'll be able to see how God was with us the entire time. He's going to use what we've done, and what we've been thru, to get the glory out of our story.

I heard the Lord say, "joy is on the way", and in just a few days, the worst season of our lives will be responsible for producing the best seasons of our lives. Joy is on the way, and everything is working together for our good. So, lift up your heads and be lifted up, because the King of glory is still in control. His plan to deliver you, make you whole and to bless you is still in play! Don't grow weary, and do not get discouraged, because joy is on the way. Jesus has come to see about us, and His plan is to protect us, and to promote us. Payday is coming and everything we've endured is going to have to pay us. So, put on your joy and be at peace, in Jesus' name, Amen!

JANUARY 24

Colossians 3:17 (NASB): And whatever you do, whether in word or deed, do it all in the name of the Lord Jesus, giving thanks to God the father through him.

WATCH YOUR MOUTH

Watch your mouth and stop saying what you didn't hear God say. God's word over your life is still true. So please know that whatever you've done, and however you feel, can never change it. Let's pray together: Father help us to govern our mouths and stop us from saying things that don't echo what You've already spoken. I pray for strength to withstand the negative words, thoughts, and images that the enemy is using to try to get us to forfeit our future.

Help us, Holy Spirit to keep saying what You've already said and help us to keep the enemy's words out of our mouths and minds, in Jesus' name. "Let the words of our mouths, and the meditation of our hearts be acceptable in thy sight," and let them be used to bring Your will to pass in our lives. We pray for grace to say what we believe, the strength, the wisdom, and the discipline not to say what we feel. This is our prayer today, in Jesus' name, Amen!

JANUARY 25

I John 1:9 (NASB): If we confess our sins, he is faithful and just and will forgive us our sins and purify us from all unrighteousness.

DO YOUR JOB

Father, I'm praying for grace to stay in my lane. I'm praying that I won't be distracted by what other people are doing. That I won't feel any kind of pressure to compete or move at a pace, that puts my future at risk. Thank you, Father, for teaching me patience. And for showing me how to wait without stressing and without tripping in my mind. I pray for grace to stay on task, for the discipline to keep my eyes on my assignment and on my prize. Thank you for the grace that's on my life and that I can't be intimidated by someone else's grace or the assignment they've been given.

Thank you, Lord, for helping me to settle into my call. For teaching me to enjoy the journey and every experience along the way. I'm going to stay the course. I'm going to stay focused. I'm going to stay in place. I'm going to stay encouraged. I'm going to overcome the disappointment. I'm going to overcome the judgment. I'm going to overcome the mistakes. I'm going to overcome the failures and the fears, in Jesus' name. I will not lose heart or sight of the big picture. I will not lose myself. I'm going to do what You've called me to do, without anxiety, hesitation and without looking back, in Jesus' name, Amen!

JANUARY 26

Galatians 5:22-23 & 25 (NASB): But the fruit of the Spirit is love, joy, peace, forbearance, kindness, goodness, faithfulness, gentleness, and self-control. Against such things there is no law. Since we live by the Spirit, let us keep in step with the Spirit.

GOD'S ALREADY MOVING

Don't trip, don't quit and don't you dare back down! It's already done. It's already getting better. It's already getting easier. And God's already moving on your behalf. Now get your good cry out, wipe your face and let's go. There's way too much in front of us for us to get stuck, fooling with something or somebody that represents an old place.

So, my prayer is now Lord come! Do what You've promised You'd do and lift us up where we belong! Keep us together, emotionally, mentally, spiritually, and financially. Rebuke the devourer for our name's sake. Bless us so good until all our doubters have no choice but to acknowledge that You are God, and You are good! We give You praise that it's finished. We give You praise that it's done. We lift our heads, and we lift our eyes to the hills, from whence cometh our help. Our help comes from You Lord. Our strength comes from You. It's in You, that we live, we move, and we have our being. In Jesus' name, Amen!

JANUARY 27

Psalms 40:1 (NASB): I waited patiently for the Lord; He inclined to me and heard my cry.

YOU'VE GOT THE RIGHT QUARTERBACK

I heard this during my weekend prep, and I heard it again this morning; "You've got the right quarterback (YOUR PASTOR) and you definitely have the right coach (HOLY SPIRIT)." So, stop letting the devil play tricks with your mind and have you contemplating leaving your church just because your quarterback has gotten into some trouble. He or she, only did what they did because they were trying not to lose their grip. So, trust Holy Spirit, who is the reason you are where you are. Stay the course because you're about to be a part of the greatest comeback ever. Holy Spirit has put together a masterful game plan and if we stick with it, there is no way we can lose.

We have the right quarterback and we for sure have the right coach. My prayer is that we learn to be loyal and forgiving. While at the same time holding people accountable to the bible. I pray for patience, endurance and for extended strength to finish. I pray that love will cover you, your church and that Matthew 16 will become your reality. That the gates of hell will not prevail against you, in Jesus' name.

I pray for prophetic insight. That Holy Spirit would cause you to see beyond the offense and beyond how you feel. I pray for

the fruit of the spirit to show up strong in your life, family, and church in Jesus' name. May goodness, kindness, joy, and peace be our portion. May love, patience, faithfulness, and self-control overtake us and become the river by which we navigate the course of our lives. May we find rest for our minds and souls today. It's in Jesus' name I pray, AMEN!

JANUARY 28

John 5:26 (NASB): For just as the Father has life in Himself, even so He gave to the Son also to have life in Himself

ANY DAY NOW

Good morning Holy Spirit! I'm ready! I wasn't before, but I'm ready now! I set my affections on things above and I intentionally elevate my expectations. I refuse to allow pride and fear to dictate my desire or to choose what I believe for. I'm expecting a miracle, any day now!

I'm expecting God to do something so big for me, that the bankers, doctors, lawyers, legislators and every one of my haters will have to say that God is good. They will have to acknowledge that God is on my side. I decree and declare breakthrough for the believer!

I call that old season of waiting and warfare to an end. I prophesy a win, in Jesus' name. I speak life to your dReam! Life to your body! Life to your family! Life to your business! Life to your savings and checking accounts! Life to your reputation! Life to your mind! Life to your bones! Life to your bloodstream, and your cardiovascular system! In Jesus' name I pray, Amen!

JANUARY 29

Psalms 138:3 (NASB): When I called, you answered me; you greatly emboldened me.

PRAY FOR STRENGTH

We're stronger than we think we are. We can take way more than we think we can take. Today, let's be strong in the Lord and in the power of His might. Let's ask Holy Spirit to once again strengthen us in the places where our strength is failing. Let's choose to focus on what's ahead. I pray for mental strength to let the past remain in the past. Father make us strong again and build us up in every area that's been worn down. Renew our strength and restore our joy. Father don't let anything steal our strength. Make us strong again and don't let the pressures of living alone or in a troubled relationship push us into a place of compromise.

Father build us up in our self-esteem and in our own estimation of our self-worth. Make us strong again and don't let our mistakes or other people's opinions about us move us away from Your thoughts toward us. Because Your thoughts of us are beautiful. Your plans accommodate our humanity and give us a future and living hope. Thank you for increasing our strength and restoring our desire to glorify You in everything we do. We declare, "You are my strength, strength like no other, strength like no other reaches to me!" It's in Jesus' name, we declare these things to be so, Amen!

JANUARY 30

Psalms 51:1 (NASB): Have mercy upon me O Lord, according to thy lovingkindness: according to the multitude of thy tender mercies blot out my transgressions.

PRAY FOR STRUCTURE

What you're doing is working. Don't let the devil pressure you into abandoning the game plan that you know God gave you, just because you're behind in points and you feel like you're losing. Your feelings can't be trusted. So today, I pray for endurance and that you will find peace in God's will, even though His will seems to have taken you the long way around! I pray that Holy Spirit will give you a sneak peek into your future and cause you to see what He sees. I pray that you don't grow weary in doing well. I pray that you will stay the course and continue following the instructions given to you by Holy Spirit. What you're doing is working. The gaps are beginning to close. Everything is finally starting to come together. The areas of vulnerability are no longer as exposed as they once were. Soon you're going to be able to see that your labor has not been in vain.

I'm praying that God continues to establish the kind of structure around you that lasts. And that He will build the kind of team, that can execute your vision, with excellence and with precision. I pray for divine help because what you're building matters. It will be a help and a blessing to people long after you're off the scene. Be encouraged and patient today. Be good and be free today. It's in Jesus' name I pray, AMEN!

JANUARY 31

Deuteronomy 28:8 (NASB): The Lord will send a blessing on your barns and on everything you put your hands to. The Lord your God will bless you in the land he has given you.

GOD'S GOING TO SHOW YOU HOW

Let's pray that we don't go another day with the wrong people in the wrong places in our lives; Amen! I'm praying that Holy Spirit would give us courage and wisdom to respectfully and responsibly reposition everything and everybody, who's in the wrong place. Holy Spirit show us how and show us where. Help us to know that the time is now. Don't let us waste another day trying to force things. Don't let us waste another moment trying to make things work that are out of order. And Holy Spirit remove those things that are no longer pleasing to You.

Show us how, show us where and then give us the courage to make the changes we need to make. Give us the wherewithal to do it now! Let the words of our mouths and the meditation of our hearts and every relationship we have be pleasing unto You. It's in Jesus' name we pray, Amen!

FEBRUARY

FEBRUARY 1

2 Thessalonians 3:3 (NASB): But the Lord is faithful, and He will strengthen and protect you from the evil one.

FIGHT

You're not depressed! You're not alone! You are loved and you are valuable. So, fight! Fight what you feel with the truth. Fight what you feel with the word. Stop letting the devil play the same tricks on you every weekend. I'm praying that the truth will make you free. And despite what your flesh keeps suggesting, I pray that you will choose to believe what you know you heard God s about you.

I pray for you today, that you will find the will and the desire to fight. I pray for the courage to fight the lies with the truth, in Jesus' name. I pray that wallowing in guilt, shame and settling for misery will become intolerable. I pray that tonight will be the night that you decide to think yourself happy. You're not crying yourself to sleep tonight! I command you to put on your joy and be free! I speak peace and sweet sleep over you tonight. I pray for the mental strength to stay free and to stay at peace, in Jesus' name I pray, Amen!

FEBRUARY 2

Ephesians 2:8 (NASB): For it is by grace you have been saved, through faith- and this is not from yourselves, it is a gift from God.

YOUR ANGELS ARE STRONGER

This is going to be the best week of our year, thus far! So, get your mind right and get focused on what God has promised. The battle is still the Lord's. Our fight is more mental and emotional. But we already know how to win in these areas. Father help us and help us to keep our eyes on you. Don't allow us to remain distracted by drama and demons. Holy Spirit teach us how to pray and what to pray for.

We pray according to Revelation, chapter 12, verse 8, and we decree and declare that the fallen angels that are fighting against us, are not strong enough to defeat the angels that are fighting for us. They cannot maintain their place in our lives because we continue to trust in You. So, let yesterday be the last day that we stress over the plan of the enemy. From today forward let us find hope in the plans of our God. Father increase our faith. Help our unbelief and cause us to set our hope in You again. We cannot lose! In Jesus' name, AMEN!

FEBRUARY 3

Colossians 3:10 (NASB): And have put on the new self, which is being renewed in knowledge in the image of its Creator

SHOUT NOW!

Don't wait until the battle is over, shout now! This is not a question of if, this is a question of when. The truth is, God has already given you the victory. Victory over every enemy and over everything that opposes His plan for your life. It may not feel like it right now, but I need you to say this, "God has, smiled on me, He has, set me free," Hallelujah! So, Father we praise You for the victory and we thank you for making all things well. Today we put on our strength and we put on the garment of praise. Knowing that even though we're still in the fight, the end result is already guaranteed.

We cannot lose because we are on the winning side. We will not stress because the blood of Jesus was and still is enough. We win because of Jesus. We win because of Calvary. Father we choose to lift up our heads and be encouraged. We choose to trust in the Lord with all of our hearts and lean not to our own understanding. We choose to trust You and praise You along the way. Victory is mine. Victory today is mine. So, I'm going to tell my story and I'm going to give You glory. For it was You alone, who healed my body, touched my mind, and brought me out. It was You alone, who defeated my enemies, and delivered my soul. Oh, I give You praise today, and I'll tell the world that You did it for me. It's in Jesus' name I pray, Amen!

FEBRUARY 4

Revelation 21:4 (NASB): and He will wipe away every tear from their eyes; and there will no longer be any death; there will no longer be any mourning, or crying, or pain; the first things have passed away."

FIX OUR HEARTS

I am praying for God's will to be done in the United States of America. I'm praying that senseless, satanic murders will somehow be used to birth a lasting movement of love and genuine care for one another. I'm praying that generations will come together. And that wisdom, passion and purpose will be used collectively, in Jesus' name!

I pray for all pastors and politicians. I pray that they will finally acknowledge and find the courage to confront the cancer of racism, as it breaks the heart of God.

Father fix our hearts and change our minds. Help us to love our neighbors, as we love ourselves. We cry out for justice, but more importantly, we cry out for Your presence. We want You. We need You. We love You! Now show Yourself strong! In Jesus' name I pray, Amen!

FEBRUARY 5

Isaiah 26:3 (NASB): You will keep in perfect peace, those whose minds are steadfast, because they trust in you.

A FRESH START

Read Matthew chapter 8, verses 1 thru 4, and let Holy Spirit minister peace to your soul. I know it's a stretch. But listen to me, "Jesus is about to touch you and make you clean from the inside out." God said to tell you, "I'm ready, I'm willing and I'm able to do exceedingly, abundantly, above all that you can ask or think." So, my prayer for you today, is that you would find the courage to come to Jesus just as you are. That you would discover that you haven't been waiting on Jesus, but that Jesus has been waiting on you.

I pray for miracles, signs, and wonders today. I pray that an immediately would hit your life today. I pray that God would cleanse you and wipe away everything in your past, that would've made a mess of your future. I plead the blood over your credit report, over your reputation, over your good name, over your conscience, and over your criminal history, and I declare you clean, in Jesus' name! Be free today, and let your test become your testimony. It's in Jesus' name I pray, Amen!

FEBRUARY 6

James 1:26 (NASB): If anyone thinks himself to be religious, and yet does not bridle his tongue but deceives his own heart, this man's religion is worthless.

BRIDLE MY TONGUE

Father, I pray you don't allow any corrupt communication to come out of my mouth. Cause my thoughts and my words to be gracious, kind, loving, and reflective of a person who's in relationship with Jesus Christ.

Help my mind! Help my mouth! And don't let me say anything I'll regret or have to apologize for later.

Father, don't let anything, come out of my mouth that You haven't put in my mouth or approved! Let the words of my mouth and the meditation of my heart be acceptable to you. Let them please you. And let them open doors today to something big!

I decree and declare, "The next thing God does for me is going to be big!" It's in Jesus' name I pray, Amen!

FEBRUARY 7

Luke 17:1 (NASB): "Things that cause people to stumble are bound to come, but woe to anyone through whom they come.

FREE FROM OFFENSE

Today I'm praying for the grace to be our authentic selves. That Holy Spirit will help us to continue being who we genuinely are at our core. I pray that the way we're treated and the way we've felt, will not be the determining factor in what we do. I pray for grace to keep being who we are and who God's made us to be. I pray that Holy Spirit will help us to not be affected by how we've been made to feel; nor by what they've said and done to us. I pray that truth will prevail. I pray that our feelings will have to submit to the truth and not the other way around. I pray for discernment to identify when the devil is trying to play us. Or trying to use our emotions and our unmet needs and desires against us.

Holy Spirit show us what is real and don't let the devil play games with our minds and our emotions anymore! Don't let the disappointment and the perceived rejection change us. Don't let us wall off the people we want and need in our intimate space for fear of rejection and disappointment. Show us where we're off. And show us how we've allowed the enemy to use our circumstances to change who we are at our core. We decree and declare; we are changing for the better and not for the worst. I am changing, but not because of what they did, or didn't do. But because of what You did at Calvary.

Father we praise you today, for bringing the emotional torture to an end. Thank you for casting down the accuser of the brethren. And thank you for making life and doing the right thing easier. We declare today to be the day, that we begin a new chapter of emotional freedom and peace. Today is the day, that we don't let them change us, but Your unconditional love, changes them. It's in Jesus' name we pray, Amen!

FEBRUARY 8

Psalms 138:8 (NASB): The Lord will vindicate me; your love, Lord, endures forever – do not abandon the works of your hands

NO MORE OFFENSE

We've been off without even knowing it, we've been living in offense. And as a result, everything we see, hear, and feel gets processed through the filter of offense. I heard the Lord say, "I'm breaking it off your life." God is breaking offense from our lives and the hold of rejection that has kept us locked in the cycle of fear, guilt, and shame. Today, God calls the chaos into divine order and the truth of who we really are, is making us free. No more living life offended and repeating the same destructive cycles. Today we declare our freedom! We walk away from the generational behavioral patterns that have boxed us in, limited us and restricted our joy. In Jesus' name, we are free.

It's time for you to bust a move! You've been around this mountain way too many times. I'm praying that God will give you the wisdom, to know when to make your move. I pray that this week, will be the week that you decide to do something different. I pray that today will be the day that we finally realize that we do deserve better. Holy Spirit show us when and teach us how. Don't let us live another day in fear or offended. Give us the courage to take a step today and don't allow us to be restricted by the people we know. Reprogram our feet and grant us grace to start making moves and taking steps towards our destiny. Break us through. Break us out. Don't let yesterday bind us or box us in. In Jesus' name we pray, amen!

FEBRUARY 9

Matthew 5:14-15 (NASB): You are the light of the world. A town built on a hill cannot be hidden.

DREAM AGAIN

A dream hasn't ever hurt anybody! So why don't you stop tripping and start dreaming again. Picture yourself doing it. See yourself running it. Envision yourself walking in it. Start preparing your surroundings for it and give God some faith to work with. It's time and you feel it too.

So, let's make this day. Let's start something, that God will have to finish. Let's launch out into the deep and do something that nobody we know has ever done. Amen! Go get it. It's got your name on it anyway! I believe in you. God trusts you and purpose and destiny awaits you. Be bigger today. Be better today. In Jesus' name, amen!

FEBRUARY 10

Matthew 18:21-22 (NASB): Then Peter came to Jesus and asked, "Lord, how many times shall I forgive my brother or sister who sins against me? Up to seven times?" Jesus answered, "I tell you, not seven times, but seventy-seven times"

ORDER MY STEPS

Today, you're going to stare life in the face and you're going to stop settling for stuff you know you don't want. I'm praying that we all find courage. That we rediscover and regain the mental strength to acknowledge and confront our fears. I'm praying that Holy Spirit would quicken our bodies, hearts and cause us to come alive again, in Jesus' name. I pray for a holy boldness to overtake us and I pray that waiting becomes inappropriate and unacceptable.

I pray for spirit led, spirit filled and spirit metered patience. I pray that we find wisdom and grace to make moves, while we're waiting. Father don't let us waste another day hanging around the wrong people or sitting around wasting time in the wrong places. Order our steps today and by tomorrow, Holy Spirit help us to be back on track. Help us to be back in place and set up for the best days we've had all year. Don't let us run away. Don't let us miss our moments. Don't let us live another day in yesterday. Don't let us waste another minute entertaining guilt, fear, and shame. Grace us to confront our fears. Grace us to confront our failures. Father grace us to accept, embrace and to pursue our future. Not the future the devil showed us, but the future You secured for us. It's in Jesus' name I pray, AMEN!

FEBRUARY 11

Nahum 1:7 (NASB): The LORD is good, A stronghold in the day of trouble, And He knows those who take refuge in Him

GIVE US STRENGTH

Father, I give you praise, but I do not understand. I was told you were sovereign and in control of all things. But the older I get, the more I realize that you've given men free will and the ability to choose.

So today Father, I praise you for peace, strength, and the ability to stay focused. Help us to not be distracted by the pain and the disappointment inflicted by other people's choices.

I praise you today, that even though your will is not automatic, it is causing "all things" to work together for our good!

I do not understand this, but I praise you through the pain and anger, knowing that things are already getting better! Touch the families of the lost, our communities at large and God, please bless America. It's in Jesus' name I pray, amen!

FEBRUARY 12

Psalms 34:17 (NASB): The righteous cry out, and the Lord hears them; He delivers them from all their troubles

---

YOUR GIFT WILL MAKE ROOM

Proverbs chapter 18, verse 16 says, "A man's gift makes room for him and brings him before great men." Well, I'm a living witness, that if you trust and serve God, He'll open doors that no man can close. So that's my prayer for you today; that your gift would clear a path for you to move forward. That the grace of God on your life would finally take you to the place in your life, that God has ordained for you to be.

I pray that God would open double doors and that He would enlarge your territory, in Jesus' name. I pray for favor with men, for favor with God and that all stumbling blocks would become steppingstones. I pray that what you used to trip over; God would grace you to leap over. And that you would come to know what it's like to live your life without fear. Get ready to turn up because you're about to testify. It's in Jesus' name I pray, Amen!

FEBRUARY 13

Proverbs 3:26 (NASB): For the Lord will be at your side and will keep your foot from being snared

GOD IS WAITING

Forgiveness begins with you. Moving on and moving forward with your life starts and stops with you. So, let's choose to believe and trust God today. It's time we get on with kingdom business. We've got way too much to do, to let the devil keep us focused on yesterday. Father give us the strength to pick up where we left off. And don't let us live another day in condemnation or in defeat. Help us to see your love and your provision as we go throughout the day. Remove the sting out of the devil's accusations. Guard our hearts, minds and give us peace, as we forget those things that are behind, and we reach for what is ahead.

Psalms 30 and 5 says, "For His anger is but for a moment, His favor is for life; Weeping may endure for a night, but joy comes in the morning." We thank you for Calvary and for a life full of favor. We thank you for Jesus, and we give you praise for a journey full of joy. You're not mad, you're ready. You're not indifferent, you're excited about our future. You're not done, your plan is just being revealed. We're forgiven, our future is secure and better is coming. No eye has seen it and no ear has heard it, the things that you've prepared for those who love you. So, we turn our hearts back to you, we set our affections on things above and we say yes! We expect a miracle today. In Jesus' name, Amen!

FEBRUARY 14

Proverbs 3:5 (NASB): Trust in the Lord with all your heart and lean not on your own understanding

HUMAN BEING

Don't be so hard on yourself, you're not God! You're human and your being is still being restored. The grace of God is yet working in us, on us and the 2nd Adam in us is being renewed. The spirit of the Lord, Jesus Christ is living in us. His image and likeness are becoming the dominant influences in everything we say and do. I pray for grace to keep growing. I pray for the courage to confront our own selves and for the wisdom to make the necessary adjustments.

Holy Spirit teach us your ways and show us how to self-correct before we make a mess of everything we hold near and dear to our hearts. Help us to manage our humanity, while walking in our divinity. And don't let our flesh get the best of us. Order our steps and don't let the devil deceive us ever again. Don't let our humanity diminish our true being. Help us to be all that you've called and equipped us to be. In Jesus' name, Amen!

FEBRUARY 15

Psalms 19:1 (NASB): The heavens are telling of the glory of God; And their expanse is declaring the work of His hands.

STAYING THE COURSE

What God has for you; it is still for you! I'm praying for you this morning, that Holy Spirit would grace you to stay focused. That not by power, not by might but by His spirit, that God would help you to stay the course.

I curse every distraction and I pray that your discernment would kick into overdrive. And that you will be able to see every snake and every person sent into your life by the enemy to keep you off course.

I'm praying the power of God shows up in your life in such a manner that nothing and nobody, not even you, would be able to hold up God's plan any longer. I declare breakthrough and overflow for you today! In the name of Jesus, I speak supernatural acceleration and progress today. That the things you've been in faith for would manifest today.

I pray that this day, in this year, of this month would be a new beginning for you. I pray that God would do for you, what He did for Hezekiah and add 15 more big years to your life! It's in Jesus' name, Amen!

FEBRUARY 16

I John 3:19-20 (NASB): This is how we know that we belong to the truth and how we set our hearts at rest in his presence: if our hearts condemn us, we know that

YOUR EARS ARE ABOUT TO POP

I declare you do have an ear to hear. You are not off, nor dull of hearing and your ears are in tune to what God is saying. You've spent your last day wandering in the wilderness. You've spent your last day chasing somebody else's dReam! Today marks the beginning of a new season for you. No more distractions. No more meaningless fights and conflicts with people are a part of your future. I speak peace over this year, and I call forth divine protection, in the name of Jesus. I pray that your ears would start popping and the voice of the Lord would become clearer than you've ever heard Him before. Your ears have been prepared and I declare you can hear what the spirit of the Lord is saying.

You've been lost, left for dead, lied on and lived a less than life. But that all started changing as soon as you connected with this God moment. So, I pray for grace to tune out the haters because God is talking. Turn the radio down, God is talking. Stop scrolling, God is talking. This is your season to hear and to write the vision; because God's about to accelerate the pace of your come up. God is about to speed up the processes, remove the barriers and the red tape, in Jesus' name.

So ready yourself. Prepare your house. Tell your family. Start collecting boxes. Start purging your closet and your friends list. Clean up. Get rid of everything broken and no longer of use to you, God is talking. He's speaking clearly, and what He's saying is about to shift your position. He that hath an ear, let him hear. In Jesus' name, Amen!

FEBRUARY 17

Job 42:2 (NASB): "I know that you can do all things, and that no purpose of yours can be thwarted.

SEASON OF THE TURN

I heard the Lord say, "tell them, this is the season that I turn it! This is the season that I turn them, again!" So today I prophesy to every situation, circumstance and I command them to agree with the word of the Lord.

I plead the blood of Jesus, over your body, over every issue that's caused you stress and mental trauma. I call your mind into perfect alignment with God's word and pray for peace to flood your soul. In the name of Jesus, I declare, "This is the season of the turn!"

Today things start shifting in your favor. I command every missing piece to fall into place, in Jesus' name! I declare, by the Holy Ghost that it's turning. That this turn agrees with God's plan. It's getting better! The drama, misunderstandings and strife are gone. I decree that every day this week, you will have peace. It's in the mighty name of Jesus I pray, Amen!

FEBRUARY 18

Romans 10:17 (NASB): So, faith comes from hearing, and hearing by the word of Christ.

FAITH CARRIES ME

Father, it's in the name of Jesus that I humbly come before You, thanking you for another day! I thank you for Jesus! I thank you for Holy Spirit! And I thank you for peace in my mind!

Thank you, Father, that even though I'm under attack, I will not lose my cool. Thank you, Lord, that my faith is carrying me and that I will not waver! Thank you, Lord, for peace, patience and for the God given ability to persevere until the end. I'm not a quitter. I will not give up. I will not be intimidated.

I praise you for holy boldness. Thank you for the courage to face the enemy without fear, any added stress or anxiety. I cast my cares on you! I set my hope on your love. I declare today is the day of breakthrough, in Jesus' name I pray, and it is so, Amen!

FEBRUARY 19

Hebrews 4:16 (NASB) Let us then approach God's throne of grace with confidence, so that we may receive mercy and grace to help us in our time of need.

EYES ON JESUS

We are not ignorant of the devil's vices. We already know how he works. We've seen the same lame strategy over and over again. Yet, for whatever reason we keep stressing over a wasted weapon. Listen to me, the word of God is still true, and it still works, even if you're wrong. So, don't let the devil use guilt and shame to back you into a corner. Nor cause you to forget that the word is still your best option. Father, in the name of Jesus, we plead the blood and we release our faith for a way of escape. We thank you for paying our ransom, and for sending Jesus as the propitiation for our sins. Our hearts cry out for you today! We look to the hills and we declare that all our help comes from you.

Father we stretch our hands to thee, no other help do we know of. Not only are you our last option, you're our best and only option. So, we set our hope on you. We set our hope on your love. Even when we we're dead wrong, we refuse to cast off our confidence. We will see the goodness of the Lord. We will see the power of God demonstrated on our behalf. We will see you show yourself strong on our behalf. We decree and declare that we will not sink, and we will not go under. We will not succumb to the chatter, nor to the voices in the wind. Because we will not take our eyes off you.

We're going to stay on course. And we will not waste any moment of your time, tripping over something you've already handled. No distractions and no fear! It's in Jesus' name Amen!

FEBRUARY 20

Deuteronomy 10:14 (NASB) Behold, to the Lord your God belong heaven and the highest heavens, the earth and all that is in it.

MORE THAN YOU NEED

This is my prayer for you today. That the days of living with leftovers would end and the days of living in overflow would begin now. Father bless your children, give them strategies to eliminate debt and build wealth. Your word says you've given us power to get wealth (Deut. 8:18). So, we call forth every idea, song, script, solution, book, recipe, and business concept in the name of Jesus.

We call forth divine assistance and we release the angels to work on our behalf. We expect more. We expect double. We expect money miracles, supernatural turnarounds, and comebacks. Father show yourself strong on our behalf. Make the devil a liar concerning our families and our future. It's in the mighty name of Jesus' we pray, Amen!

FEBRUARY 21

1 Samuel 15:22 (NASB): Samuel said, "Does the Lord have as much delight in burnt offerings and sacrifices As in obeying the voice of the Lord? Behold, to obey is better than a sacrifice, And to pay attention is better than the fat of rams.

DON'T CHOKE

You've lived in fear and beneath your privilege for way too long. It's time to do something about what you don't like about your life. You already have enough in your hand to make something happen. Please don't let the devil talk you out of your miracle. Obey God!

Trust what you heard the first time. And don't let circumstances push you into disobedience. What you're considering doing is a distraction. The enemy is trying to get you to throw better days in the trash. So, don't choke! Do what God told you to do and watch Him respond to your faith. I'm praying for you! I believe in you! I'm excited about your future! In Jesus' name, Amen!

FEBRUARY 22

James 1:4 (NASB): And let endurance have its perfect result, so that you may be [c]perfect and complete, lacking in nothing.

I'M IN CONTROL

I'm praying for patience, again! I pray for the right frame of mind and calm to your spirit; to help you deal with the people in your life, who aren't where you are professionally nor spiritually.

I pray that the issues in your life won't have you off your game emotionally, that you find yourself going off and exploding on people for no justifiable reason. I pray against road rage. I pray against the spirit of anger. I pray for peace and release.

I pray against rage and the spirit that seeks revenge. In the name of Jesus! I pray for self-control and that the power of God comes on you in such a way, that you will be able to control your thoughts, mouth, and actions!

May the Holy Ghost become the motivating force behind everything you say and do! In Jesus' name I pray, Amen.

FEBRUARY 23

Jeremiah 29:11 (NASB): For I know the plans that I have for you,' declares the LORD, 'plans for prosperity and not for disaster, to give you a future and a hope.

THEY WILL CALL YOU

Be encouraged. The days of begging people to help you and support you are over. Your gift is making room for you. Selah! Now Father, we declare that we trust you. Even though we've had some difficult days; we believe your plan is still good. We believe that your plan includes the people who've been where we're going and the people who have what we need. We decree and declare; that you're turning the hearts of the owners, managers and the people who make things happen, to call the shots in our direction, in Jesus' name.

We believe that you're raising up people, who will use their power, influence, and all of their resources to make sure we have everything we need to go to our next level. Father we trust your plan and believe it's good. And that it's already secured our future. We decree, we have an ear to hear what you're saying. We declare, we will never be locked out or left behind again. We hear greater in our inner ear and we will answer the call. It's in the mighty name of Jesus we pray, Amen!

FEBRUARY 24

Psalm 139:14 (NASB): I praise you because I am fearfully and wonderfully made; your works are wonderful, I know that full well.

BIG FAITH

I break the hold of that competing and comparing spirit that has you looking at other people, and their "stuff", wishing you had their life. I pray for you today, that your faith won't fail. I pray that this anointing, released in this song, reignites your fire, and your faith, and causes you to believe God again for everything He promised you.

I pray for NOW faith! I pray for BIG faith! I pray for childlike faith, so you'll go back to believing that anything is possible, and that God really can do anything but fail! I pray you go to sleep and wake up to a miracle! I pray that by the time you go to rest tonight, and open your eyes, you'll be seeing signs. I pray that you wake up to a wonder, in Jesus' name! God is no respecter of persons, but He is a respecter of faith. So go to sleep knowing that God is about to do something while you're asleep! It's in Jesus' mighty name we pray, Amen!

FEBRUARY 25

Judges 7: 20-22 (NASB): When the three units blew the trumpets and broke the pitchers, they held the torches in their left hands and the trumpets in their right hands for blowing, and shouted, "A sword for the Lord and for Gideon!" And each stood in his place around the camp; and all the army ran, crying out as they fled. And when they blew the three hundred trumpets, the Lord set the sword of one against another even throughout the entire army; and the army fled as far as Beth-shittah toward Zererah, as far as the edge of Abel-meholah, by Tabbath.

GET OVER PEOPLE

There are people around you whom you love and trust, who do not want you to do better. And they definitely don't want you to do better than them. Get over it! You cannot allow them to make you feel bad about wanting something more or something different. That desire to do better and be better is from God. The push that you feel is God's hand motivating you to move forward. To forget those people, places and those things that represent who you once were. Get over it! You're not who they want you to be and you'll never be that person again.

So, I pray for the wherewithal and the wisdom to decide to let people be miserable, all by themselves. I pray for the courage to go it alone if you have to. I pray for the grace to stay focused, even if you have no one present to bounce things off. I pray that Holy Spirit would become your very present help. And that obeying, trusting, and following God's lead in the face of adversity, would be your first and only viable option. So, they left you. Get over it! So, they talked about you behind your back, get over it. So they called you stupid and crazy, get over it! You're headed to a place that no one in your family has ever been. I pray that their lack of revelation, experience, and exposure, would not become a stumbling block or a delay to God's will coming to pass in your life. In Jesus' name, I pray for grace to get over people, Amen!

FEBRUARY 26

Matthew 17:20 (NASB): And He said to them, "Because of your meager faith; for truly I say to you, if you have faith the size of a mustard seed, you will say to this mountain, 'Move from here to there,' and it will move; and nothing will be impossible for you.

NOW FAITH

I'm praying for stubborn faith! That we are not moved by what we can see, but only by what we believe! I pray for NOW FAITH, and that we are not held hostage by our senses.

I pray, that we choose to believe that regardless of how things appear or how we feel our faith won't waver. And despite what we can't touch and what seems to be impossible; I still believe that with God, all things are possible. I still believe, even after some prayers did not manifest what I wanted.

I still believe that there's nothing my God cannot do! So, I'm going to keep praying, fasting, and placing a demand on the power and the promise of God, to do miracles on behalf of the believer!

I'm going to keep praying until prayer stops the enemy's attack, and releases God's yes on my behalf! It's in Jesus' name I pray, AMEN!

FEBRUARY 27

1 Corinthians 15:57 (NASB): but thanks be to God, who gives us the victory through our Lord Jesus Christ.

THE DEVIL IS A LIAR

Father it's a new day! The devil's been trying me. Trying to get me to accept that things are what they are and that they are beyond fixing, but the devil is a liar!

Today I accept the truth. And the truth is, my steps are ordered by the Lord. I'm justified by faith! I'm washed in the blood of Jesus! And no weapon formed against me shall prosper!

So, I'm declaring this a fear free day. And today, I take a stand and say, "enough is enough." Today I sound an alarm, and declare, "what God has for me, is for me." Nobody can stop it! Nobody can steal it! So, all day today I'm going to be singing, "Victory is mine! Victory is mine! Victory today, is mine! I told Satan, get thee behind, because Victory, today, is mine!" It's in Jesus' name I pray, AMEN!

FEBRUARY 28

Matthew 20:28 (NASB): just as the Son of Man did not come to be served, but to serve and to give his life as a ransom for many

STOP FALLING FOR IT

You've seen this attack before. This isn't the first time the devil has come at you like this. Don't fall for it. Don't let him control you emotionally, and don't let him mess up your flow. You have authority and you possess the mental strength to choose to be unbothered.

You don't have to go to bed angry or frustrated, because you have the grace, to choose peace. In the name of Jesus, I command you to be the bigger and better person. I command your soul to take joy and to be at peace. No cussing, no fighting, no paranoia, and no more acting like somebody who's not in a real relationship with God. Enjoy your day and the rest of your night. Sleep well, knowing that if God be for you, He's more than enough, and He's all you really need. That's my prayer for you today. It's in Jesus' name I pray, Amen!

MARCH

MARCH 1

Isaiah 41:10 (NASB): Do not fear, for I am with you; Do not be afraid, for I am your God. I will strengthen you, I will also help you, I will also uphold you with My righteous right hand.'

GET OUT OF FEAR

DO NOT GET IN FEAR! God's got way too much of himself invested in you for you to lose. If God weren't with you and for you, you would be dead by now!

You need to get up, get out of fear and get over people and what they've said to you. Jesus died for us. He loves us. He cares for us. His plan is good and he's right here with us. Despite what we've done and how we've behaved. He has not left us, and his love for us remains. Hallelujah!

We have nothing to fear. First John chapter 4, verse 18 says, "There is no fear in love; but perfect love casts out fear." His love for us is perfect, it expels, throws away and puts down every negative thought. It removes the guilt and the shame. So, get out of fear, because your faith won't work there! And God's hands are tied while you're living in fear. Get out of fear, so God can finish what He started. Get out of fear, so the devil's plan to detour you and destroy you, can't work. Get out of fear because today is a new day and anything is possible. Glory to God! That's our prayer today. In Jesus' name, Amen!

MARCH 2

Matthew 5:16 (NASB): Your light must shine before people in such a way that they may see your good works and glorify your Father who is in heaven.

YOU CAN'T HIDE

You are who you are, and nothing that's happened to you and nothing you've done can change that. In Matthew chapter 5, Jesus called you the light of the world. This explains why trying to stay under the radar, never works for you. They didn't choose you; God did. And that's why you've been unable to hide. It all makes sense now. My prayer is, that you'll focus on the wide doors and trust God to deal with your many adversaries.

I pray that trouble doesn't change your mind. And that running away would no longer be an option for you. I pray that hiding out and trying to stay "out of the way, would become impossible for you. That your light would shine brighter than it's ever shined before. I pray for favor with resourceful people and that the ears of the decision makers would be yours. I pray that you'd know the difference between leading and being stubborn and arrogant. Holy Spirit teach us to shine, without coming under the influence of pride, in Jesus' name. Grant us the grace to glow, grow and go into every area that you've called us to illuminate for the sake of the kingdom. And we say, all glory belongs to you! It's in the matchless name of Jesus we pray, Amen!

MARCH 3

1 Timothy 6:12 (NASB): Fight the good fight of faith; take hold of the eternal life to which you were called, and for which you made the good confession in the presence of many witnesses.

FIGHTS MEAN GROWTH

Grow up. Stop fighting the process. Let God do, what He's trying to do and stop stressing over stuff that's already under your feet. Some fights just have to be fought, so fight. Not people and not in your flesh but fight the fight of faith. Use what you're going thru and what you feel as fuel. Don't let it hold you back, but let it push you forward. And stop questioning whether or not God heard you.

This fight, you're just going to have to fight! The difference this time is, you're coming out with scars and spoils. This time you're coming out with a cause and with cash. So, stop tripping. Hold your head up. Be encouraged and trust God to do everything He promised. I'm praying for you, and I believe in you. Grow up! In Jesus' name I pray, Amen, Amen, and Amen!

MARCH 4

Philippians 4:4 (NASB): Rejoice in the Lord always; again, I will say, rejoice!

TO GOD BE THE GLORY

Good morning Holy Spirit. Today is going to be the best day I've had this quarter! This is the day, that the Lord has made and the way my mental strength is set up; there is nothing that can happen, nothing that anybody can say, or do to keep me from rejoicing in it!

I praise you early because I believe that by the end of the day, you will have done something for me, that only El'Shaddai, God our creator, could've done! I declare my God is making ways, today! My God is opening doors, today! My God is healing the sick, today! My God is shutting the mouth of the accuser, today!

So, I praise you early, because I believe that by the end of the day, that only Jehovah Jireh, the provider, will have supplied all my needs! I will not end this day with a deficit. I'm coming out of this day in overflow! This day will not end with me needing anything, but by the end of the day I'll have everything I need! By day's end, the only thing left to do will be to raise my hands, and say, to God be the glory. In Jesus' name I pray, Amen.

MARCH 5

Romans 13:1 (NASB): Every person is to be subject to the governing authorities. For there is no authority except [b]from God, and those which exist are established by God.

PRAY FOR THE USA

Holy Spirit, we need your help. Touch our hearts and heal us from the bitterness, birthed by racism in America. Help us to be better. Show us how to effectively love our enemies and those who spitefully try to use us. Give us peace in the process. And don't let our broken hearts, become hard hearts. Keep our minds and ears open, so anger and disgust doesn't shape our response nor frame our perspectives. Help us to keep our eyes on you, and don't let us get distracted by the things that can't change anything.

Father we need you. We need grace to cope, strategy to know what to do now, and how to move forward. Help us so we don't react in our flesh. Show us what to do and when to do it. And help us, so this time doesn't end up like the last time, and we don't walk away feeling defeated or thinking things will never change. We're not moved by what we see, but only by what we believe. Father increase our faith and our influence. Touch and turn the hearts of the legislatures, those who administer justice, and those who enforce the law. Cause them to come subject to your will for Black America and the hood. We will keep praying and seeking your wisdom for what we must do, to make living in America, while being black, safer than what it is now.

Guide our preachers, pastors, youth leaders and teachers. Cover our sons, our daughters and father be a fence around the Hood! In Jesus' name I pray, Amen.

MARCH 6

Psalm 141:3 (NASB): Set a guard, LORD, [a]over my mouth; Keep watch over the door of my lips.

GUARD MY LIPS

God's been too good to us, for us to let this passing season of pain and difficulty cause us to forget all that the Lord has done. My prayer is, that you'll forget what they did to you and remember what God's done for you. I pray for courage to look ahead, and for grace to press our way forward. I pray that we learn to remember and that we find the strength to remind ourselves, and to remind God of what He promised. I pray that we remember that trouble don't last always. And that we find peace in the fact that better is already on the way. I pray for disciplined mouths, and that "keeping it real" won't make us curse what God has already blessed. I pray that the grace of Job comes upon us. That no matter what happens, and no matter what people say we will not sin with our lips. I pray for courage to control what we say. And that how we feel won't be what determines what we say.

Thank you, Holy Spirit, for guarding my mouth. Thank you, Holy Spirit, for giving me the wisdom to get out of my feelings before I start talking. Thank you, Holy Spirit, for giving me what to say, how to say it, and when to say it. Thank you, for making my words count. And for giving me the authority to declare a thing and that thing be established. I shall have, whatever I say!

So today, I refuse to waste my words. I refuse to allow the enemy to make me say things about myself and about my situation, that God hasn't already said. Yes, I'm hurt. Yes, I'm confused.

Yes, I'm angry, but I will not sin with my lips. I want to cuss but I can't because I still trust God. I live for God, and come what may, I will praise God! I will not sin with my lips, but I will bless the Lord at all times, and His praise will forever be in my mouth. It's in Jesus' name I pray today, Amen!

MARCH 7

2 Corinthians 4:8-9 (NASB): *we are* afflicted in every way, but not crushed; perplexed, but not despairing; persecuted, but not abandoned; struck down, but not destroyed;

WE WILL WORSHIP

Good morning guys! This is the day that the Lord has made, and He's fashioned this day in such a way, where we cannot be defeated!

We are hurting, but we are not losing. The victory is ours! It's already been decided in eternity and we fully accept the finished work in time. We weep, but we still worship! We hurt, but we continue to look to the hills, from whence cometh our help, our help, comes from the Lord!

So, Father I thank you for peace in our hearts and our minds. I thank you for giving us peace. Your peace, the kind of peace that surpasses all understanding. And frees us from anger and from guilt. I thank you Holy Spirit, that you are with us. That the God of all comfort is prepared and has prepared us to endure this hardship as good soldiers.

We will not faint! We will not fail to trust you! And we won't ever cease to give you praise! Have your way today. In Jesus' name I pray, Amen!

MARCH 8

Luke 5:4-6 (NASB): Simon responded and said, "Master, we worked hard all night and caught nothing, but will do as You say and let down the nets." And when they had done this, they caught a great quantity of fish, and their nets began to tear;

LIVE FULL

You've settled, we've settled, but today, I feel God stretching us into something bigger. I feel God pulling us out of yesterday and pushing us into today. I sense the Spirit of God calling us up and calling us into something greater. My prayer today, is that we'll find the courage to let go of what we're used to. That Holy Spirit will show us what's been prepared, and what's going to be available to us, in the near future. Show us what's in front of us and show us what you've set in place. Give us the courage, to reach for it, and the patience to wait on it. Make settling for less an unacceptable option. Make living beneath our privilege a thing of the past. Give us the means and the wherewithal to live full.

Holy Spirit, don't let us go back to living on E. Don't let us look at yesterday and because of the work required to live on a higher level, start to desire what was. Grant us the grace to see better, to want better, to do better and to be better. We want more, and we're not satisfied with who we were, where we were, and with what we had. That was not what you'd given to us. So, help us to live full, to stop running off fumes and the residue of past victories. In Jesus' name, AMEN!

MARCH 9

Psalm 911:11 (NASB): For He will give His angels orders concerning you, To protect you in all your ways.

NO FREAK ACCIDENTS

I plead the blood over every car, plane, train, bus, and any other means of transportation, and pray for divine protection against any and all freak accidents. No slip and falls, no bone breaks, fractures, joint or ligament damage, in Jesus' name!

I cover God's people with the blood, and pray against everything the devil plans to use, to upset our day, in Jesus' name I pray Amen!

MARCH 10

Psalm 118:17 (NASB): I will not die, but live, and tell of the works of the Lord.

I WILL NOT DIE

I set my faith in agreement with every person who's dealing with sickness and disease, and I release my faith for miracles! Today is as good a day as any, for God to heal my body. So, I choose, to believe, the report of the Lord! Father, your report says I am healed from breast cancer, HIV and Aids. Healed from every genetic, and hereditary illness! Healed from every disease to which mankind has no cure! I decree and declare; I WILL NOT DIE!

Today, I choose to believe, the report of the Lord! Your report says, I am filled! Filled with now faith! Filled with your spirit! Your report says I am free! Free from my past! Free from what I did! Free from what they did and from the pain and disappointment of what they didn't do!

I choose to believe, and I speak victory, over every situation today, in Jesus' name! I expect a miracle today! I expect the Lord who heals, Jehovah Rapha, to make a way, out of no way! I WILL NOT DIE!

Everywhere I go and everywhere I am today, I'm looking for miracles, signs, and wonders. It's in the mighty name of Jesus I pray, Amen! Amen! AMEN!

MARCH 11

Isaiah 43:18,19 (NASB): "Do not call to mind the former things, Or ponder things of the past. Behold, I will do something new, Now it will spring forth; Will you not be aware of it? I will even make a roadway in the wilderness, Rivers in the desert.

YOUR NAME IS ON IT

God's got a blessing with your name on it! So be still, Selah. Be still, so you can see that everything that's happening to you, is really working for you. That's my prayer today, that you won't be so busy running and doing, that you fail to see the small details, that God's put in your path to reassure you, that He's still with you. I pray for clear vision in the midst of warfare. I pray that the stuff that's blowing up around you; and the things that've lost their life, and their value won't distract you. I pray that they won't cause you to miss what God has set before you.

Be still and know! Be still and grow! Be still and go forward, with no fear. And you'll know the difference between what's God and what's a demonic decoy. Because what God has given you, will have your name on it. No fear. No regret. No guilt. No shame. This is your season to get over it. This is your season for a do over. This is your season to clapback, bounce back, and get back, everything you lost, squandered, and straight messed up. In Jesus' name, Amen, Amen and Amen!

MARCH 12

Colossians 3:17 (NASB): Whatever you do in word or deed, do all in the name of the Lord Jesus, giving thanks through Him to God the Father.

IF IT HAD NOT BEEN

Father I'm stopping, in the middle of attending to my business, to say "Thank you!" Thank you for helping me maintain my focus, and for keeping me on the cutting edge of my industry. Thank you, Holy Spirit, for giving me insight, wisdom, and for teaching me how to do everything I do with excellence.

Thank you, Father, for sending the teacher and for filling me with your spirit. It's the anointing that's making the difference! It's your presence that's on my life and your grace that's prevailing in everything I do, that's making the difference.

If it had not been, for the Lord, God Jehovah, who was on my side; I'd be unemployed and uninspired. Had it not been for you Lord, I'd be lost and losing. But thank God for favor!

I'm stopping to pray, I'm taking a break to praise because you just keep on, doing great things for me! Every time I turn around you keep blessing me! And for this, I give you praise! It's in Jesus' name I pray, AMEN!

MARCH 13

1 John 4:1 (NASB): Beloved, do not believe every spirit, but test the spirits to see whether they are from God, for many false prophets have gone out into the world.

FAKE NEWS

What the devil is trying to get you to accept, and respond to, is not the truth! It's fake news, and the question Holy Spirit is asking us is, "whose report will you believe?" How you approach today, will answer that million-dollar question. My prayer today is for patience, and that we will let patience, as James chapter 1, verse 4 says, "have its perfect work, that you may be perfect and complete, lacking nothing." I pray for an increase of faith, and that Holy Spirit would help our unbelief. I pray for refreshed discernment and that Holy Spirit would once again enable us to know the truth. And set the truth apart from the lies, and the fake news that the enemy is so desperately trying to get us to embrace.

I pray for endurance and fresh revelation; so that the enemy can no longer use our eyes to discourage us and shrink wrap our faith. I pray for refreshed discernment. I ask Holy Spirit to show us what's real, and what's a lie. Separate the truth from the lies and cause us to believe God again.

Don't let us settle because we're tired of fighting and weary of the struggle. Increase our faith and cause us to hope against hope again.

Uncover and expose every lie, and don't let the enemy use a bad report or fake news to draw us away from your word. Remind us. Say what you said about us, to us again. Cause your report to be thee report, that we hold on to. It's in Jesus' name we pray, Amen!

MARCH 14

Matthew 21:22 (NASB): And all things you ask in prayer, believing, you will receive."

GOD'S GOING TO DO IT

Miracles are assigned to this day! So, Father, in the name of Jesus, I thank you for healing my body and for touching my mind. I thank you for your healing and for using our family and our testimony to glorify you. I praise you for this place of grace, that's been created by the body of Christ. I praise you for allowing us to access your presence in such a way, that our bodies and our lives will manifest something miraculous and produce something supernatural.

We declare by faith, that we are walking in a season of miracles, signs, and wonders. And that not many days from now, the doctors will confirm medically, what we already know has happened spiritually! Healing is our birthright as believers, and so today we claim what rightfully belongs to us!

We plead the blood of Jesus, over every sickness, and over every disease, and we command it to go, in the name of Jesus! We curse cancer at the root! We curse every hereditary disease, and every disease that's been passed thru the blood!

We command arteries to open up, sugar levels, and blood pressure to regulate! We declare the power of God is present to heal, and we command miracles to manifest today, In the name of Jesus!

God's going to do it. God's going to make an open show of the enemy's defeat. God's going to restore the years we lost, fighting sickness. God's going to give us back every dollar we spent on medications and treatment.

I declare the words of Isaiah chapter 61, verse 7, over The Believer, "Instead of your shame you will have a double portion, and instead of humiliation they will shout for joy over their portion. Therefore, they will possess a double portion in their land, everlasting joy will be theirs." It's in Jesus' name I pray, Amen, Amen, and Amen!

MARCH 15

Ephesians 6:12 (NASB): For our struggle is not against flesh and blood, but against the rulers, against the powers, against the world forces of this darkness, against the spiritual forces of wickedness in the heavenly places.

WE ONLY HAVE ONE ENEMY

We only have one enemy, and if you can see them with your physical eye, they're not it. The accuser of the brethren is our enemy and my prayer is for revelation of truth. I pray that Holy Spirit would open our eyes, so we don't waste our time coming against people and flesh, instead of taking authority over our one enemy. Christians call his name way too much, so I intentionally refrain from saying it. But you know exactly who I'm referring to. We have but one enemy and it's not your boss, your ex and it's definitely not another Christian. So today I'm praying for Christians, who've been seduced into attacking one another. I pray for freedom from every seducing spirit that would illegitimately give you cause to fight against another believer. I pray that the spirit of truth would prevail. And that we do not continue to be lulled into fighting.

I know relationships aren't always easy, but I pray that we won't allow the commonalities of life to mislead us into making enemies out of our brothers and sisters. I pray for the church; that she would awake out of sleep and begin to cover and love one another, as Christ loves us all. I pray that love would prevail. That the same spirit that raised Jesus from the dead, would overtake Christians again. And cause us to see that we've been played, tricked, bamboozled, run amuck, led astray, and fooled into fighting the wrong fight. Holy Spirit refocus our energy and show us where the real fight is. Teach us to war and don't let us war against flesh and blood, but against our one and only enemy. In Jesus' name, Amen!

MARCH 16

1 Peter 3:9 (NASB): Not returning evil for evil or insult for insult, but giving a blessing instead; for you were called for the very purpose that you might inherit a blessing.

IT DID NOT TAKE YOU DOWN

It may have taken you through, but it did not take you down. Everything you've been through and everything that's happened to you, lifted you. It lifted your perspective, elevated your thinking, and birthed a commitment to self to never go back there ever again. I pray now, for the conviction to stay lifted, to keep your perspective higher and your thinking elevated, I pray that the only thing you'll be thirsty for is righteousness, and that you'll never chase after anybody else, but God.

Stay up there. Stay lifted. And let God turn every attack of the enemy, into an escalator! Let God use every hardship, and every bit of drama, to lift you up. Trust that God will not let it bring you down. Stay lifted in your heart, in your mind and in your soul. Don't let the enemy get you to thinking about payback and revenge. Stay up here, and let God deal with your enemies, because they can't fight you and not end up fighting God. Stay lifted in your thinking and in your approach to life, love, and the pursuit of happiness. That's my prayer for you today. That's my prayer for me today and for everybody connected to me. It's in Jesus' name I pray, Amen!

MARCH 17

1 Peter 2:2 (NASB): Like newborn infants, long for the pure spiritual milk, that by it you may grow up into salvation

---

LET IT GO

First Corinthians chapter 13, verse 11 says, "When I was a child, I used to speak like a child, think like a child, reason like a child; when I became a man, I did away with childish things." My prayer today, is that Holy Spirit would help us to grow up and that everything we've carried from childhood, into adulthood, would lose its grip on our lives, in the name of Jesus.

I pray for exponential growth, spiritually, socially, mentally, and financially. I pray that the issues of blood, that have passed from one generation to the next, would be broken off your life. I pray that the power of God would touch you, like never before. I pray for an encounter with God today, that gives you the strength to say, not anymore. I pray for the courage to tell your past, never again. I pray that the grace to let it go would be your portion, and that this time it'll take root!

I pray that God shuts every door, that would send you back into yesterday. I pray that the power of God comes on you so strong, that you have the strength to say I'm done. I pray for your spirit's eye, and that God would give you another glimpse of your future. I pray that that you will finally see for yourself, that your past and the stuff you're leaving behind, doesn't even come close to what's ahead. It's in Jesus' mighty name I pray, AMEN!

MARCH 18

Isaiah 54:17 (NASB) "No weapon that is formed against you will prosper; And every tongue that accuses you in judgment you will condemn. This is the heritage of the servants of the Lord, and their vindication is from me," declares the Lord.

ALL THINGS WORKING

I'm praying that every hard thing, and that every hard area of your life, would have to submit to the power of sacrifice, in Jesus' name. I pray that the power of God is demonstrated on your behalf quickly, and that what the enemy had purposed to work against you, would work for you, in Jesus' name. I pray for a quick breakthrough, speedy relief, and recovery, in Jesus' name!

Let God arise and His enemies be scattered. And let every weapon that was formed against you, cause those who'd previously judged you to become compassionate, loving and forgiving towards you. I pray for your heart and mind, and ask Holy Spirit to restore your focus, your spiritual and mental stamina, and your joy, in Jesus' name. We declare breakthrough, release, and elevation, today. It's in Jesus' name we pray, Amen!

MARCH 19

1 Peter 1:13 (NASB): Therefore, prepare your minds for action, keep sober in spirit, fix your hope completely on the grace to be brought to you at the revelation of Jesus Christ.

STAY ON GUARD

Holy Spirit, I need you and I'm praying that you would remove every distraction and anything that would cause me to miss what's coming. Don't let anything, good or bad, catch me sleeping. Don't let me be so entangled in "stuff", that I fail to see what's coming at me that could potentially set me back. Cause me to be sober, vigilant and show me what I need to do, to prepare myself for what's ahead. Sanctify my mind, remove the mental clutter, and the emotional baggage that would lull me to sleep causing me to come into a fight unprepared for my opponent. Show me what's about to hit my life. Show me who, or what I'm about to have to withstand. Give me strategy, and the structure needed to overcome the opposition.

Holy Spirit I need you and I trust you to keep me alert, aware and prepared! Help me and don't let the devil catch me off guard. Show me who I need to connect to. Show me what I need to do to thwart the coming attack. Please Lord, hide me in your presence. Don't let me get attacked without already being fully prepared to win. Don't give the devil opportunity to surprise me, sneak attack me or overwhelm me. Give me the tools and the resources I need, to make an open show of the enemy's defeat. Don't let anything, catch me off guard. In Jesus' name I pray, Amen!

MARCH 20

1 Corinthians 1:10 (NASB): Now I exhort you, brethren, by the name of our Lord Jesus Christ, that you all agree and that there be no divisions among you, but that you be made complete in the same mind and in the same judgment

UNITE THE CHURCH

This is my prayer for the body of Christ today, that we will not be ignorant of the devil's vices and keep attacking one another. I pray for wisdom, self-control, and that we'll learn how to love one another. That we'll pray for each other, before launching vicious attacks that are motivated by the accuser of the brethren.

Holy Spirit help us to model patience and love. Help us to afford other Christians the same mercy, that we would want for ourselves or for our children. Please Father, don't let us mistreat your children, or mishandle your purpose in their lives. Teach us to pray, prior to putting our mouths on people, that we didn't die for. Help us to model mercy and love and teach us to pray.

Father we need you, we need your wisdom, and we need your grace; so, the devil doesn't destroy us from the inside. Make us one, and don't let the devil pit churches against churches or preachers against preachers. Help the church and keep us out of the drama that the devil is using to turn people's hearts away from Jesus, and His Bride.

Help us to correct our behavior and change our minds, as it relates to how we deal with one another. Holy Spirit help the body of Christ, be the body, and keep us from fighting against one another, in Jesus' name! Don't let the way we've treated other Christians, be the reason why people won't receive the gospel of Jesus. Please Lord, Amen.

MARCH 21

2 Samuel 22:36 (NASB): "You have also given me the shield of Your salvation, And Your help makes me great.

HELP IS ON THE WAY

I pray your strength today, and that Holy Spirit keeps us in the right place, at the right time, surrounded by the right people. I pray for a drama free day today. And that the grace on your life would repel every negative voice from your space.

I pray for an ear to hear, and that you be so in tune to God's voice, that nothing gets by you today! I pray for help and that qualified, passionate, and compassionate people would be drawn to you.

I pray that the grace on your life would expel the life suckers. And the strength stealers from your work environment. I pray that people outside of your normal scope of influence would take to you.

I pray for unexpected help! I pray for unsolicited partners! And I declare strength, to every area where you've always been weak, today! It's in Jesus' name I pray, Amen.

MARCH 22

Proverbs 2:6 (NASB): For the LORD gives wisdom; from his mouth come knowledge and understanding.

YOU ARE SMARTER

I know the way I said it is crazy, but you get the point! Now pray this prayer with me; I have the mind of God! I'm created in His image and likeness, and the spirit of the almighty God, Elohim, dwells richly within me. This means I'm instinctively creative and innovative. I'm a creative genius! And what others have to begin creating with their hands and with their funds, I create with my faith, and with the words of my mouth. I'm not afraid of hard work, and my life is a testament to that. But this is the season of my life, where I work smarter and not harder. I'm a creative genius, and the spirit of the living God dwells richly within me.

Therefore, I call forth every idea, every necessary thought, and strategy. I pray for wisdom, for witty inventions, and business ideas. I pray for the eyes and ears of the learned. And that Holy Spirit would teach me how to think and not just process facts. Holy Spirit help me to think better and deeper. Teach me how to create with my mind, and with your spirit. Cause this anointing that's on my life, to produce something to better my life. Don't let me go another month, anointed, and not in my vein or in my lane! Teach me how to prosper. Show me how to win. Expand my thinking. Increase my capacity to reason and resolve. Let this mind be in me, that was also in Christ Jesus. Don't let anybody outthink me ever again! In Jesus', Amen!

MARCH 23

2 Corinthians 9:8 (NASB): And God is able to make all grace abound to you, so that always having all sufficiency in everything, you may have an abundance for every good deed;

MY BRAND IS BLESSED

Father I thank you for getting me through another day. For giving me the mental and spiritual strength to press past how I feel physically and emotionally. Thank you, Holy Spirit, for keeping me focused and giving me the inner strength to handle my business with excellence.

Thank you, Lord, for trusting me to represent your interests in the Earth. Thank you for making it impossible for me to fail! I give you praise, for the grace to be at the top of my game. A leader in my industry. And one of your best options on the planet.

I speak to my calendar, I speak to my clientele, and I command you to increase in quality, and not in quantity. I declare grace to work smarter and not harder! I decree and declare grace, for an increase in the value and the demand of my brand. My fees are increasing, and so is the stature of the people I serve and service, in Jesus' name! I'm getting better, not cheaper.

My brand, my anointing, my gift, and the grace that's on my life are in demand globally. In Jesus' name, AMEN!

MARCH 24

II Corinthians 1:20 (NASB): For no matter how many promises God has made, they are "Yes" in Christ. And so through him the "Amen" is spoken by us to the glory of God.

IT'S GETTING BETTER

I pray that you don't let the drama, or the stresses associated with growth to become distractions. You're headed in the right direction! You can get done what you need to get done, with the people who are already with you. All you need to do now, is stay focused, keep the main thing the main thing, and make a few minor adjustments.

Now Holy Spirit help us to stay focused and give us the strength to fight fear and the spirit of fatigue. Strengthen us where we're weak. And open our eyes so we can see the areas where we need to make the adjustments. Don't let us stay discouraged another day and restore our joy, in Jesus' name. We decree, and we declare, "things are getting better!" In Jesus' name I pray. Amen!

MARCH 25

Deuteronomy 28:7 (NASB): The LORD shall cause your enemies who rise up against you to be defeated before you; they will come out against you one way and will flee before you seven ways

THIS IS WAR

Don't expect the devil to play fair. This is war, and nothing about this journey is going to be fair. The God of all grace, according to First Peter chapter 5, verse 10, "Who called you to His eternal glory in Christ, after you have suffered for a little while, will Himself perfect, confirm, strengthen and establish you." So, hold on, because the trouble you're in, might be self-inflicted and it might be lingering, but the truth is, it won't last always. So, hold on to your faith, and keep your head up, because God's promised to never leave you, nor will He forsake you. Stop buying into the lie that you're alone or that nobody cares enough to walk you through it. That's a lie. You're God's child, and even though you've made mistake after mistake, He's right here with you. There is no temptation that's overtaken you, that He hasn't already made a way of escape.

The devil's a liar, but he can't beat you. This is war, and it isn't fair, but God told me to remind you whose side you're on. You're on the winning side. You're already on the winning side. Although you may have lost a battle or two, or three, you cannot lose, because Jesus has already won for you. To God be the glory. Don't expect the fight to be fair. You just stay sober and vigilant.

Stay in God's presence and keep your eyes on Jesus. Let Holy Spirit keep you, and don't let your feelings lead you astray. In the name of Jesus, we have the victory, Amen!

MARCH 26

Psalms 34:4 (NASB): I sought the LORD, and He answered me, And delivered me from all my fears.

BETTER IS HERE

Good morning Holy Spirit! I'm so glad that you're here! I'm so glad, that I can sense your presence, and that you've once again, kept your word. The promise is that you will never leave me, nor forsake me. So, I thank you today, that for the rest of the day, you will be right here with me. I praise you for your abiding presence and that I don't have to ask or beg you to come, because you're already here! Thank you for sustaining our relationship. For being consistent in it, even when I was tripping, and acting out. I don't know why you love me like you do, but I'm so glad that you do! And so, I praise you today, that our relationship only gets better from here!

I bless your name and I know my life can only get better from here! My confession of faith, and my prophetic prayer is, "BETTER IS HERE!" It's not coming, it's already here! And things are going to get better! I decree, and I declare, "It only, gets better from here!" Better is my daily bread! Better is my portion! Better is my inheritance! Better is my endgame! Better is my mantle! Better is what I produce! Better is what I release! And my life must align itself with what I'm carrying. So, my health is BETTER! My finances are BETTER! Every one of my relationships are BETTER! Today is already BETTER, than yesterday! And it's in Jesus' name I pray, AMEN!

MARCH 27

Romans 12:12 (NASB): Rejoice in hope, be patient in tribulation, be constant in prayer.

THINK, THEN SPEAK

Your words matter. What you say is law. So please be on the watch for words, that are dictated by your feelings and by what you see with your natural eye. You cannot afford to say anything that's contrary to what God has said and opposite of what your faith is about to produce. You are much closer than you think you are. The enemy of your soul wants to use your mouth to cancel or postpone the manifestation of what God's got planned for your future. Please know that "keeping it real", is overrated and immature at times. It is a tactic that the enemy uses to hold you captive in your past. Don't fall for the trick of the enemy, again. You've been thru enough now to know when you're being set up, and when you're about to walk into something that's going to change your life for the better.

I command you to think before you speak. I call your mouth subject to God's word and to God's will. Keep it real but speak from revelation and truth and not from frustration and hurt. Keep it real, but say what God has said, not your competition. Keep it real, but don't let your faith succumb to your flesh. Think and think again. Think like God thinks, and then speak, like God spoke. I command your creative genius to flow, and I decree and declare that this is the season you create your reality, with the words of your mouth. In Jesus' name, Amen!

MARCH 28

I Corinthians 15:57 (NASB): But thanks [be] to God, which giveth us the victory through our Lord Jesus Christ.

THEY MUST RESPOND

Nothing is safe, and it feels like everything is under attack, but I don't believe God brought us this far to leave us. God's got a plan, and as we fast, pray and obey His voice, our obedience is going to provoke the power of God on our behalf. These storms are God's way of getting the nation back at His feet. My prayer is that no one who obeys, will lose anything that cannot be replaced, in Jesus' name. I pray for divine intervention, and for divine interruption of the enemy's plans. I pray for wisdom to survive and for grace to overcome. I declare that our obedience is causing a shift in the direction of the wind. I decree that our willingness to obey God is turning the eye of the storm. And the only things that will be lost, will be the things we didn't need, want, and could no longer use.

Nothing valuable, nor precious to us will be lost in the storm, in Jesus' name. When this storm is over, we'll be able to move forward and into what God's promised us, without the anxiety, without the fear and without the pressure, that running from Pharaoh added to our lives. The waters must respond to our obedience and what became a "way out of no way" for us, will become a dead end for all our enemies. It's in Jesus' mighty name I pray, Amen!

MARCH 29

Romans 8:31 (NASB): What then shall we say to these things? If God is for us, who is against us?

I WILL NOT BE BROKEN

Father I thank you, for waking me up this morning, and for making sure I have my right mind! Thank you, Holy Spirit, for keeping me, and for not allowing what I'm dealing with to break my spirit.

Thank you, Lord, that the pressure didn't make me snap. And that the pain didn't make me lose my sanity. Thank you, Holy Spirit, for showing yourself strong on my behalf, and for rebuking the devil for my sake! Thank you, for exposing the lies, that the enemy has been trying to pass off as the truth.

Thank you, Father, for keeping the whole truth before me and for making sure I never settled for half-truths and whole lies! The truth has made me free! Free from depression! Free from suicidal thoughts! Free from sickness! Free from anger! Free from jealousy, and envy! Free from poverty! Free from what they did to me! Free from what they say to me! Free from what they've said about me!

I AM FREE! My mind is free! My spirit is free, and because I'm free, now I choose to believe the report of The Lord! His report says I'm healed! His report says I'm free! And that's what I'm going to be, In Jesus' name I pray, AMEN!

MARCH 30

Psalm 34:8 (NASB): But thanks be to God, which giveth us the victory through our Lord Jesus Christ.

ISSA TRAP

I know people you've trusted have turned on you and I know the attacks came unexpectedly. But you cannot fall apart and go back to doing things in your flesh! Issa trap and the enemy is using the possibility of you losing everything, to try to pressure you into leaving everything that God's assigned you to. God told me to tell you, Issa distraction, not a dead end, and you are not going to lose anything by taking a stand for God.

I'm asking Holy Spirit to give you peace in the fire. I pray for grace to hold it together and that even though you're still tied up, you won't burn up. I pray for grace to pass the fear test. And that watching others be consumed by what was set up to consume you, will cause you to recognize that Issa trap. Holy Spirit don't let the fire burn us up, but make it lift us up in the eyes of those that have attacked us and turned on us.

Let's pray for one another today, expecting to see miracles, signs, and wonders, believing that this moment of distraction, will become an "ahha" moment. We pray for grace to endure the heat, understanding that God is cooking something.

God's using the fire to elevate us in the eyes of a nation. I pray for grace to hold it together, while everybody else around us is being consumed. I pray that the person, place, or thing that attacked us, will have to bless us and our God. Whatever tried to take us out, will have to take us in, and cause to us prosper. It's in Jesus' name, Amen!

MARCH 31

Romans 8:26-27 (NASB): "In the same way, the Spirit helps us in our weakness. We do not know what we ought to pray for, but the Spirit himself intercedes for us with groans that words cannot express. And he who searches our hearts knows the mind of the Spirit, because the Spirit intercedes for the saints in accordance with God's will"

PRAY FOR ME

Pray for me as I pray for you, that Holy Spirit will cleanse our natural and spiritual pallets. And refresh the desires of our hearts, so that we desire only what His will is for our lives. I pray that Holy Spirit open my eyes and scrubs my inner ear of everything religious, and wrong, in Jesus' name. I pray that our ability to hear without any mental clutter will increase exponentially and overnight, so that our next move, is the right move.

I pray that all people distractions be removed and replaced by the people who are assigned to this season of our lives to cover us and bless us. I pray that every mistake, becomes an opportunity for God to demonstrate His sovereignty, mercy, and love toward us. What should've locked us out, will be overcome by purpose, destiny, grace, and mercy. It's in Jesus' name we pray, Amen!

APRIL

APRIL 1

Isaiah 41:13 (NASB): For the Lord thy God will hold thy right hand, saying unto thee, Fear not; I will help thee.

PRESS YOUR WAY

Turning around has to become a non-option! You are too vested and too close to consider going back to Pharaoh. Your promise is not back there, it's up here. So, press your way. I pray that pressing becomes your determination, and that the promise of the Father becomes your motivation. I pray for grace to resist, grace to stand, and an increase of your ability to tolerate pain, without distraction. I pray for a laser focus on the promise, and the grace to professionally manage the pain.

I pray for patience, perseverance, and the voluntary increase in our prayer life. The word of the Lord to us is, "Press your way!" So, we praise God for strength, for clear minds, and clean hearts. We gird up our loins with truth, cover our hearts with righteousness, our feet with the gospel and we take up the shield of faith as we cover our minds with the realities of what Jesus did at Calvary. We put on the full armor of God, and we press, because the promise has already been secured. It's in Jesus' name we pray, Amen!

APRIL 2

Matthew 21:22 (NASB): If you believe, you will receive whatever you ask for in prayer.

IT'S ABOUT TO BREAK

I woke up this morning and I heard the Lord say, "Wait, it's about to break!" This word is your word. I'm not sure what it is or how long it's been dragging on, but if you just hold on, things are about to get better. Say it, so you can have it, "It's about to break!" We speak to every stronghold and negative, low-line mindset and way of thinking, and we command you to break! We speak to lack, and to the spirit of poverty, and "just enough", and we command you to break. We put on the garment of praise and we speak to the spirit of heaviness, and depression, and we command you to break.

We speak to the spirit of infirmity, that has attacked our bodies and gained access to us physically, generationally, and culturally, and we command you to break! We speak to the spirit of lasciviousness and low self-esteem, and we command you to break! Set the captives free today, in Jesus' name. Pharaoh, we command you to lose God's people, and let His sons and daughters go free, in Jesus' name. We decree and declare that patience will have its perfect work today, that the fruits of frustration wither away today, and the children of God walk in joy, and in peace today. In Jesus' name we pray, Amen!

APRIL 3

Proverbs 18:21NASB): Death and life are in the power of the tongue, And those who love it will eat its fruit.

GUARD MY TONGUE

Please Lord, cover and control my tongue today, and don't let me say anything I don't mean, or anything that's going to hurt somebody I love.

Holy Spirit guard my heart, my mind, and my mouth, and do not, I'm begging Lord, do not allow to me to cuss anybody out today! In fact, Father, expand my vocabulary, and give me the grace to say what I need to say, but like a Christian would say it.

Thank you, Lord, that today you're going to help me twice! Power's coming on my thoughts, and my tongue! Power's coming on my mind and my mouth!

Power is coming to my family, and my finances! Today! I pray for your help again! I'm praying for your help Lord, in a double portion! In Jesus' name I pray, Amen! Amen! AMEN!

APRIL 4

Philippians 3:10 (NASB): that I may know Him and the power of His resurrection and the fellowship of His sufferings, being conformed to His death;

RESSURECTION

The same spirit that raised Jesus from the dead, is the same spirit, and the same grace that is upon my life. So, I speak to my body, my spirit, my soul, and I command you to live! In the name of Jesus, I speak life and resurrection power to everything in my life that died prematurely. I decree and declare life to everything God wants to live, and I prophesy turn arounds in every situation and in every circumstance, NOW!

This is my season to come back from the dead. This is my season to shut the mouth of every naysayer and every doubter. This is the season of my life where what should've killed me, is going to make my name great.

So, I endure my Gethsemane, and I endure my Calvary, for the joy that is set before me, this is NOT the end! I will rise again, and the next time I get up, I'm getting up with power. I'm getting up with power and I'll be walking in purpose. It's in Jesus' name I pray, AMEN!

APRIL 5

I Samuel 12:24 (NASB): Only fear the LORD and serve him in truth with all your heart: for consider how great [things] he hath done for you.

PHARAOH'S LAST DAY

The running, the living in fear and the contemplating going back to Egypt is over. God told Moses in Exodus chapter 14, verse 13, to speak to the Israelites, and to tell them, "Do not fear! Stand by and see the salvation of the Lord which He will accomplish for you today; for the Egyptians whom you have seen today, you will never see them again forever." I claim that same grace for you, for your family and for everything and everybody connected to your future. I decree and declare; this is Pharaoh's last day. The enemy you have seen, you will never see again. And whatever has been pursuing you, trying to force you back into who, and where you used to be, is about to encounter the power of God, and they, or it will not survive.

So, no fear because not only is God with you, but God is for you! Start preparing yourself mentally to possess what God promised you. Set your spiritual house in order, because you're about to come into health, wealth, and prosperity, like you could've never imagined. You're about to hit your overflow, and life as you once knew it, will never be the same. Today is your Pharaoh's last day, so I pray that you don't start missing living life on the run. I pray that the thrill of the chase doesn't become your drug of choice.

I pray that living free from the past, and from how it was attractive to you, and that you find contentment with living in peace. The fights and the foolishness end today. And I pray that freedom doesn't bore you, but that it pushes you closer to God. In Jesus' name I pray. Amen, and Amen!

APRIL 6

Proverbs 14:27 (NASB): The fear of the LORD is a fountain of life, turning a man from the snares of death.

DON'T QUIT

You are closer now than when you first believed. So now is not the time to be thinking about settling or quitting. If it's not what God promised, if you're not where God promised, then it's time to dig in, get your mind right and walk by faith. God is not a liar. Everything He said to you, is still the truth. Every word He's spoken to you, and over you, will come to pass. So, I'm praying that patience will have her perfect work and that you never feel incomplete, or uncovered, ever again.

I pray for endurance, and increased spiritual stamina, so that you stay the course. I rebuke the spirit of the quitter and I command you to stand fast in the faith. I command you to put on your strength, and to push back against every negative, discouraging report, in the name of Jesus. Don't quit, be strong and very courageous. Don't quit, be sober, and in everything give thanks. If you do not faint, if you do not grow weary, if you do not quit, you will reap in due season. It's in Jesus' name I pray, AMEN!

APRIL 7

James 1:5 (NASB): But if any of you lacks wisdom, let him ask of God, who gives to all generously and without reproach, and it will be given to him.

I HAVE THE KNOW HOW

You do have options, choose better, you really do! I pray that Holy Spirit would open your eyes and cause you to see that you are not trapped, and that God has already made a way of escape!

I pray for revelation and for wisdom! I pray that your mind would explode with creativity, and that your gifts would continue to make room for you! I pray for favor with the kings, and with the decision makers. I pray that God would place you on the hearts of the people who control the purse. And that Holy Spirit would lead them to help you, and to help fund your dreams!

I speak a season of grace over you, and that the power of God would touch you, and give you "know how", and skills beyond what you've been trained to do! I pray that supernaturally, The Spirit of God would overtake you, and cause you to know what to do, and to know what to say!

It's in Jesus' name I pray, that you would never again feel out of options, or like the walls are closing in on you! In Jesus' name, Amen, Amen, and Amen!

APRIL 8

Psalms 65:11 (NASB): You have crowned the year with Your bounty, And Your paths drip with fatness.

BLESS MY BUSINESS

Father, I thank you for the gifts and talents that you have given me to make a business for myself. I declare today over strategic alignment for my business. I declare that I will generate revenue from every continent, and from multiple countries.

I'm in demand! People are looking for me, to bless me, and to secure my services from all over the world!

My gift is crossing genres, causing industries to collab, and birthing new products and innovative concepts and ideas. What God's graced me to do: helps people, encourages people, rescues people, preserves people, and generates millions of dollars! In Jesus' name!

I'm going to work my grace without distraction. I will not struggle emotionally, nor financially, ever again! It's in the mighty name of Jesus I pray, AMEN!

APRIL 9

*Jeremiah 29:11 (NASB): For I know the plans that I have for you,'
declares the LORD, 'plans for welfare and not for calamity to
give you a future and a hope.*

HIS PERFECT PLAN

Father I thank you for providing a window of time for me to sit
and reflect, and to appreciate just how good my life truly is.
Things may not be perfect, but your plan is. I just wanted to
pause for a minute to say thank you!

I'm just pressing my way through, but I just want to thank you,
because my life is way better than so many people, who are
smarter than me. People who are better connected than me,
better behaved than me, and better at what they do than me.
But because my relationship with you is growing, I'm at peace,
and I have joy down in my soul!

Thank you! Things aren't perfect, but your plan is! So tonight,
and for the rest of my days, I choose your peace. I choose your
joy. I choose your way, over my way, and I say "YES", again, and
again, and again! And Father let my "yes" please your heart, till
we're both satisfied! In Jesus' name I pray, AMEN!

APRIL 10

Kings 17:8-16 (NASB): Wait on the Lord: be of good courage, and he shall strengthen thine heart: wait, I say, on the Lord.

I HAVE GOOD IDEAS

Because we trust the principle of honoring spiritual leadership with our seed and because we trust the prophet who has been divinely assigned to our lives, and because we've decided to trust the provider who has never failed us. Let's confess this together, "I will never run out of God ideas!" We claim the grace of Elijah, decreeing and declaring that God is going to command somebody to provide for me, in Jesus' name. Because we have a seed in the ground and because we choose to trust the principle, we believe God Is raising up somebody to use their power, influence, resources, and ability to help us. This is the season where what's in our hands, never runs out. This is the season where what's on our life, never runs dry.

I speak a river of creative genius and wisdom over the faithful. I speak to your creative juice and I command it to flow without hindrance. I speak to the creator in you and I command him to flow, in Jesus' name. I speak to your ability to think, reason, discover solutions and solve problems, and I command it to increase and go flow like water. You will never run out of God ideas. What you use to make money with, will never be exhausted, and the oil on your life will never run dry. You're creative, attractive to the shot callers and anointed by God! Your gifts are making room for you. Your gifts are making money for you. Your gift is making your name great. So, be at peace, change is coming. Reclaim your joy, help is on the way, and trust the provider to supply all your needs, according to His riches in glory. It's in Jesus' name I pray, Amen!

APRIL 11

John 16:13 (NASB): But when He, the Spirit of truth, comes, He will guide you into all the truth; for He will not speak on His own initiative, but whatever He hears, He will speak; and He will disclose to you what is to come.

SPEAK HOLY SPIRIT

Good morning Holy Spirit, this is my official invitation to you, for you to walk with me all day today. I give you permission to speak up, and to butt in, whenever you deem it necessary. Don't let me think, or say, or do, anything that's out of your will for my life today.

Fix my broken heart today! Regulate my mind today and cause my thoughts to say "YES" to everything that you're doing. Give me the courage to "think myself happy", through every challenge, and through every hardship.

Holy Spirit cause me to be clear about your will for my life, and then cause me to remain focused. Let me not be distracted by the things that do not matter. In Jesus' name I pray, AMEN

APRIL 12

Proverbs 18:10 (NASB): The name of the Lord is a fortified tower, the righteous run to it and are safe.

BY THE TIME YOU WAKE UP

By the time you wake up, things are going to be different. By the time you get up, things are going to be better. So, go to sleep knowing that He never sleeps nor slumbers. And while you're sleeping, God's going to be moving things and people into place so that tomorrow is a better day than today. Go to sleep encouraged tonight, knowing that while you're asleep, God's plan to bless you, will be providentially shifting things in your favor. So, go to sleep, get some rest, and expect to wake up to a miracle.

Be at peace tonight, and let your mind rest for once, because all night long, the hand of God will be at work on your behalf. Wake up expecting to see signs and wonders. Wake up expecting to see something you've never seen. Stop scrolling, stop lurking and close your eyes, free from fear and anxiety. By the time you wake up, it'll already be done, now go to sleep. In Jesus' name I pray, Amen!

APRIL 13

I Corinthians 15:3-4 (NASB): For what I received I passed on to you as of first importance: that Christ died for our sins according to the Scriptures, that he was buried, that he was raised on the third day according to the Scriptures.

NO MORE FEAR

Today begins your fear free season, in Jesus' name! Everything that had you in a holding pattern and stuck in yesterday, is being broken off your life. Today is a breakthrough kind of day, and everything that used to hold you back and hold you captive, loses its fake authority over your life, today. I pray that the power of God becomes real to you again, and that today you have an encounter with God that changes you, from the inside out. I pray for an awakening in your spirit and that you finally realize that what you thought you saw, was False Evidence Appearing Real!

Your enemy cannot defeat you. Your enemy cannot win. So, confess this with me, "I have no reason to fear! I have no reason to consider losing, ever again. Every time they see me, they're going to see me winning, in Jesus' name." So be encouraged today. Walk by faith today. Take a chance today. Believe God again today. Be free today because the false evidence has been debunked. The report of the enemy has been proven wrong. God's about to make you a miracle, a sign, and a wonder, before the year is over. In Jesus' name, Amen!

APRIL 14

Ephesians 6:13 (NASB): Therefore put on the full armor of God, so that when the day of evil comes, you may be able to stand your ground, and after you have done everything, to stand.

GOD SPOKE IT

Numbers chapter 23, verse 19 says, "God is not a man, that He should lie", and that settles the issue. If He spoke it, it will come to pass. So today, I pray for a fresh ear and that we won't allow impatience to cause us to start questioning what we know we heard. I pray that patience will have her perfect work and that waiting on the Lord becomes easier for us.

I pray for our eyes and ears to come open again, so we can hear and see what we need to in order to maintain our posture of faith. I pray that the word He spoke gets louder and clearer, every day, until all fear and doubt is gone. In Jesus' name I pray, Amen!

APRIL 15

Exodus 30:31 (NASB): You shall speak to the sons of Israel, saying, 'This shall be a holy anointing oil to Me throughout your generations.

ANOINT MY GIFTS

Everybody wants to be successful, but everybody's not willing to do, what the successful have done. So, I'm praying that God will give you wisdom, and a willing heart. I'm praying that God connects you with a true spiritual father, who will confirm and cover the grace that's on your life. I'm praying for you today, that your soul be free from the spiritual abuse, and the misuse of your gift. And that Holy Spirit would make you free from any and all church hurt, and any emotional baggage you're still carrying, in Jesus' name.

I pray that the grace on your life, finds it way home. To that place and that money, or unforgiveness, never again be the thing that prevents you from serving your real spiritual father's vision.

I pray that the work of Malachi chapter 4, be accomplished in your heart, and that God will turn the hearts of the fathers to the children, and the hearts of the children to their fathers, in Jesus' name. So that whatever pain remains from your childhood, or your past relationships, would be consumed in the safety of the Father's love. It's in Jesus' name I pray, Amen!

APRIL 16

Proverbs 21:1 (NASB): In the Lord's hand the king's heart is a stream of water that he channels

NO MORE TEARS

I heard the Lord say, "stop weeping! You're crying over something that's about to become your claim to fame! You're depressed over something that I'm about to completely turn around, in just a matter of days!" So, get yourself together, as best as you can, because God is about to make you a miracle, a sign, and a wonder. Stop your crying, because although your situation is bad, it is not beyond the scope of what God is able to do.

I pray for peace to persevere, until Jesus gets to your house. I pray that Holy Spirit will protect your ears, and not allow the bad news, nor the negativity to penetrate your soul. I pray for revelation, and patience. I pray that the truth will make you free. So those tears of sorrow and sadness, will be transformed in God's presence, in Jesus' name. I pray that those who have sown in tears, will reap in joy and that before this calendar year is over, that Jesus will have turned your mourning into dancing. I speak to every situation and circumstance, and I command it to come under God's will. I decree and declare, "no more fears and no more tears, because God's going to wipe, all of our tears away." It's in Jesus' name I pray, Amen!

APRIL 17

Acts 20:24 (NASB): But I do not consider my life of any account as dear to myself, so that I may finish my course and the ministry which I received from the Lord Jesus, to testify solemnly of the gospel of the grace of God.

FINISH STRONG

I pray your strength today and I pray for the wisdom, and the courage, to separate yourself from everything, and everybody that consistently takes from you, and never gives anything in return. I pray for freedom from ever leach, and from every bloodsucking relationship, that robs you of quality of life.

I pray for the will to break free from, and the desire to want to be free from, every person that you care for, but the feelings are not reciprocated. I pray for discernment to know when someone's trying to play you, and for the wisdom to use their ill intentions as fuel for the journey ahead.

I pray you find peace in God's will, and that nothing will be able to steal your joy, nor rob you of your energy. I speak strength to you, and I declare, "You are not going to finish this year exhausted, nor beaten down, and you are not going to end the year without any money!"

You're going to finish this year strong! I speak strength to your faith! Strength to your mind! Strength to your bones! Strength to your body! Strength to your finances! Strength to your family!

I speak strength, grace, and favor to your hands. I declare that whatever you put your hands to, will prosper. It's in Jesus' name I pray, Amen!

APRIL 18

Psalms 77:14 (NASB): You are the God who performs miracles; you display your power among the peoples.

I DECLARE MIRACLES

The next 3 months will be filled with miracles, with signs, and with wonders, and what God does for you in the next 3 months, is going to make up for what happened to you, over the last 12 years. I heard the Lord clearly, and He said to tell you to expect a miracle, everyday! God's about to restore the years and revive everything that you thought was dead.

So, be encouraged, Jesus is in your house. He's about to take you by the hand and walk you out of that dead, dark place, into a supernatural place and make you a sign to your circle, that Jesus is real and He's still working miracles. No more bad years. No more living in fear and in torment. This is your time to live, and to be free. In Jesus' name I pray, Amen!

APRIL 19

Ephesians 2:8 (NASB): For it is by grace you have been saved, through faith--and this is not from yourselves, it is the gift of God

FOCUS ON MY FUTURE

Yesterday is over and there isn't anything we can do about it. So, let's commit to one another tonight. That starting right now, we're going to take our attention away from what's behind us, away from what they did, what we did, and set our affections on things above and what God has prepared for us. Let's cover one other and pray that we'll find the courage to let go of the pain, shifting our attention from the negativity, and turning our hearts to God. Knowing that His thoughts of us are good, and His plans have eternally secured our future.

I pray that you go to sleep tonight, knowing that tomorrow is going to be better than today. That you walk thru your day tomorrow with your head up high, knowing that you are loved and set up for something supernatural, in Jesus' name. What's coming is better. What's behind you is done with and nothing they throw in your face can stop God's will for your life from coming to pass! I pray that you'll agree to focus forward and forget. I pray that you'll resolve to let it go and pick up what you've been sleeping on and walk it out, because God's about to blow your mind. Your life will never be the same if you will only believe. It's in Jesus' name I declare these things to be. Amen!

APRIL 20

James 1:2-4 (NASB): Consider it pure joy, my brothers and sisters, whenever you face trials of many kinds, because you know that the testing of your faith produces perseverance. Let perseverance finish its work so that you

YOU'RE NOT LEFT OUT

Holy Spirit just told me to tell you, you will not be left out! Yes, you've made mistakes. Yes, you've ran out of gas. And yes, you couldn't do everything that everybody else did, but you will not lose your place in line. God's going to put you in the hearts of the people who control the resources. He's going to cause them to look upon you favorably. So, don't let the devil keep you all up in arms, over a lie. What you did do, meant something to somebody, and that somebody is about to come back and bless you for what you did. So, stop tripping in your mind and stop stressing over what was taken away from you, because God's about to give it all back, plus some.

Holy Spirit help us to hold on to our faith, even though technically we didn't finish. Help us Holy Spirit to stay in faith, and not lose heart. Help us to stop comparing ourselves to other people and to what they did, or what we didn't do. Help us to stay in faith and stop blaming ourselves and other people, for what hasn't happened. Help our unbelief, teach us to still believe, and stay in faith for miracles, even after we've blown it. We got left behind, but because you're leaning in our direction, we will not be left out. It's in Jesus name I pray, Amen!

APRIL 21

Hebrews 10:35-36 (NASB): Therefore, do not throw away your confidence, which has a great reward. For you have need of endurance, so that when you have done the will of God, you may receive what was promised.

COMING BACK STRONG

You are not finished, because what God's done for you, is not finished being revealed. So, quitting, giving up, settling, or going back, is not something that you're going to consider. Hebrews chapter 10, verse 35 and 36 says this, "...Therefore, do not throw away your confidence, which has a great reward. For you have need of endurance, so that when you have done the will of God, you may receive what was promised." The promise is that God will never leave you, nor forsake you. That He will never, put more on you, than you're able to bare. That He'll make a way of escape. And that even though He's allowed the enemy to sift you as wheat I pray that your faith will not fail and that you will bounce back, better!

I pray for you today, that your faith will flow like a river. That your confidence in our God will well up in your soul and overflow. It's not over. You're coming back. The devil hasn't seen the last of you. You are not going to die; you're coming back strong! So, I command you to be strong, and very courageous!

I command you to rise up and get back in your place! Be strong! In Jesus' name I pray!

APRIL 22

Psalm 107:28-30 (NASB): Then they cried to the LORD in their trouble, and he delivered them from their distress. He made the storm be still, and the waves of the sea were

NEVER OUT OF GRACE

You may have run out of gas, but you never ran out of grace! God has already put preemptive measures in place to secure your future. So be encouraged today, because even though you're exhausted, you will not be excluded. So, I'll be praying for you today and praying with you, believing for favor with the king. Praying that when people attempt to blackball you and convince others that you shouldn't participate when the harvest comes in, that Holy Spirit will turn the heart of the shot caller in your favor. I pray that what you did do, counts for something, and that the enemy doesn't take away the effects of what you've already done.

I pray for favor with the king and the shot caller, so that your name stays on the list. I pray for the fruits of faithfulness to come to bare and that God restores everything that was lost or stolen, plus some. I pray that this season of restoration, ends with you refreshed and with more in your hands than you started with. I pray for overflow and renewed strength. I pray that God upsets every hater and every judge. And that God uses your life as a present demonstration of His mercy and love.

Have a super day today, knowing that you're already in the season of plus some. Smile at your haters today, and anybody who tries to push your buttons, because they're only indicators that you're closer now than you've ever been before. That's your portion in this season. In Jesus' name I pray, Amen!

APRIL 23

Philippians 4:19 (NASB): And my God will meet all your needs according to the riches of his glory in Christ Jesus

---

PLUS SOME

I know you ran out of gas, and others have judged you, and counted you unworthy, but God. I know you feel like you blew it. Like you don't deserve anything more because you didn't have the strength to fight, but God said to tell you, "fighting isn't your assignment in this season." Your assignment is to stand guard over what remains. To protect what's left, even if it doesn't belong to you. This is the season of your life where God sends people to fight for you. And not only to retrieve what was lost or stolen, but to bring back some things that you've never had.

I pray that you overcome the spirit of grief and low self- esteem. I pray that Holy Spirit shines a light on your path. That you fully understand your assignment for this season. And that you don't get caught up in other people's opinions about what they think you should be doing. I pray for clarity, as relates to the grace that you have for today and that you don't start doing stuff you have no grace for, because of peer pressure. I pray that you get clear on your call to protect the baggage and that God raises up somebody to use their power, influence and ability, to help you and to bless you. I speak the blessing of the Lord over the fatigued, over the forsaken and most importantly, over the faithful, in Jesus' name. You will not just get what's coming to you, but I heard the Lord say, "plus some!" The spoils from your enemy's camp is coming to your house, and even though you didn't fight the last fight; you will get the next harvest, and it's going to put you in overflow. You've been faithful to that which God gave you to do and now you're about to have something you've never had. Everything you lost and everything that was stolen, plus some! It's in Jesus' name we pray, Amen!

APRIL 24

Proverbs 1:5 (NASB): A wise man will hear and increase in learning, And a man of understanding will acquire wise counsel

TAKE TIME TO LISTEN

Shhhh, slow down and be still. Holy Spirit is speaking, and if you will be intentional about listening, you're going to hear God's voice like you've never heard Him before. Now let's agree that every distraction, every contrary voice, every negative and outside influence, would lose its grip on your heart and on your mind. Let's agree for a fresh ear and the ability to block out alternative sounds and voices. I set my faith in agreement with you, that in the next couple of weeks, you will have heard God's voice so clearly, that all fear and uncertainty about God's plan for your life and your future, will be gone.

I pray that Holy Spirit speaks above the fray and above the frustration. I pray for a renewed passion to pursue God and to spend time alone in His presence. I pray that the fear of being alone with God goes away and that you find yourself at peace every time He shows up for you. God speak clearly. Let your voice drown out every other voice, especially the voice of our flesh. Increase our ability to discern your voice as we take the time to listen, and to weed thru the noises of life. Speak to our hearts. Talk to us until we choose to never listen to fear again. Speak to us until we choose to live and walk by faith. Don't let anything contrary to your promise escape the filter of Holy Spirit. Protect our ears, guard our hearts, and renew our strength, as we purposefully listen for your voice In Jesus', Amen!

APRIL 25

Psalms 46:10 (NASB): He says, "Be still, and know that I am God; I will be exalted among the nations, I will be exalted in the earth."

YOU'RE GOING TO SEE ME WINNING

This is your winning season. So, don't let what you see with your natural eye dictate how you feel about your future. This is your season to win. This is your season to overcome. This is your season to breakthrough. So, I pray that your faith won't fail and that you will stop making plans to lose. Losing may be a part of your testimony, but it is not a part of your future. So, I pray for you today, that your feelings won't cause your faith to fade and stop making plans to lose. Your situation is not going to end up like the devil wants you to believe.

I pray that Holy Spirit will help your unbelief and that the opposition backfires, and causes your faith to increase, in Jesus' name. I pray that you'll find the strength of will, to look to the hills and to look to the author and the finisher of your faith. I command you to look up. I command you to lift up your head. I command your spirit to rise up, speak up, and grow up, in Jesus' name. Your test is producing a testimony and soon you'll be able to tell the doubters, "every time you look up, you gone see me winning!" It's in Jesus' name I pray, AMEN!

APRIL 26

Ecclesiastes 7:8 (NASB): The end of a matter is better than its beginning; Patience of spirit is better than haughtiness of spirit.

GRACE TO BE ME

I'm praying that you have the courage to fully express yourself, and to share your truth, and your honest perspective with the people you love, without offending them. I'm praying that Holy Spirit gives you the grace to articulate your heart, how you feel, and how you've been made to feel by their actions, without pointing the finger or making everything their fault.

I pray that you finally have the courage to look at yourself, and that Holy Spirit would lovingly show you the "real" you. The you that He loves. The you that Jesus died for. The you that's still worth saving. I pray that you would embrace you and begin to unconditionally love yourself and begin to treat yourself better.

I pray for an awakening in your soul, and that you don't waste another day beating yourself up, for how you look, or for how you're shaped, or for what you can't do, or for what you've done. I pray for the courage to forgive yourself, and the people in your life, and in your past life who've hurt you. I pray that what they've done, never affects you in a negative way or what you do, ever again. Thank you for fixing our hearts, and changing our minds, before allowing us to cross over into the New Year, it's in Jesus' mighty name I pray, Amen!

APRIL 27

Ecclesiastes 3:1 (NASB): There is a time for everything, and a season for every activity under the heavens:

WE MUST WORSHIP YOU

It's time to put on the garment of praise, in exchange for the spirit of heaviness. It's time for you to get that weight off of you and find peace in the presence of the Lord. So Holy Spirit we say yes, and we invite you into our personal space again. We say yes, Holy Spirit and we give you permission to have your way and do whatever you need to do, to help us get our joy back. In Jesus' name, we set our affections on you again and we set on hope on you. We focus on you, and we take our attention away from the pressure and the pain, and we make you our focus again. No more distractions. No more pity parties. No more blaming others. No more feeling sorry for ourselves. We're going to use our perfected praise to shut the enemy down. We've been through too much, and we've seen you do too much, not to worship.

We cast down the spirit of weariness and defeat, and we choose to believe your report. We praise you in advance. We bless you before we see it. We honor you, before we actually have it. Our souls make their boasts in you, and the humble will hear our praise, and get glad. We've been through too much, not to worship you. We've seen too much, not to give you praise. We sing your praise and declare every day, is a day of Thanksgiving. In Jesus' name we pray, Amen.

APRIL 28

Nehemiah 8:10 (NASB): Nehemiah said, "Go and enjoy choice food and sweet drinks, and send some to those who have nothing prepared. This day is holy to our Lord. Do not grieve, for the joy of the LORD is your strength."

RIGHT PLACE, RIGHT TIME

I saw this, and immediately got stirred in my spirit! I heard Holy Spirit say, "You have the grace, to be in the right place, at the right time." And then I heard Him say, "And you are not going to drop the ball." Whew! That's what I want us to get in agreement for, the grace to be in the right place at the right time. I pray for laser focus, so that no matter what's going on around us, we won't ever take our eyes off of the ball. I pray for a persistent spirit and that even though you're behind in points and you're running out of time that you will keep your eyes on the prize. I pray for grace to seize the moment. I pray for grace to rise to the occasion. I pray for grace to keep the ball in your hands and for help to advance it once you get your footing.

Holy Spirit strengthen our hands and give peace to our feet. Block every enemy and anything that would cause us to fall before crossing the goal line. Help us to maintain our balance and don't allow anything or anybody to trip us up before we finish. Help us to press thru the bumps, and the bruises. Help us to stay focused, even though we're exhausted, and hurting all over. Don't let us lose sight of the goal line, and grant us the grace to finish strong, in Jesus' name. We will not miss our moment, and we cannot lose because this is our winning season. This is our season to make the game changing, history making play, that will make Jesus famous and our name great. This is our season to win and win again. This is our season of consecutive championships and accolades, so be glorified in us. Get the glory out of our story, and thru our lives Father. Let the world know that Jesus lives. It's in Jesus' name we pray, Amen!

APRIL 29

II Peter 1:3 (NASB): His divine power has given us everything we need for a godly life through our knowledge of him who called us by his own glory and goodness.

MY WINNING SEASON

Everything attached to me wins. Everything I put my hands to prospers, and every tongue that rises against me in judgment, according to Isaiah chapter 54, verse 17, God will condemn. So, I approach this day believing that no weapon formed against me shall prosper, in Jesus' name. I set myself in agreement with the word, and with the blood and I cast off fear, guilt, and shame. I remind myself that the blood was enough. I remind myself that Jesus paid it all, and I restart the process of pressing toward the mark. I choose to have selective amnesia, and to forget those things that are behind.

I ask for your help Holy Spirit, to bring to my remembrance, everything that you've spoken and everything you've promised to do. I thank you for my past, and I praise you for not wasting any of those days, the good ones, and the bad ones. Thank you for turning my mess into my message and thank you Holy Spirit for using everything I did, and everything they did to me, to build your case for mercy and love. Thank you now, that everyday day was useful and that everything was working together for my good! I boldly declare, that either way, I cannot lose. I cannot lose because the season won't allow it. I cannot lose because you've already won the victory and secured my future. This is my winning season, and I decree and declare, that everything attached to me wins! I am on the winning side, and in the name of Jesus, I have the victory. Victory is mine; victory today is mine. Now be glorified in my life. Be pleased, and be praised by my story, and I will forever bless your name. It's in Jesus' name I pray, Amen!

APRIL 30

Hebrews 12:28 (NASB): Therefore, since we receive a kingdom which cannot be shaken, let us show gratitude, by which we may offer to God an acceptable service with reverence and awe;

GOD HEARD YOU

He heard you so stop tripping. Don't be anxious. Don't grow weary. Don't lose your faith. Don't quit. Don't go back. He heard you, so fix your face. Fix your attitude. Act like you know.

Put a praise on it and stop tripping and set your attention on the truth. He heard you. His nature won't allow Him to sit idle and do nothing. As a matter of fact, according to Isaiah 65:24, He heard you before you even called and while you were still speaking His plan to rescue you went full throttle.

Hold on to your faith because God heard your prayers. Stop tripping, because in a few days, things will be better. In a few days, things will have turned in your favor. The devil's a liar, God heard your prayers. The Lord of Hosts has gone to work on your behalf. So, I pray that you receive patience, that you might inherit the promise, after you've done the will of God. It's in Jesus' name I pray, Amen!

MAY

MAY 1

John 14:26 (NASB): But the Advocate, the Holy Spirit, whom the Father will send in my name, will teach you all things and will remind you of everything I have said to you.

IT DIDN'T WORK

The devil tried it, but it didn't work. So, let's stay focused on the failed attempts, instead of the formed weapons and decide within ourselves that no matter what he tries, we're going laugh. In Jesus' name, I pray that you find the wherewithal to choose peace today and that you keep smiling even when your feelings want you to keep crying. I pray for peace in your mind and joy in your spirit.

I pray that despite the screaming distractions that surround you, that you'll have the mental capacity to choose the truth over the lies that the enemy keeps throwing at you. I pray that you'll be able to sift through what you see, how you feel and be able to embrace your future with joy; even if it seems farther away than you'd like. I pray for strength to keep going, until you hit your overflow. I pray for courage to keep pressing towards the mark, until everything connected to you wins. Stay the course! Enjoy the ride. Don't let people, or passing circumstances, make you miserable while you wait. In Jesus' name I pray, Amen!

MAY 2

Psalms 41:2 (NASB): The LORD will protect him and keep him alive, And he shall be called blessed upon the earth; And do not give him over to the desire of his enemies.

REAL FRIENDS COVER

Father, I thank you sending people into my life, who'll tell me the truth in love. I thank you for planting people in my life, who genuinely, and sincerely care about my wellbeing. Thank you, Lord, for sending real friends.

I pray for my friends today, and I lift up the people in my life who are here by divine assignment. I pray for the people you've placed around me to make me better. Thank you, Father, for keeping me around people who challenge me, and hold me accountable, even when I don't really want to be responsible. Thank you for planting people in my life who refuse to let me be trifling. And who refuse to let me settle for stuff that you've not given to me.

I give you praise for showing me how much you want for me, by consistently putting people in my face who stretch me and pull out the better me. Thank you for the people in my life who'll talk to me, and not about me. Thank you for the straight shooters, who don't sugarcoat the truth, and give it to me like it really is.

MAY 3

Proverbs 18:10 (NASB): The name of the LORD is a fortified tower; the righteous run to it and are safe.

MY PRAISE, COVERED

I don't care how many friends, likes, and reposts you get. How popular you become. How much money you make. You will never be able to afford to lose your praise. Don't get it twisted, it's your praise that moved God to keep you and to cover you. It's your praise that kept drawing God's attention and provoking God's power, so whatever you do my friend, please don't lose your praise.

I pray even now that Holy Spirit helps you to remember what He's done and what He's promised. I pray that your soul looks back and gets happy all over again, about the word of the Lord concerning your future. I pray for Holy Spirit motivated flashbacks, and that the promise of God would light a fresh fire in your heart, mind, and soul. I call every thought captive and subject to the spirit of the Lord, and I release a fresh wind over your house. I pray for a praise to come up out of your soul and that you would recognize that praise is how you fight back. Holy Spirit, touch our hearts, restore our joy, refresh our memory, and renew our praise. Receive our praise and use it to stop the enemy in his tracks. Use it as the legal justification to cover us when the enemy would try to expose us. Receive our praise, and use it to break us free, today. Let this day, be the first day, in a new season of praise, power and protection. It's in Jesus' name I pray, Amen!

MAY 4

Proverbs 16:3 (NASB): Commit your works to the Lord And your plans will be established.

I WILL PERSIST

Father today I'm praying for uninterrupted focus, and clarity of thought. I pray for tunnel vision that allows me to stay on task, and focused on the job at hand, and yet not lose focus of the big picture, and everything that's going on around me.

I thank you Lord, that despite the noise, and the distractions that exist, and persist, in my space, that I have the grace to block them out! I praise you, for an ear to hear what I'm supposed to hear. What I need to hear, and the grace to tune out every other negative, contrary, distractive voice and sound. I speak peace over my space!

I speak joy over my days, and I will no longer be bothered or in unrest because of other people, who most times don't even know how they're affecting me. I praise you for the grace to coexist. I thank you that from today forward, I won't lose sleep, I won't lose focus, and I won't miss my moment, focusing on other people, and their behavior.

I'm at peace! I'm focused! I'm on task! I'm in sync with God! I am! Even with the noise, and the distractions that won't go away. In Jesus' name I pray! Misery is a choice. Choose better. Amen!

MAY 5

Romans 8:28 (NASB): And we know that in all things God works for the good of those who love him, who have been called according to his purpose.

MY PRAISE, CHOSEN

God didn't choose you because of your gift. He chose you because of His grace, Selah. God didn't choose you because you were perfect. He chose you because your praise was. So, whatever you do, please don't let the enemy pressure you into abandoning your praise. It's because of your praise, that you were not consumed. It's because of your praise, that you were not exposed. It's because of your praise, that even though you almost lost everything, you're about to get back everything, plus some.

So, I pray for you today, I pray for us, that no matter how much pressure we're under and how personal the attack is, that somehow, we will always manage to find our praise. I pray that we never lose our voice, and that Holy Spirit gives us the strength to praise our way through whatever. I pray that the sound of freedom would come out of our bellies, even when we're hurting and confused. I pray that we'd find our voice today and that the sound of our praise would provoke the power of God to move on our behalf. I pray that the host of Heaven would respond to our praise, immediately. I pray that the sound of our praise would become the soundtrack of our enemy's defeat, in Jesus' name!

Now Holy Spirit have your way and use our praise to eliminate everything that would stand between us and the fulfillment of your will. Take our praise and destroy every yoke. Take our praise, and wipe out every demonic band, that would stand against us. Holy Spirit have your way today and tear down every stronghold. Have your way today and set us free in our minds and in our spirits. Don't let the enemy keep us silent anymore but fill our hearts and our mouths with your praise. It's in Jesus' name I pray, Amen!

MAY 6

Psalms 118:17 (NASB): I will not die, but live, And tell of the works of the Lord.

TRUTH IS, I'M FREE

Thank you, Holy Spirit, for the grace to overcome and for the wisdom to filter the facts the truth. I'm so glad I know the truth, and because I know the truth, I'm free, and I walk in the joy of the Lord, in Jesus' name!

I'm not so consumed with survival and not dying, that I let days and weeks go by, without actually living! I declare I have the grace to enjoy my life, and not just endure my life! I decree and declare, that I'm living abundantly, and not just barely! I commit to myself, that I will not waste another day, solely focused on my enemy.

I will not die! Not before I've lived! I might be in a fight, but I'm going to enjoy my days! I might not have everything I want, but I'm going to enjoy what I have! I might not be exactly where I want to be, or where I think I should be, but I'm going to enjoy my life where I am! In Jesus' name! I pray for peace, and for wisdom, and for courage, and for strength, and for freedom, from negative perspectives, and from negative people. In Jesus' name, Amen!

MAY 7

Hebrews 4:16 (NASB): Let us then with confidence draw near to the throne of grace, that we may receive mercy and find grace to help in time of need.

STOP TRIPPING

Stop tripping. You've got God on your side and you're filled with Holy Spirit. The Spirit of the living God is on you, in you and with you and this makes you unbeatable. So, my prayer for you today is that you do not grow weary in doing well. I pray that you receive the work of Holy Spirit in your life and refuse to let the challenges of the season wear you down.

I decree and declare, you are strong. You are focused. You are unbreakable. You are the one that God is using to restore credibility and significance to your family. I declare you're going to be stronger. You're going to be wiser. You're going to be who God's created you to be. You're going to be better. You're going to be bigger. You're going to be everything you dreamt of being, and you're "being", begins today. It's in Jesus' name I pray, Amen!

MAY 8

Matthew 6:10 (NASB): your kingdom come, your will be done, on earth as it is in heaven.

MY PRAISE, KEPT ME

I'm going to say this again, "you cannot afford to lose your praise!" So, get out of your feelings, and get back in faith. Let's praise God for what He's done. For what He's promised to do. And for everything else He's already done, that we just haven't lived long enough to see yet. I promise you; He can't lie, and I promise you, He wasn't lying! When He told you what He told you. When He showed you what He showed you. Both what He told you, and what He showed you, were already done. So, let's not get selective amnesia and start to forget that He's never failed us yet. Let's not let what we see now, rob us of our faith, for what we saw back then.

The truth is that God's not a man, that He should lie, and whatever He told you, and whatever He showed you, it is coming to pass. So, let's go into the day with our hands lifted up and our mouths filled with praise, knowing that our praise is why He kept us. Let's go into the day expecting a miracle, a sign, or a wonder. Let's go into this day in worship, knowing that it's our praise, and our worship, that's keeping us alive!

That's my prayer for both of us, that our praise would shift some things, today. I pray for a shaking to take place, and that by your spirit Lord, you would rearrange and realign, everything and everybody in my life, that's out of place, or out of order.

Shut my flesh down, and don't let me do anything that'll set me back or hinder your will. Use my praise to wipe the slate clean! Use my praise to set things in proper order! Use my praise, to preserve my place in line and don't let me lose my joy or my peace while I complete the process. Do something supernatural, today. Take my praise and use it to do something that'll make a believer out of my haters. Be glorified in my life. It's in Jesus' name I pray, Amen!

MAY 9

Joshua 1:9 (NASB): Have I not commanded you? Be strong and courageous! Do not tremble or be dismayed, for the LORD your God is with you wherever you go."

BE ENCOURAGED

I'm praying for patience tonight and that you do not get weary in doing the right thing. I pray for endurance, and that God would supernaturally increase your stamina, and your desire to finish what you started.

I pray that Holy Spirit would take the quit out of your mind, and that He would give you the thoughts and the determination of a finisher. I pray your strength, and that every source of frustration be expelled from your space.

I pray that your ear gate shut down to every negative voice, and that your eye gate becomes as the eyes of God! I pray for a 3rd wind, a 10th wind, and that the wind of God would blow how many ever times you need Him to! In Jesus' name! I pray that you get encouraged without any visible changes in your situation.

I pray that God sends somebody into your life who'll make your baby leap, and who'll cause every dormant dReam to live, and burst forth speedily! I pray that this be the best day you've ever had, in Jesus' name, AMEN!

MAY 10

II Chronicles 7:14 (NASB): If my people, who are called by my name, will humble themselves and pray and seek my face and turn from their wicked ways, then I will hear from heaven, and I will forgive their sin and will heal their land.

RIGHT CONNECTIONS

Father I thank you for blessing me with the right connections. I praise you for bringing me into the company of the people who have what I need, and I thank you for turning their hearts towards me. I declare I've stepped into a new season and a fresh dispensation of grace, and some things I won't even have to ask for. People are going to begin offering me exactly what I need, and I will not be too proud to accept it. People who have the gifts, talents, resources, and relationships that I need, are about to come looking for me and I will not be unprepared when we meet.

This is my season for grace, for favor. This is my season to be connected to the right people, at the right time. Everything I need, is now ready. In Jesus' name I pray, Amen!

MAY 11

Colossians 2:8 (NASB): See to it that no one takes you captive through hollow and deceptive philosophy, which depends on human tradition and the elemental spiritual forces of this world rather than on Christ.

EVERYTHING I TOUCH

The blessing of the Lord is on me. God is with me and I have nothing to fear. I do not operate in fear, but I live by faith, and it's by faith and because of the blood that I am justified. I'm made right because of the sacrifice of Jesus and because I'm a believer, the blessing of the Lord is making me rich and removing everything and everybody that would add sorrow to my life. Hallelujah. God is with me.

Jesus is growing on me and in me, and because I choose to walk by faith, and not by sight, God has and is blessing my womb. Luke chapter 1, verse 42 establishes this principle in my life and I declare, "God's going to bless everything that comes out of me!" My womb is blessed, and I produce the blessing of the Lord for my life, and for my family. In Jesus' name I pray, Amen!

MAY 12

1 Corinthians 15:57 (NASB): but thanks be to God, who gives us the victory through our Lord Jesus Christ.

I AM VICTORIOUS

I confess today, it is your will, that I prosper! It's your will Father, that I have more money than I need. It is your will Father, that I be in good health, healthy in my body, and in my soul!

So, in the name of Jesus, I rebuke the spirit of infirmity, I take authority over the spirit of sickness and disease, and I declare, "I'm healed in my body, in my mind, and in my emotions! My thoughts are healthy! I make healthy decisions! And emotionally, I'm good! I'm good because the blood of Jesus made me good!

Everything bad, in my past life, in my present life, and in the history of my family's life, and in my future life, is under the blood! Victory today is mine! It's in Jesus' name I pray, Amen, Amen, and AMEN!

MAY 13

Psalm 66:12 (NASB): *You made men ride over our heads; We went through fire and through water, Yet You brought us out into a place of abundance.*

BLESS WHAT I BELIEVE

Father I thank you for giving me a dReam. I thank you for not allowing how I grew up or the environment that I was brought up in, to stop me from believing for something big. I stand on Ephesians chapter 3, verse 20, and I believe that you're going to do something far more abundantly beyond all that I can ask or think. Thank you, Lord, for giving me the desires of my heart, and then setting in motion plans to bring your will to pass in my life. I give you praise for not allowing me to be content with things that you haven't given me. Thank you, Jesus, that I'll never be satisfied with settling for less. I pray for the revelation of your will and the wisdom and the strength of will to align my life. My soul says yes and because I'm in agreement with what you're doing, I declare you're going to bless everything I'm believing for.

In the name of Jesus, I declare favor and provision, on everything I put my hands to! I pray that Holy Spirit would connect me with the people who have what I need and then make them bless me. I pray that you would relax the rules for me and cause decision makers to make exceptions for me. Supernaturally, you're reducing the price for me that what was beyond my budget, would come under my budget, leaving me in overflow and with a surplus. Father I still believe that there will be a fulfillment of those things that you spoke to me. It's in the name of Jesus I pray, Amen!

MAY 14

John 10:27-28 (NASB): My sheep hear my voice, and I know them, and they follow me :28 And I give unto them eternal life; and they shall never perish, neither shall any man pluck them out of my hand.

LISTEN

I declare you have the grace to pay attention. I pray that your ears will remain open to what God has spoken concerning your life. I declare you have an ear to hear what the spirit of the Lord is saying, and that the distractions of life will not be able to stop you from hearing. I command you to listen. I command you to be open and willing to let go of everything you thought was God, and now you realize was sent by the devil to steer you in the wrong direction. I pray for courage to drop it. I pray against that proud spirit, that would keep you hanging on to people and things that you now know are not God's will for your life.

Father, in the name of Jesus, I break the hold of everything that's become a stronghold and I speak freedom over the believer. In the name of Jesus, I rebuke every unnecessary distraction and I pray for the desire and the grace to pay attention. I pray for the grace to listen and hear, and I declare you will never be full of hearing, ever again. What you hear today changes your life for the better, forever. It's in Jesus' name I pray, Amen.

MAY 15

Romans 8:1-2 (NASB) Therefore there is now no condemnation for those who are in Christ Jesus. For the law of the Spirit of life in Christ Jesus has set you free from the law of sin and of death.

STOP TRIPPING

Stop tripping! You've already done it your way, now God is about to answer your prayer, and do it his way. So, my prayer for you today, is that your heart, your mind, and your spirit will remain open to what God is doing in this season.

I pray that you are not so locked into what He did, that you miss what He's doing. I pray for the strength, and the courage to let it go. I pray that your yes would be constant, and immediate, and that you will not struggle to obey the voice of God.

I pray that you will finally know that what God has for you is bigger, and better than anything you've ever had. I pray that your eyes will pop open, and that you'll be able to finally see, that what you're holding on to, is killing you, hindering you, and keeping you away from the biggest season you've ever known, emotionally, spiritually, and financially.

I command you to let it go. I declare that you've come into the season of your life where God's going to give you what HE wants you to have! I decree and declare that God's giving you the desires of your heart, and that life for you is about to get better. In Jesus' name I pray!

MAY 16

Ezekiel 37:3-5 (NASB): He asked me, "Son of man, can these bones live?" I said, "O Sovereign Lord, you alone know." Then he said to me, "Prophesy to these bones and say to them, `Dry bones, hear the word of the Lord! This is what the Sovereign LORD says to these bones: I will make breath [1] *enter you, and you will come to life.*

MOVE FORWARD

I pray that you find the courage to move forward! I pray that every failure, would fuel your faith, and cause you to believe God for something even bigger! I pray that you dReam big again, and that you find the strength to grab hold of everything that time pushed you to let go of. I pray that Holy Spirit would bring every idea, and plan, and vision, back to your remembrance. And that the power of God would touch you in a real way, gently reminding you that you can do better.

I pray that the thought of going back would make you nauseous, and that moving forward would become your medicine. I pray that you decide to do better, today, and that you'd develop spiritual allergies to anything and everything average. Be good to your spirit and refuse to settle for safe. It's in the mighty name of Jesus I pray, Amen!

MAY 17

1 Corinthians 2:16 (NASB): for who has known the mind of the Lord, that He will instruct him? but we have the mind of Christ.

I AM A MASTERMIND

I am not slow. I'm not dumb. I'm not stupid, neither am I undiscerning or insensitive to the truth. I am filled with the Holy Ghost, the Spirit of the living God lives on the inside of me, and I know the truth. I'm God's child, I have His DNA, I have His mind, and from today forward I declare I'm going to think like my father. My father is omniscient, He knows everything, and there's nothing He cannot do. He thinks beforehand, He's not reactive, in any way because He knows the end, from the beginning.

I decree and declare, "I have the mind of God!" I'm not uninformed, I'm not intimidated and I'm not settling for less, ever, again. God calls me thoughtful. God calls me skilled. God calls me talented. God calls me His and there's nothing I can't think my way out of. My mind is sharp, my spirit is strong, my eye is focused, and I see what I need to do. So, in the name of Jesus, I pray for wisdom and for favor. I pray for a divine download of information that will put me atop of my field. I pray for the mind of the master, for an immediate transfer of revelation and truth, that will set me apart from the pack. I agree with God today, I am a mastermind. I'm smart. I'm clever. I'm righteous. I'm forgiven. I'm next. I'm now. It's in Jesus' name I pray, Amen!

MAY 18

Psalms 126:3 (NASB): The Lord has done great things for us; We are glad.

DO SOMETHING BIG

Good morning Holy Spirit, I'm up, and I'm ready, for you to do whatever it is you've planned to do through me, and for me on today. I praise you for my life, and I thank you for having a plan. I'm confident in the fact that nothing in my past, present, or future, was, nor will they ever be random or a coincidence. Everything that happens, only happens because you're prepared for it, and because you've prepared me for it! I'm prepared for whatever, and I can handle whatever. That's the truth.

I say yes Lord. Yes, to your will, and this is hard for me Father, but I say it anyway, yes to your way. I submit to your way, and I'm praying for grace to get out of your way, so you can do what you've planned to do in Jesus' name! My soul says, "YES" again. My mind, my will, and my emotions, say," do it however you want to do it. Use whoever you want to use, and I'll be content, knowing that I'm finally in your will! Do something jaw-dropping today! Do something today, that'll shut the mouth of the naysayers and the people assigned to me by the enemy to discourage me. Do something immediately! Do something quick, fast, and in a hurry so that the time this day is over, I'll be bigger, better, and blessed forever. It's in Jesus' name I pray, Amen!

MAY 19

Romans 8:1-2 (NASB): Therefore there is now no condemnation for those who are in Christ Jesus. For the law of the Spirit of life in Christ Jesus has set you free from the law of sin and of death.

I'M THE CHOSEN ONE

Father, I thank you that I have victory over my life. I thank you that I have dominion over my parents' past and for their parent's past. The generational curse has been broken, and the blessing of the Lord, a generational blessing, is upon me, and upon my family.

I haven't been perfect, but I am the one that God's chosen to release the blessing in my family! I have a guaranteed future, and I have hope!

Hope that's built on nothing less, than Jesus' blood, and righteousness! So, I dare not trust, the sweetest frame, but wholly lean on Jesus' name! It's on Christ, the lamb of God, the propitiation for my sins, the one who was, and is to come, it's on Christ, the solid rock I still stand.

I declare my foot will not slip, I shall not be moved, and everything God promised, will come to pass! It's in Jesus' name I pray, Amen, Amen, and AMEN!

MAY 20

Romans 8:31 (NASB): What, then, shall we say in response to these things? If God is for us, who can be against us?

YOU'RE BETTER THAN THAT

I'm praying for you today, that Holy Spirit will open your eyes and cause you to see just how valuable and precious you really are, in Jesus' name. I pray that your self-esteem explodes, and you never allow yourself to be taken advantage of again. I pray that Holy Spirit increases your discernment, so you know every time somebody's trying to play you. I pray that you begin to see yourself as God's child, as God's investment and as the reason that Jesus sacrificed His life.

I break the hold of rejection on your life. I break the power of every soul tie, and I declare your freedom tonight, in the name of Jesus! You will never settle again! You will never offer your body for acceptance again! You will never chase a man again! You will never compromise your morals, or your integrity, or your relationship with God again, ever. I declare your freedom tonight, and I release the strength of God upon you, in Jesus' name I pray, Amen!

MAY 21

Hebrews 12:11 (NASB): All discipline for the moment seems not to be joyful, but sorrowful; yet to those who have been trained by it, afterwards it yields the peaceful fruit of righteousness.

I'M NOT DOING IT

I confess that I am God's child. My life has purpose. God is heavily invested in my past life, my present life, and my future life! God is with me. God is for me. And God wants me to live, abundantly. So today I choose God. I choose his will for my life. I say yes to what he's planned, and I refuse to allow my flesh, and my feelings to control my life another day! Today I choose righteousness, and for the first time in my life, I choose it, believing God's going to help me sustain my choice, hallelujah! By faith I declare, some things I'm just not doing, not anymore.

Enough is enough, and I will no longer allow the enemy to use my behavior, as justification for the hold up of what God's planned for my life in this season. Some things I'm just not doing. Not anymore! I'm going to honor God with my mouth and with my body. No more overeating. No more walking around bitter, mad, and angry. No more clinging to relationships that dishonor my faith and offend my father. Not anymore. Some things, I'm just not doing. Not anymore, so Father, I pray for your help and for your wisdom to sustain my confession. It's in Jesus' name I pray, Amen!

MAY 22

Mark 9:23 (NASB): 'If you can question" said Jesus. "Everything is possible for one who believes."

MAKE ME A MIRACLE

Father, I love you! I love you, and I thank you for giving me another day to pursue my purpose in life. I thank you Lord that my past cannot hinder, or alter my future, in any way, and that my present situation, is being used to position me to do what I've always dReamed of doing!

Thank you, Lord! My best days are ahead of me! My latter days, according to Haggai chapter 2, and verse 9, will be way better than my former days, and I'm declaring THIS IS, my season for miracles, signs, and wonders! THIS IS, the season, that I see the hand of God, fully functional and in operation in my life.

Make me a miracle! That's my prayer Lord and shut the mouth of every demon who said I'd never make it! Glorify yourself in my situation! Show yourself strong, on my behalf! And I'll forever give you the glory, the honor, and the praise! It's in Jesus' name I pray, AMEN!

MAY 23

*Jeremiah 29:11 (NASB): For I know the plans I have for you,"
declares the LORD, "plans to prosper you and not to harm
you, plans to give you hope and a future.*

IT'LL BE BIGGER

The next thing God does for me, is going to be BIG!!! So, I set
my affections on Him. I refuse to give my attention to anything,
or to anyone, that's not focused on Jesus. This season I'm in,
requires focus, and faith, and sanctification. I commit to myself,
to pursue your presence. I commit to chase you again, even
though I'm disappointed about where I am, and what hasn't
happened, and what did happen, and how I was treated by
the people I thought had my back! In spite of it all, Lord I still
choose you. I choose you when I'm hurting, and I choose you
when I'm good. Because I finally realize what you've been
trying to do for me, is bigger than me.

Your plan for my life is bigger than I thought it was and now that
I know the truth, I can make better choices. Now that I know
the truth, my behavior will reflect that of a man who's got
generations depending on his yes thank you for showing me
the truth. The truth about who I am, the truth about who you
are, and the truth about what's really going on in my life.

Truth is, it's bigger than I thought it was. I just didn't know, but
now that I know better, I'm going to do better. Father give me
the strength, and the courage to do better, and to be better.
It's in Jesus' name I pray, Amen!

MAY 24

Isaiah 55:11 (NASB): so is my word that goes out from my mouth:
It will not return to me empty, but will accomplish what I desire
and achieve the purpose for which I sent it.

GOD IS NOT A LIAR

Father I trust you and I choose to stand firm on your word. I realize that I have a choice. I can allow the facts to frame my faith or I can choose to base what I believe for on your word. So today, I choose your word. You are not a liar. You can't lie, and everything you've spoken is still true. I choose the truth over the facts. I choose what I believe over how I feel.

I trust you, more than I trust the doctors. I trust you, more than I trust the banker, or the lawyer, or the teacher. I set my hope on you, and I set my hope on your love; knowing that once you begin a thing, in the spirit, that thing, is already finished. You are the author and the finisher of my faith. My situation is going to end better than it began. I am not afraid, and I will not die, because I'm living by faith. It's in Jesus' name I pray, Amen!

MAY 25

Galatians 5:1 (NASB): It is for freedom that Christ has set us free. Stand firm, then, and do not let yourselves be burdened again by a yoke of slavery.

NO LONGER BOUND

Father I praise you today for breaking the chains that have held me bound. I thank you for delivering me from the things that I got myself caught up in that had nothing to do with glorifying you.

Thank you for loving me through it all. Thank you for your mercy and the grace to overcome. Father I had some stuff. I was in some mess, but today I am free. Because of your love, I am free.

I am free from oppressive behavior. I am free from ungratefulness. I am free from every perverse thought in my mind. I am free from generational curses and negative soul ties. Father I thank you because today I am no longer bound. There are no more chains that hold me and keep me shackled to the stuff that held me hostage for so long. I am free. I thank you. In Jesus' name, Amen!

MAY 26

Psalms 1:3 (NASB): He shall be like a tree Planted by the rivers of water, That brings forth its fruit in its season, Whose leaf also shall not wither; And whatever he does shall prosper.

TROUBLE WON'T CHANGE ME

Trouble will not change me. I will not allow life and circumstance to change who I am. I am who God says I am, and it's my choice to remain authentic and true. I'm not changing just because my life is not what I wanted it to be. I'm not going to become some watered down, diluted version of my true self just because I've gotten a bad report. I am who God says I am, and I'm not going to let what's sent to make me, break me. The devil is a lie! Trouble is my friend, and it's going to produce the wisdom and the compassion, and the anointing I need, to do what God's called me to do.

So, I'm going to face this trouble with a smile on my face, and with a heart full of faith! I'm going to filter the bad report through the blood and with the word. I'm going to keep on being who God made me to be. I'm just a few days away from the biggest season of my life, and I'm going to enjoy this ride. It's in Jesus' name I pray, Amen.

MAY 27

Romans 8:28 (NASB): And we know that in all things God works for the good of those who love him, who have been called according to his purpose.

DISAPPOINTED

Life can be a trip sometimes, but I'm not going to lose my joy or change who I've always been just because something didn't go the way I wanted it to, the devil is a lie. I'm going to keep being and doing, and I'm going to keep dReaming. I'm not going to stop living and I'm not going to allow the disappointment to keep me from believing. So, Father, I pray for peace this morning. I pray that you'll settle my spirit, and give me proper perspective, your perspective regarding my situation. Give me revelation of the truth and allow me to see what's really going on so that the disappointment, doesn't become discouragement.

Cause me to discern your will so that I can embrace the truth. So, the lies of the devil won't affect me like they have in the past. Increase my ability to hear your voice and make me super sensitive to your spirit, in Jesus' name. And Father, I pray that this let down, won't break me down, but cause it to be the thing that builds me up, and draws me closer to you! Let this moment of disappointment mature me and make me better, and stronger, and wiser, in Jesus' name. Cause it to give me the boldness I need to move forward. I'm disappointed, but I'm not dead. I declare, "I shall live!" It's in Jesus' name I pray, Amen!

MAY 28

Psalms 113:7-8
He raises the poor from the dust and lifts the needy from the ash heap; he seats them with princes, with the princes of his people.

GOD HEARD YOU

This is what I heard to tell you, He heard you, so stop tripping. Don't be anxious. Don't grow weary. Don't lose your faith. Don't quit. Don't go back. He heard you, so fix your face. Fix your attitude. Act like you know. Stop tripping and set your attention on the truth. He heard you and His nature won't allow Him to sit idle and do nothing. As a matter of fact, according to Isaiah 65:24, He heard you before you even called, and while you were still speaking His plan to rescue you went full throttle.

Hold on to your faith, because God heard your prayers! Stop tripping, because in a few days, things will be better. In a few days, things will have turned in your favor! The devil's a liar, God heard your prayers, and the Lord of Hosts has gone to work on your behalf. I pray that you receive patience, that you might inherit the promise, after you've done the will of God. It's in Jesus' name I pray, Amen!

MAY 29

Jeremiah 18:6 (NASB): "Can I not, O house of Israel, deal with you as this potter does?" declares the LORD. "Behold, like the clay in the potter's hand, so are you in My hand, O house of Israel.

I'M GETTING BETTER

I am getting better! I am changing! The spirit of the Lord is upon me, and He's confirming me to the image of His son. I'm getting better every day.

My choices are getting better, and my desire to please God with my life is growing, by the minute. I'm getting better and the way I see myself, reflects this mega change that happening in my heart, mind, and spirit.

I'm becoming more and more like Jesus, every day, and the things that I used to be bound by, are dropping off of my life daily. I'm changing, and I can see the change. Confess it, it's not a lie, you're prophesying. I'm getting better. Better is on me. Better is in me and it's showing up in the way I treat my family, and my friends.

I'm getting better and I can see it reflected in the way I treat the people who've hurt me and tried to play me. What the devil meant for evil, God uses it for my good. Today I decree and declare, better is my new norm. It's what I'm presently walking in, and it's waiting for me in my future! It's in Jesus' name I pray, Amen!

MAY 30

Psalm 51:12 (NASB): Restore to me the joy of Your salvation And sustain me with a willing spirit.

I'M TAKING IT BACK

Good morning Holy Spirit! Today's going to be a big day for us! It's a new day, and today Jesus is going to make me go "wow"!

Answers to my prayers are going to manifest today, and the things that I've been in faith for are just going to fall into my hands. My faith, and my refusal to quit, is going to produce fruit today, and I'll never be afraid to trust God again. I cannot be discouraged, I cannot be defeated, and I will not be denied because this is my season!

So, I'm going to look adversity straight in the eye, and say, "don't even try it!" No weapon formed against me shall prosper, and God's going to shut the mouths of my enemies! Today I'm going to Holla, "I got my joy back! I got my peace back! I got my swag back! I took it back! In Jesus' name, it is so! Amen!

MAY 31

Deuteronomy 30:9 (NASB): "Then the LORD your God will prosper you abundantly in all the work of your hand, in the offspring of your body and in the offspring of your cattle and in the produce of your ground, for the LORD will again rejoice over you for good, just as He rejoiced over your fathers;

BETTER BEGINS NOW

Better begins again for me, today! So, I position myself and I prepare myself for what God is doing. I set myself in agreement with God's will and I align myself to move in His time. I will no longer be the cause of my setback. I refuse to continue to be the reason why God's will and plan for my life remains on hold. I set myself in agreement with God. I choose your will Father, and I say yes all over again. I want what you want for my life. I'm praying for wisdom to live better, and to make better choices. I choose better. Better chooses me, and my life will never be under again. I pray for courage to choose what's best, and what's right, over what's comfortable and convenient. I thank you Father, for the wisdom and the discernment to know the difference between them.

I choose to move forward, praying for the strength to never go back, or desire anything ever again, that's beneath me. I pray for friends who want to live right. I pray that you'll bring me into close company with people who are committed to living for you, and that you'll separate me from everything and everybody who jeopardizes my relationship with you. Better begins today! It's in Jesus' name I pray, Amen!

JUNE

JUNE 1

Psalm 86:11 (NASB): Teach me Your way, O LORD; I will walk in Your truth; Unite my heart to fear Your name.

TEACH ME YOUR WAYS

Today I make a conscious decision to walk by faith, and NOT by sight! Despite what I see on TV or what I hear in these social media streets, I will not mix my worship with worry, and I refuse to mix my praise with perturbation! In other words, I'm NOT going to let this thing scare or detour my dReam. I choose to take precautions, and yet not be distracted, but I WILL not put my dReam on hold!

I'm going to take this time to revisit the stuff you gave me, that the devil told me I didn't have time for. I'm going to use my "down time" wisely and start plans according to the blueprint. I will not fall prey to lurking and scrolling all day. I pray that Holy Spirit's going to use these weeks to teach me how to discipline myself with no need for outside oversight, or accountability! This is MY dReam, and it's time I start making moves, and making things happen instead of waiting on someone from the outside to come inside, to help me!

Starting today, I reset my focus. Starting today, I reclaim my time. Starting today, I revisit my future on the canvas of my imagination. TODAY, I start to dReam AGAIN! The word of the Lord as spoken over my life and my family is, "God's got SOMETHING to prove" to this generation of unbelievers.

I declare and decree, "You're going to use my life, my family and my story to do it, in Jesus' name!"

So today I pray for wisdom, I pray for insight and I pray for grace to prepare for what's ahead. I pray for the truth about my future to be uncovered and made extremely visible, so that I don't get in a hurry, and run right by it! Open my eyes and cause me to see, and grace me to see deeper, beneath and beyond the surface so I can move in truth, despite the facts! My prayer today is, teach me your ways oh Lord. Show me how to please you with my everyday walking around life! I promise I'll tell everybody it was you, and NOT me! It's in Jesus' mighty name I pray, Amen!

JUNE 2

Psalm 57:6 (NASB): My enemies have set a trap for me. I am weary from distress. They have dug a deep pit in my path, but they themselves have fallen into it.

HE BLOCKED IT

Father, I thank you for the good, for the bad, and for the downright ugly! I thank for being the God who uses everything, for the good of your people. I thank you for what you blocked, for the things you just wouldn't let happen, and then for the things you did let happen.

I'm grateful for everything, and everybody you allowed in my life, because I see it's making me better! They tried to kill me, but it made me better! They thought they'd set me up to fail, when actually they were being used to teach me how to love my enemies.

Thank you, Lord, for everything that should've reduced me, but actually increased me. Thank you for every mistake that I learned from! Thank you for teaching me how to discern your voice and then giving me the courage, and the confirmation I needed to obey you.

I declare this week coming will be filled with multiple victories, and full of wins! In Jesus' name I pray, AMEN!

JUNE 3

Proverbs 16:3 (NASB): Commit your works to the LORD And your plans will be established.

BUILD YOUR ALTAR

I pray that as you build God an altar, that every ungodly attachment would burn off because of His presence. I pray that every unfruitful connection would drop off, as you continue to pursue God's presence. I pray that any and everything you're vested in and committed to, that God isn't behind or didn't ordain, that it would fall by the wayside, in Jesus' name.

I pray that everything and everybody you're connected to, would be the manifestation of God's plan for your life. No more mistake relationships. No more unproductive exchanges or interactions. I pray for divine connections, that will connect me to everything God's willed me to have. I pray for people, process and for patience. I'm asking Holy Spirit to help you sanctify your mind, your mouth, and your motives. In the name of Jesus, I decree and declare that the next 48 hours belong to God! The next 2 days belong to the kingdom and even now, God is repositioning you. He's correcting your posture, purifying your soul, and setting you in place for the release of glory that's about to elevate your life forever! The charge is, "guard the next 48 hours!" No fear! No foolishness! It's in Jesus' name we pray, Amen!

JUNE 4

Galatians 5:22-23 22 (NASB): But the fruit of the Spirit is love, joy, peace, forbearance, kindness, goodness, faithfulness, 23 gentleness and self-control. Against such things there is no law

---

IT'S TIME

It's time for you to stop tripping and get better! Ecclesiastes chapter 3, verse 1 says, "There is an appointed time for everything and there is a time for every "event" under heaven", so I align myself with scripture, and I decree and declare, it's time! It's time for me to stop allowing what happened and what didn't happen, to steal my joy. It's time for you to experience something good and for God to do something big. It's time for me to uproot, tear down and throw away some stuff, and put an end to every ungodly relationship that kept me depressed and in shame, wishing I had somebody else's life.

It's time for me to do something big, something the devil and my haters never expected me to do. It's time for my event. It's time for me to enjoy my righteous life, without the inclusion of anything or anybody that represents my old rachet life. It's time for me to be me and live. It's time for me to enjoy my family and my children. It's time for me to know what it feels like to life my life stress free, and drama free. It's time for me to make some changes to my attitude and my circle. It's time for me to obey God and live an abundant life, debt free! Time for me to be a blessing and launch my business. It's time for me to be, who God's called me to be! Time for me to be myself and love myself. It's TIME. Father, I pray that what You've already finished in eternity, will manifest itself in time, today. In Jesus' name I pray, Amen!

JUNE 5

Psalms 37:23 (NASB): The steps of a man are established by the Lord, And He delights in his way.

NOT OUT OF PLACE

I will never, be out of place again and I will never be out of grace again. Father I give you praise today, for divine placement! I thank you for showing me where. I praise you for showing me when, and I bless you for the courage to obey, even if I don't know why. I pray for an obedient spirit, and a consistent yes. I pray for signs and wonders that will affirm my obedience and cause me to know that I'm in Your will.

I pray Holy Spirit, that you'll begin to send people into my life to make my transition easier, and that staying where I was, will no longer be a viable option. Make moving easy for me. Take my "yes Lord" and use it against my enemies! Take my "yes Lord" and use it to make the way plain for me. My soul says yes, to your will, and to your way. I give you praise that I'll not waste another day trying to figure out where I'm supposed to be. That I'll not waste another year of my life trying to work somebody else's grace, and in somebody else's lane.

Thank you, Lord, for showing me where I'm supposed to be, and when I'm supposed to be there. I'll never be out of place again because the spirit of the living God is with me. I'll never be on the wrong job again or pursuing the wrong people or the wrong things again because Jesus walks with me, and He talks with me, and He tells me what to do, and when to do it. I'm on my way to something exceedingly, and abundantly! I'm stepping into something big, something above everything I've asked for and thought about. And can't no devil in hell hold me down. In Jesus' name I pray, AMEN!

JUNE 6

Psalm 25:5 (NASB): Lead me in Your truth and teach me, For You are the God of my salvation; For You I wait all the day.

LORD SHOW ME HOW

Father I thank you for giving me divine strategy. I thank you for showing me how, why, when, and where. Thank you for showing me what I have to work with, and who I'm supposed to walk with. Thank you, Father, for not leaving me in the dark to fend for myself, even when I was tripping and in my flesh. Thank you, Holy Spirit, for revealing yourself as my very present help, and for giving me strategies that are beyond my experiences, and unlike anything I've ever seen. I pray now for courage to walk in the thing that I've never seen done before. Thank you, Holy Spirit, for showing me how and for giving me the mental capacity to think it through and document the process, in its entirety.

I pray for a sober spirit and for the grace to write it down without fatigue or frustration. Thank you for the patience to endure the process of development and for the strength of will to document my strategy. I will never again be without strategy. I will never again be without a carefully thought through game plan or design. I decree and declare, that the power of God is upon me afresh, giving me designs, blueprints, road maps, schemes, systems, master plans, arrangements, and strategy, to affect change in culture. I decree and declare, that the spirit of the Lord is upon me, and He's anointed me and given me strategy to infiltrate systems and cultures, for the glory of God. I have compounded, generational wisdom! I have the mind of Christ, and there's nothing I cannot think my way out of. It's in Jesus' name I pray, Amen!

JUNE 7

Psalm 31:3 (NASB): For You are my rock and my fortress; For Your name's sake You will lead me and guide me.

LORD SHOW ME WHY

Lord show me why I had to go thru that. Show me why I didn't die and why I can't die. Show me why I'm really here. Show me why I'm living in this city and not some other town. Show me why my relationships won't work. Show me myself and show me what I need to change about me. Show me why I keep attracting the same kind of people. Show me why I'm single. Show me why I'm not further along in my career and business. Show me why my children are the way they are and why they act the way the act. Show me why you won't kill all my enemies and why they're still here and necessary. Show me myself and show me why I need to change. Show me why I don't have a lot of friends. Show me why I'm your favorite and why you still love me. Show me why you saved me and why you keep blocking the enemy's attempts to destroy me.

Show me why you're committed to my life, and my future. Show me why you won't give up on me, and why you still believe in me. Show me why your plans for me, are way bigger than mine. Show me why you sacrificed Jesus for me and why you choose me every single day, despite my faults and my failures. Show me why I can't quit and why giving up is foolish. Show me the real me and why I have to keep moving forward, then give me the courage to embrace your purpose and your plan for my life. In Jesus' name, AMEN

JUNE 8

Exodus 15:13 (NASB): In your loving kindness, You have led the people whom you have redeemed; In your strength you have guided them to your holy habitation.

LET IT GO

First Corinthians chapter 13, verse 11 says, "When I was a child, I used to speak like a child, think like a child, reason like a child; when I became a man, I did away with childish things." My prayer today, is that Holy Spirit would help us to grow up and that everything we've carried from childhood into adulthood, would lose its grip on our lives, in the name of Jesus. I pray for exponential growth, spiritually, socially, mentally, and financially. I pray that the issues of blood that have passed from one generation to the next, would be broken off your life, and that the power of God would touch you, like never before.

I pray for an encounter with God today, that gives you the strength to say, "not anymore!" I pray for the courage to tell your past, "never again!" I pray that the grace to let it go would be your portion, and that this time it'll take root. I pray that God shuts every door, that would send you back into yesterday. I pray that the power of God comes on you so strong, that you have the strength to say, "I'm done!" I pray for your spirit's eye, and that God would give you another glimpse of your future, so that finally see for yourself, that your past, and the stuff you're leaving behind, doesn't even come close to what's ahead. It's in Jesus' mighty name I pray, Amen!

JUNE 9

Romans 15:13 (NASB): Now may the God of hope fill you with all joy and peace in believing, so that you will abound in hope by the power of the Holy Spirit.

LORD SHOW ME

Lord show me, so I don't waste another year trying to figure my life out. Show me, so I don't waste another year in a relationship I was never supposed to be in, in the first place. Show me what your will is and what you desire for my life. Show me your plan so I don't go another 12 months chasing something I was never supposed to have. Reveal your will and make it clear and undeniable so that I'll have the courage I need to tell my flesh, "no!" Show me how to help myself, and what I need to do to make myself better. Show me how to increase my value in my industry, and in my area of passion, and gifting.

Show me how to get out of debt. Show me how to have a happy marriage. Show me how to raise my kids. Show me Lord and then give me the peace of mind and the strength of will to obey. Show me what to do next. Show me where to go, when to go and who to ask when I get there. Don't let me waste another year of my life fishing, or walking around in the dark, show me. Show me, and then cause my mind and my spirit to agree, so that I'm not 2 completely different people, walking around in 1 body. Don't let me be double minded and unstable another day but show me how to balance my day-to-day life. Show me where to plant my business. Show me the area of my expertise and then help me to choose it. Show me who I can trust. Show me who's for me and then help to stay focused on and committed to them. Show me Lord, where my sweet spot is, and the city and state I'm supposed to be in. Show me, me, and then show me how to love me. Show me how to dress without compromising my integrity or losing my personality. Change my mind, wash my mouth out, and show me how to talk like an intelligent Christian. Show me who I need to hang around. Show me who's connected to my destiny, and who belongs in my future. Show me, so I can see and know what my next move is, in Jesus' name! I declare I will see, Amen!

JUNE 10

Proverbs 3:5-6: (NASB): Trust in the Lord with all your heart and lean not to your own understanding in all your way acknowledge him and he will make your paths straight.

WHAT GOD WANTS

Stop tripping! You've already done it your way, now God is about to answer your prayer, and do it HIS way! So, my prayer for you today, is that your heart, your mind, and your spirit will remain open to what God is doing in this season. I pray that you are not so locked into what He did, that you miss what He's doing. I pray for the strength, and the courage to let it go. I pray that your "yes" would be constant and immediate, and that you will not struggle to obey the voice of God. I pray that you will finally know that what God has for you is bigger and better than anything you've ever had.

I pray that your eyes will pop open and that you'll be able to finally see, that what you're holding on to, is killing you, hindering you, and keeping you away from the biggest season you've ever known, emotionally, spiritually, and financially. I command you to let it go. I declare that you've come into the season of your life where God's going to give you what He wants you to have. I decree and declare that God's giving you the desires of your heart, and that life for you is about to get better. In Jesus' name I pray, Amen!

JUNE 11

1 Corinthians 9:8 (NASB): And God is able to make all grace abound to you, so that always having all sufficiency in everything, you may have an abundance for every good deed.

WALK IT OUT

Father I thank you for another good day. I thank you, for orchestrating the perfect set of circumstances, that would cause me to be strong, and focused.

I praise you for strengthening my soul, and for giving me the grace to win. I don't lose. I don't quit. And I do not faint! I walk in the grace to finish what I started. So, I've pulled aside from my grind, and from my routine, for a prayer stop to say, thank you Lord, for the grace to walk it out.

I declare strength to my bones, and strength to my spiritual feet and ankles! I decree and declare, that I have the presence of mind, and the strength of will, to make the moves I need to make! I have the grace to walk it out! I will not back down! I will not turn around! And I will not settle for something beneath me, and lesser than what You promised!

I have the grace to walk it out, and the grace to walk away. In Jesus' name I pray, AMEN!

JUNE 12

2 Thessalonians 5:23 (NASB): Now may the God of peace himself sanctify you entirely; and may your spirit and soul and body be preserved complete, without blame at the coming of our Lord Jesus Christ.

GOD WILL PROTECT

Stop tripping and stop making what you did, and who you did it with, bigger than God. It's time to let it go. It's time for you to move on to something divine, and something that God's chosen, and prepared for you, but you will never do that, as long as you're afraid of what might happen if you leave. So, Father, in the name of Jesus, I pray for the courage to obey you. I pray that we'll realize once and for all, that there is nobody greater than you, and that whenever you give instructions, they're always accompanied by divine protection.

We do not have to be afraid of what we know we have to walk away from, it cannot hurt us. We do not have to fear satanic retaliation, because whatever the enemy tries to do, in response to our obedience, will not work. The promise of Isaiah chapter 54, verse 17 is this, "no weapon that is formed against you will prosper; And every tongue that accuses you in judgment you will condemn."

So, Father I claim that promise for my life, and I praise you for protecting me from my past. I give you praise for covering me, and for helping me to stop tripping over what didn't work.

Greater is coming. And I have nothing to fear. I have nothing, and nobody to be afraid of because you are with me. Psalms 3 says, " But you, O Lord, are a shield about me, My glory, and the one who lifts my head." I claim that promise for my life, that whatever the enemy tries to do to me, that you've already blocked it, and that you're causing everything to work together for my good. It's in the name of Jesus I pray, Amen!

JUNE 13

Isaiah 41:10 (NASB): Do not fear, for I am with you; do not anxiously look about you, for You're your God. I will strengthen you, surely I will help you.

UNBOTHERED

The effectual fervent prayer of a righteous man availeth much, so Father I thank you that my prayers have not been in vain. I thank you for providing me with the weapon of prayer and praise, and that because I've been stopping to pray, that my prayers stopped whatever that thing was, that was fighting against me.

My prayers have stopped it! And my praise has broken it! I have the victory tonight, in the name of Jesus! And I declare that for the rest of this year, I will be unbothered!

The peace of God, that surpasses all understanding, is guarding my heart, and my mind, and I remain unbothered! Things aren't perfect, and they're not exactly how I want them to be, but I refuse to stress, and I refuse to get out of character. I speak peace over my house, over my kids, over my family, and over my mind, in Jesus' name!

I choose the joy of the Lord! I choose to be at peace, with myself, and with everybody else in my circle. And I'm going to spend the rest of this night enjoying my salvation. It's in Jesus' name I pray, AMEN!

JUNE 14

Philippians 1:9-10 (NASB): And this I pray, that your love may abound still more and more in real knowledge and all discernment, 10so that you may approve the things that are excellent, in order to be sincere and blameless until the day of Christ

HELP IS ON THE WAY

I pray for consistency, in your determination to want to do better. I pray for courage to make the tough decisions, that I know must be made.

I pray for unexpected help, for help to come to you from the outside, and that God would turn the hearts of the shot callers, and the people with the influence and resources, in your direction!

I pray for Holy Spirit to breathe over everything connected to you and give you another wind! In Jesus' name and I pray that by the time you wake up, that the grace of God will have been released to you, over and over again!

I praise God that you'll awake refreshed, and ready to do it big! I praise God that you'll awake un-intimidated, unbothered, and under an open Heaven. It's in Jesus' name I pray, AMEN!

JUNE 15

Psalm 32:11 (NASB): *Be glad in the Lord and rejoice, you righteous ones; And shout for joy, all you who are upright in heart.*

DEFENSE WINS

I'm praying for you today...that Holy Spirit would teach you to guard your heart, and how to guard your mind. I pray that the wisdom of God would overwhelm your thought processes, and make being vulnerable, and susceptible to sneak attacks from the enemy, an impossibility. I pray that you learn how to protect your eye gates, and your ear gates, and that you don't allow anything in your spirit, and anyone in your space, that would put at risk, the thing that God has promised you! I pray for X-ray vision...and that your discernment would increase by the minute. I pray that your snake radar goes crazy, every time the enemy sends a viper, disguised as a friend.

I pray that Holy Spirit helps you to plan your defense, and that He walks you through the strategy to keep your heart pure. I pray that your ability to defend your faith, and your future blows up. And that the power of God comes on you in such a way that the enemy backs off you, and off your family. I pray that you take full advantage of the season you're in, and that you enjoy the ride to the top.

I pray for focus of mind and that you are not so consumed with defending your life, that you forget to enjoy your life. Have a good day today, in Jesus' name. Make some new money today, in Jesus' name. Create a new business venture today, in Jesus' name. Work your genius today, in Jesus' name. Fight for what you believe in today, in Jesus' name. Do you today, the righteous you, in Jesus' name, and may God get all the glory, and all the honor today. It's in Jesus' name I pray, Amen!

JUNE 16

Ezekiel 36:26 (NASB): Moreover, I will give you a new heart and put a new spirit within you; and I will remove the heart of stone from your flesh and give you a heart of flesh

I'LL NEVER BE THE SAME

Father, what a day! And all I can say is, "I will never be the same again!" The way you set things up today, was incredible, and my life will never be the same!

I felt myself changing today, for the better, and I feel like the chains were broken in Jesus' name! Father I thank you that what I felt was real! The power of God touched me today, and I'm going to sleep, with my mind made up to never go back to being who I was!

I'm not the same! I feel different! And I know that something supernatural happened for me today, and with the help of the Holy Ghost, I'm never going back! So, Father I pray for strength, and for wisdom, to maintain this move that took place.

I pray for grace to go forward, and the courage to never look back, in Jesus' name! And when I rise in the morning, I'll be ok with the new me, comfortable with this new place, and I won't be afraid to be better. It's in Jesus' name I pray, Amen!

JUNE 17

Galatians 6:9 (NASB): Let us not lose heart in doing good, for in due time we will reap if not grow weary.

NOT TODAY

I'm not dying. Not today! I'm not quitting, and I'm not about to give up, not today. Father I pray for strength to endure, and the wisdom to make the necessary adjustments, to sustain my peace.

I pray for patience to stay the course, and for the mental toughness, to honor my righteous choice. I've made mistakes in the past and done some things simply because they felt good, and I wanted to, but I've changed and I'm still changing. I'm not who I once was, and do I possess the wherewithal to say to everything I once fell to, not today.

I'm free because the Son has made me free. So, I won't be falling today. I won't be walking in fear today. I won't be losing my faith today. And I for sure won't be giving up on God, not today. It's in Jesus' name I pray, Amen!

JUNE 18

Proverbs 27:9 (NASB): Oil and perfume make the heart glad, so a man's counsel is sweet to his friend.

FRIENDS PROTECT

Father, I thank you for sending people into my life, who'll tell me the truth in love. I thank you for planting people in my life who genuinely and sincerely care about my wellbeing. Thank you, Lord, for sending real friends. I pray for my friends today, and I lift up the people in my life who are here by divine assignment. I pray for the people you've placed around me to make me better. Thank you, Father, for keeping me around people who challenge me, and hold me accountable, even when I don't really want to be. Thank you for planting people in my life who refuse to let me be trifling and who refuse to let me settle for stuff that you've not given to me.

I give you praise for showing me how much you want for me, by consistently putting people in my face who stretch me and pull out the better me. Thank you for the people in my life who'll talk to me, and not about me. Thank you for the straight shooters, who don't sugarcoat the truth and give it to me like it really is. I'm better because my friends told me the truth. I'm better because of the people you planted in my life, who didn't let me get beside myself, and start tripping over the little bit of success I've gained.

Thank you for my friends for the people in my life who keep my grounded, and humble, and compassionate. Thank you, Lord, for keeping people around me, who'll tell me when I've gone too far, or when I'm doing too much. Thank you, Holy Spirit, for helping me to hear them and making it impossible for me to ignore them. Thank You!

Thank you for not allowing me to become intoxicated with my own success, or with my own failure, thank you for keeping me balanced, and consistently kind, especially to the people whose help I don't think I need. I declare today to be a sobering day a day where all things come back into proper perspective, and alignment. It's in Jesus' name I pray, amen!

JUNE 19

John 16:33 (NASB): These things I have spoken to you, so that in Me you may have peace. In the world you have tribulation, but take courage; I have overcome the world.

I'M A FINISHER

In the name of Jesus, I declare strength over my life. I declare courage in my heart, and peace in my spirit. The peace of God is my right, as a believer, and so I choose peace over panic.

I will not allow what I see with my natural eye, to take my attention away from what I've seen with my spirit's eye. I can see, and I have vision, that goes way beyond my current position.

So today I'm working on forgetting and praying that Holy Spirit would help me to remember what Jesus did at Calvary when the enemy throws what I did, back in my face! Today I'm working on forgiving myself and praying that Holy Spirit would help me to agree with God's opinion about me. It's in Jesus' name I pray, Amen!

JUNE 20

Romans 4:21 (NASB): and being fully assured that what God had promised, He was able also to perform

RAISING MY GAME

Good morning Holy Spirit today is going to be a strong day! Today, as I pursue you, and talk with you throughout the day, you're going to give me insight. And fix the way I see things, so I see them the way you see them. Thank you, Holy Spirit, for correcting my vision, and giving me the grace to see past where I am now, and beyond what's happening to me now. The truth is nothing has happened to me by accident. None of this is coincidence, or random, it's all on purpose, and it's all working to accomplish your will in my life!

So, I choose strength today! I choose your joy today, and I declare that today I will be at peace!" I'm in the middle of it, but that's not as far as I can see! I see myself in the future and I'm already better! This bump in the road, was designed to lift me, not slow me down. So, I'm going to use this day to elevate my perspective, and I'm going to intentionally raise my game! Good isn't good enough!

There's greatness on me! Being weak is no longer acceptable! The strength of God is in me, the strength of God is pushing me, and before this year is over, God will have done something so big thru me, that I'll have to ask myself, "did I do that"? It's in Jesus' mighty name I pray, Amen, Amen, and Amen!

JUNE 21

Isaiah 41:13 (NASB): For I am the Lord your God, who uphold your right hand, who says to you, 'Do not fear, I will help you'.

IT'S NOT FALLING APART

Fear is real! The fear of losing who, and what matters, is real! And if we're not careful, we'll go months and months, living in fear, and afraid to pursue anything better, for the fear of losing what we already have. My prayer is, that we overcome the spirit of fear, and find the strength to fully embrace what God has given to us. The 2nd Book of Timothy, the 1st chapter, and the 7th verse, teaches us that fear, is NOT from God, so I pray for the desire to walk in love, and power, and that we will be strong in our minds again, in Jesus' name! I heard the Lord say, "it's NOT going to fall apart!" So, I pray that our focus will shift to what God has spoken, and away from what the enemy keeps repeating. I pray for courage to keep pursuing our dreams, and the desires of our hearts.

I pray for vision to emerge out of the darkness of our regrets, and our mistakes. And that we'd practice the art of forgetting, and forgiving, and that we'd faith our way forward; knowing that God's thoughts of us are good, and that's He's given us a future, and a hope. Whoever, and whatever leaves, wasn't included in our future anyway. So, I pray that we stay focused on God, keep God first, and obey God's voice, knowing that if God started it, God will finish it. It's in Jesus' name I pray, AMEN!

JUNE 22

Psalms 34:17 (NASB): The righteous, and the Lord hears and delivers them out of all their troubles.

ELEVATE MY PERSPECTIVE

In the name of Jesus, Psalms 121 says, "I will lift up my eyes to the mountains; From where shall my help come? 2 My help comes from the Lord, who made heaven and earth." Friends...the truth is, we do have help! We are not alone! We are not forgotten! And we are not forsaken! My prayer is, that Holy Spirit helps us to elevate our perspective. And that we'd stop being so negative, and so defeated, about everything! I pray for a booster shot of faith today. And that Holy Spirit would lift up our mental view, and cause our minds, and our thoughts, to submit to our spirits.

I pray that Holy Spirit would increase our capacity to see beyond the past, and to embrace the future, as if it were already our present condition. I speak to the spirit of heaviness and weariness, and I command us to "lift up our heads"...and I decree and declare the King of Glory shall come in! Our minds are changing! Our thoughts are changing! Our perspective is changing, and now we can see our situation, the same way God sees our situation, in Jesus' Name! And Father I thank You, for thou art a shield for us, our glory, and the lifter up of our heads! Thank you, for changing the way we look at a thing! Thank you for changing the way we see it! Thank you, Father, for elevating our perspective. It's in Jesus' name I pray, Amen!

JUNE 23

James 1:2-4 (NASB): Consider it all joy, my brethren, when you encounter various trials, knowing that the testing of your faith produces endurance. And let endurance have its perfect result, so that you may be perfect and complete, lacking in nothing.

THIS TOO SHALL PASS

This is a true saying, "TROUBLE DON'T LAST ALWAYS!" But that "always" is objective...and sometimes it can seem like it's the hand that we've been dealt. When the reality is, and the truth is, that there is nothing that can stand against us, any longer than God will allow. And God will never allow anything to stand against us, that we've not already been equipped, and prepared to overcome! Hallelujah!

So, today's prayer is for vision beyond the present challenges. And that Holy Spirit would give us peace, as we wait for the manifestation of God's Word, and the demonstration of God's will, for our lives. I pray that we resolve to wait on the Lord again, and that we refuse to grow weary in well doing! I pray for insight on what's really going on, so the enemy won't be able to use the fear of losing, against us, anymore!

I pray for clear eyes, and full hearts and that we find the courage to stare the enemy in the face, while we're moving forward. This, whatever "this" is, cannot last a day longer than it's supposed to! This, whatever "this" is, cannot hurt you and it has to work for you, and not against you! So, I'm praying for grace to ride this one out! grace to endure, and grace to overcome, because this too, shall pass! It's in Jesus' name I pray, Amen!

JUNE 24

Psalms 16:11 (NASB): You make known to me the path of life; in your presence there is fullness of joy; at your right hand are pleasures forevermore.

I CLAIM JOY

I declare that I am not I'm not sad and alone. I have not missed my moment. I am not afraid to move forward because of what happened in my past.

God's plan to deliver me, from the snare of the fowler, and from the hand of the enemy is working together for my good, in Jesus' name! My testimony will be, "God brought me straight out of that, and straight into the best days of my life!" So, no fear today! No depression today! I choose the joy of the Lord! If I have to enjoy the day all by myself, then so be it!

I'm going to step into the joy of the Lord and I'll never go back to being that miserable person, ever again! I pray that God heals you, delivers you, and that God himself becomes your defender! I pray that your battle, becomes God's battle, and that your only struggle would be what to do with the overflow!

Have a strong day! Have a big day today! And know that God is with you. It's in Jesus' name I pray, Amen!

JUNE 25

Romans 12:1 (NASB): Therefore I urge you, brethren, by the mercies of God, to present your bodies a living and holy sacrifice, acceptable to God, which is your spiritual service

CLEANSE MY TEMPLE

Father I pray that Jesus will return to my physical temple today, and that He will set things in proper order. I pray that He will once again, give me the desires of my heart and that He will cause me only to desire, what He desires for me to have. I pray that my flesh won't have me out of your will, and that even though I may still desire it, that it won't control me, or render me helpless to its call.

I say "YES" to what you're doing in my life, and I recommit to laying all of my affections, and all of my devotions and desires, at your feet. Holy Spirit cleanse my temple! Wash my brain and purify my soul. Sever everything soul tie, that keeps me in yesterday. Cut everything that causes me to live outside of your will! And then Father grant me grace to overcome every temptation, and to lay aside every sin, that so easily besets me.

I decree and declare, that what I tripped over last year, I'm going to leap over this year! That what caused me to stumble, and to live in fear, and in guilt, and to bound by shame, I decree and declare that the chains are broken, and I am fRee. And from today forward, I'll be able to discern, and to see. That from today forward, my walk is right, and my heart is pure. It's in Jesus' name I pray, Amen!

JUNE 26

Hebrews 12:1 (NASB): Therefore, since we have so great a cloud of witnesses surrounding us, let us also lay aside every encumbrance and the sin which so easily entangles us, and let us run with endurance the race that is set before us.

STRENGTHEN OUR FAITH

God's about to do something! He's leaning in your direction, tipping the scales in your favor, and turning the hearts of the decision makers to you. No's are becoming yes's, supernaturally! People who were against you are about to be for you, and what used to be dreadfully difficult, is about to get supernaturally easy, in Jesus' name.

Father help our unbelief and use the resistance to strengthen our faith. Show us how to have bold faith, even in crisis, and grant us grace to stay strong. To stay steady and to stay ready, knowing that, "things are about to start happening for us SUPERNATURALLY!" Holy Spirit keep our eyes on the prize and help us to keep pressing and reaching, in Jesus' name. Show us what's ahead and don't let anything or anybody catch us off guard, or unprepared. Lean in our direction! Turn the tables in our favor and put us in a better place. Let the next few days be full of miracles, signs, wonders and unexpected blessings. Let this be the turning point, so that by next month, we have something completely different and brand new to thank you for! It's in the mighty name of Jesus we pray, Amen!

JUNE 27

Deuteronomy 31:6 (NASB): Be strong and courageous, do not be afraid or tremble at them, for the Lord your God is the one who goes with you. He will not fail you or forsake you.

FREE FROM FEAR

I declare today to be a fear free day! That you no longer be controlled, nor manipulated by what "might, could" happen, and that the thought of you losing, becomes an impossibility to you, and to the people in your circle! I pray for divine separation, from every fearful influence, and from every voice of unbelief, and that Holy Spirit would persuade you to hope against hope!

I pray for the faith of childless Abraham to come upon you, and to start growing in you, at a pace that you cannot control! I pray for faith to believe God for something supernatural! I pray that God does something big today! And that every hindrance, every hold up, everything, and everyone, that would keep you complacent, and stuck on stupid, would go, now, in the name of Jesus! I speak to every spirit, that would keep you "on hold", and I declare your freedom, in the name of Jesus!

Whatever, and whoever, has got to go now! This is our season to move forward! This is our season to go forth! This is our season to go in! This is our season to possess what we've been praying about! And we will do it, without the fear of losing anything! It's in the name of Jesus I pray, AMEN!

JUNE 28

Philippians 3:14 (NASB): I press on toward the goal for the prize of the upward call of God in Christ Jesus.

WE WON'T QUIT

I declare that you won't quit before you cross over. I'm praying you find grace and wisdom to stay the course and to course correct when needed, outliving your old reputation.

I'm praying that you are days away from changing, getting better and becoming your true self. I'm praying you don't quit on you and that you find the mental strength to keep moving forward, knowing God's about to do something for you. I pray that nothing is going to shock and convert, everybody who knew the Saul you. I call The Paul in me, out of me, and I command you to step into purpose and truth, in Jesus' name!

I call every gift, talent and skill to the forefront, and I decree and declare, you have grace to forget the foolishness, and the wherewithal to immediately change the way you walk, in Jesus' name!

JUNE 29

Proverbs 4:25 (NASB): Let your eyes look directly ahead, and let gaze be fixed straight in front of you.

FIGHTING FOR MY FUTURE

Father, I've finally made up my mind to forget those things which are behind me, and I've determined within my soul, that I'm going to reach for what is ahead. I can't do anything about what's behind me, other than leave it there. So, I choose to fight for my future, and not over my past! I choose to keep my focus forward, and not to ignore the past, but to make the past a steppingstone. There's too much in front of me, to be glued to what's behind me. So, I choose to fight for my future!

Holy Spirit help me to be present, mentally, and spiritually. Help me to stay in the moment, and yet seeing in the future. I pray for foresight, and for insight, so I don't get stuck fighting over things that don't matter anymore, and things that don't have any relevance in regard to what's ahead. I'm not wasting another minute of my life, rehashing the past. I'm not wasting another day, living in fear, because of what didn't happen, and what I did, or did not do! My fight is for what's ahead! My fight is for my future, and for what God has in store for me. I'm fasting for my future! I'm praying for His will! I'm positioning myself for something big, for something greater, for something huge, for something that cements my significance, because it's not all about me! So Holy Spirit help me to stay submitted to the process. Help me stay committed to your desires for my life. It's in Jesus' name I pray, Amen!

JUNE 30

2 Chronicles 26:5 (NASB): He continued to seek God in the days of Zechariah, who had understanding through the vision of God; and as long as he sought the Lord, God prospered him.

WINNING

Good morning Holy Spirit, thank you for waking me up this morning, and for keeping me in my right mind. Thank you for being here with me, and for keeping me, even on the days I didn't really want to be kept, thank you. Thank you for your grace, and for your mercy, and for your peace they're all sustaining me. Grace is covering me. Mercy is covering me. Peace is covering me, and because I'm covered, I can boldly declare, "WINNING"! I cannot lose because I'm covered. I cannot fail, because of the call of God that's upon me, and upon my family. I'm walking in a grace, that began decades ago, and the will of God, for my life, and for my family, is behind me, pushing me.

I cannot lose because I have the grace to overcome. I will not live in fear, because I have the grace to win. So today I use my faith, and I stir up my gift! Holy Spirit give me the wisdom and the courage to activate what's already in me! Give me the strength, to kindle afresh, that gift, that talent, that knack, that genius, that's in my blood!

Break the hold of the spirit of anger, bitterness, rejection and give me the strength I need to stir up the gift of God that's already in me. I don't waste the rest of my strong days searching for purpose and looking for something that I can prosper in.

Holy Spirit help me to see that my gift is in my blood...and then connect me to the right people, who'll help me to make my dReams, become my reality. It's in Jesus' Name I pray, and I declare, "WINNING"!

JULY

JULY 1

Luke 10:19 (NASB): Behold, I have given you authority to tread on serpents and scorpions, and over all the power of the enemy, and nothing will injure you."

I'VE GOT A PROMISE

Life's pressures are real, and there's no way of escaping them, but we do have a choice. First Corinthians chapter 16, verse 9, Paul says this, "for a wide door for effective service has opened to me, and there are many adversaries." I'm feeling the same way, as I'm sure you are to! So, my prayer today is, that we stay focused on the right thing! I pray that we overcome the temptation to make the adversity the focus, and that we choose to focus on the wide door! I pray against the spirit of anxiety, and fear, and I pray that we'll find the faith to set our affections on what God has promised. Yes, we're in a fight, but the battle is the Lord's, not ours! His name is on the line, not ours! His character is at question, not ours. So, all we have to do is obey His commands, and do what He has instructed us to do, and ALL things, will have to work together for our good!

I pray for the strength of will, to make the hard decisions. I pray for the mental fortitude, to stick to what we've committed to do. I pray that the promise, will become our focus, and NOT the pressure! I pray that we will position ourselves to LEAP, and let everything against us, push us! I pray that the pressure pushes us, and that the opposition will become the thing that guarantees the victory! It's in Jesus' name I pray, Amen!

JULY 2

Ephesians 6:10 (NASB): Finally, be strong in the Lord and in the strength of His might.

ONLY BE STRONG

Joshua chapter 1, verse 7 commands us to, "Only be strong and very courageous," so I charge you to get in agreement with the Word of God over your life, and to stop governing your life, and plotting your days, based on how you feel. We might "feel" weak, but the reality is, His strength can only be perfected in us, when ours runs out. Embrace how you feel, but then speak what you believe. I pray for the wisdom, and the discipline, to start saying what you believe, and to stop speaking things, based on how you feel.

I pray for strength in your mind, and for strength in your soul, so that your feelings don't dictate your confession. I pray for strong faith, so that your feelings don't smother your dReams, or cloud your vision. I pray for a restoration of your will to do, and to be, all that God has ordained! I pray that settling, or quitting would never again be viable options.

I pray for strength, mentally, emotionally, spiritually, and financially! I pray that our cash flow, will line up with how the anointing flows! I pray that our accounts will increase, as the grace of God on our lives increases. I pray that our private life, will be better than our public life, and that the grace, power, and strength of God, will be found in every area of our lives. It's in Jesus' name I pray, Amen!

JULY 3

Philippians 4:19 (NASB): And my God will supply all your needs according to his riches in glory in Christ Jesus.

LEAP

Father, my prayer today is, please send people into my life, who'll make my baby leap! I pray that you'll remove every hindering relationship, and disconnect me from anything, and anybody, who doesn't make what you've given me come alive.

Father show me who I'm supposed to connect to, and who I'm supposed to run to in this season. Don't let me waste another day of my life, trying to please people, and satisfy appetites, that no longer represent who I am. Disconnect me from everything that's not connected to your will for my life, and my future.

Reveal every divine connection and sever every demonic one. Remove everybody who makes my baby sleep. Get rid of every relationship that makes me comfortable being who I was never supposed to be. Cut every soul tie that binds me to my past, in the name of Jesus! I pray for revelation of divine connections and that you will make it absolutely clear, who's been sent to help me and who's been sent to set me back.

Show me and then give me the courage, the desire, and the strategy, to flush my life. Cleanse my soul, of every connection that the devil meant to destroy me, in the name of Jesus! Father send me to the people, send the people to me, who'll make my baby leap! Show me who's heard what I heard! Show me who's headed where I'm headed. And then rebuke the spirit of fear, so I won't get afraid, or intimidated, and back off, when I should be pressing in.

I decree and declare, "THIS IS THE DAY MY BABY LEAPS"! This is the day, that what God gave to me, starts moving again, in Jesus' name, Amen!

JULY 4

Psalms 143:10 (NASB): Teach me to do your will, for you are my God; let your good Spirit lead me on level ground.

FRESH START

Listen to me! The devil knows that God doesn't, and hasn't, changed His mind. So, the only option now, is to get you to change yours, DON'T! And stop letting people make you think that something's wrong, or off, because you have to make adjustments. Adjustments are the precursor to increase, and overflow, so go with it! Let Holy Spirit lead you, and trust that when He's done talking, and you're done doing, that you'll be on a path to something bigger and better, in Jesus' Name!

I'm praying now, that you won't grow weary in doing well, and that you will allow patience to perfect you, and perfect your product, in Jesus' name! I pray that Holy Spirit opens your eyes and ears, again, and that all of your days would be fruitful, and productive. It's in Jesus' name I pray, Amen!

JULY 5

Psalm 32:8 (NASB): I will instruct you and teach you in the way which you should go; I will advise you with My eye upon you.

IT WILL BE BIGGER

The next thing God does for me, is going to be big! So, I set my affections on Him, and I refuse to give my attention to anything, or to anyone, that's not focused on Jesus! This season I'm in, requires focus, and faith, and sanctification. So, I commit to myself, to pursue your presence. I commit to chase you again, even though I'm disappointed about where I am, and what hasn't happened, and what did happen, and how I was treated by the people I thought had my back! In spite of it all, Lord I still choose you!

I choose you when I am hurting, and I choose you when I'm good. Because I finally realize what you've been trying to do for me, is bigger than me. Your plan for my life is bigger than I thought it was, and now that I know the truth, I can make better choices. Now that I know the truth, my behavior will reflect that of a man who's got generations depending on his "yes", thank you for showing me the truth! The truth about who I am, the truth about who you are, and the truth about what's really going on in my life.

Truth is, it's bigger than I thought it was. I just didn't know, but now that I know better, I'm going to do better! Father give me the strength and the courage to do better and to be better. It's in Jesus' name I pray, Amen!

JULY 6

Joshua 10:8 (NASB): And the LORD said to Joshua, "Do not fear them, for I have handed them over to you; not [a]one of them will stand against you."

YOU'RE GOING TO LEAP

I'm praying that God would prevail strongly on your life to let everything that works against you, push you! I pray for wisdom and for insight, so that you don't start tripping because of the many adversaries. God has opened a wide door for us, and my prayer is, that we don't get so distracted by the adversity, that we miss the opportunity. This is our season again, so Father help us to remain focused, and confident! Help us Holy Spirit, to keep our eyes on you, and to never lose sight of what we're fighting for!

We have the grace to L.E.A.P, so we call our hearts, our minds, and our emotions, subject to God's word. No more panic attacks! No more uncontrolled episodes of anxiety, and fear! We pull down every stronghold, and every thought, that would cause us to get in fear, and to walk in unbelief. Holy Spirit help us to see beyond the present and give us another sneak peek into our future. Give us vision again and cause us to see that what's in front of us, is better than everything behind us!

Remind us, that your thoughts towards us are good, and that when you think it, that settles it! Remind us, that our latter will be greater than our former, and help us to focus forward, in Jesus' name!

Don't let us waste another day, tripping over what was! And then Father help us to forgive and help us to forget, so we don't waste another weekend tripping over something that you're going to use to make us better! Glorify yourself in my come up, and let your name be praised, as we get up, and make up, and stand up! It's in Jesus' name I pray, Amen!

JULY 7

Deuteronomy 20:4: (NASB): or the Lord your God is the One who is going with you, to fight for you against your enemies, to save you.

THE FIGHT IS FIXED

The devil's purpose in your life is to lose! And the only reason that God would even allow him to attack you, is because there is no way he can win! Your enemy is a loser! The devil's destiny is defeat! So, if you keep breathing, and keep getting up, there's absolutely no way you can lose! I know you're in a fight, but it's a fixed fight!

The outcome had been determined, and the winner had been decided upon, before the first punch was thrown. Listen to me, YOU CANNOT LOSE! Losing is not possible for you, because Jesus has already given you the victory! So, I pray for your will, and that Holy Spirit would refresh your desire to keep moving forward.

I pray for a winner's attitude and outlook! I pray for restored faith, and confidence, and that quitting becomes repulsive to you! Hear me, losing is NOT a part of your future, so keep fighting! Keep getting up! Keep believing! Keep reaching! Stretch yourself again and expect to win today! It's in Jesus' name I pray, Amen!

JULY 8

1 Peter 5:7 (NASB): He said to His disciples, It is inevitable that stumbling blocks come, but woe to him through whom they come!

GRACE TO OVERCOME

In Luke chapter 17, verse 1, Jesus says to his disciples, "It is impossible that no offenses should come." We have to stop allowing the devil to use the spirit of offense, as a means of holding us back, and keeping us trapped in the past. I pray that we finally see what anger, fear, guilt, and unforgiveness have done to us, and how they've negatively affected our lives and infected our future. I pray for the wisdom, and strength to release everything, and everybody that's kept our focus on yesterday, and on what happened, and on what they did, or did not do. I pray that the grace to forgive would overtake us, and that holding on to how we felt, and to the pain that we've grown accustomed to, would become intolerable to us! I pray for a breakthrough in the spirit, and that the power of God would break every anger chain, and every revenge chain, and every blame chain, that keeps us looking back, instead of looking ahead.

We have the grace to forgive! We have been divinely enabled to change the way we've felt, and the way we've looked at our past and our story. We have grace to forget about it. Grace to let it go and go on with our lives. Grace to see the good in the bad and grace to grow and keep it moving! We have grace to overcome. In Jesus' name, Amen!

JULY 9

1 Thessalonians 5:21 (NASB): but examine everything; hold firmly to that which is good,

DISCERNMENT

I pray for proper discernment and that we immediately be able to know when we're being lied to! I pray for an increase in our ability to identify those whom the devil has sent into our lives to set us back, and to make us miserable!

I pray for X-ray vision and that we walk in the grace to see a man's heart, before we ever hear their voice. I pray for strength to so "NO!" I pray for emotional stability, and for spiritual stamina to deny our flesh, even though everything in us says, "Do it! No one will know!" Thank you, Holy Spirit, for the desire to live right, and for the desire and the resolve to treat people right, even after they mistreated us! It's in Jesus' name I pray, AMEN!

JULY 10

Ephesians 4:23 (NASB): and that you are to be renewed in the spirit of your minds,

CHANGED THINKING

Holy Spirit help us to manage our thought life. I pray that our thinking would be framed by faith, and not by the few facts, that we have in hand. I pray that our faith would be the filter, for every "fact", and that Holy Spirit would help us to properly process every piece of information we've been given. I pray for fact proof faith, and that your future would not be altered because of stinking thinking! I pray for your mind! I pray for your mental stability, and I rebuke every demon assigned to break your mind! You are NOT going to snap! You are NOT going to lose it! You are going to walk by faith, and your thoughts are going to realign with God's will, and with God's plan for your life! You are NOT going to think yourself out of your future! You are NOT going to talk yourself into something that's beneath what God has given to you! You are NOT going to think yourself out of your destiny! And your life is about to get better because your thoughts are getting better!

Your life is changing because your thoughts are changing! Your future is secure, because you have the mind of Christ, and you think like God, and NOT like a man! Today is a new day! The first day! A better day! A destiny day! A prosperous day! A day of healing and deliverance! A day of freedom! This is the day that the Lord has made, and we're going to think like it, and act like it. It's in Jesus' name, Amen!

JULY 11

2 Corinthians 12:9 (NASB): And He has said to me, "My grace is sufficient for you, for power is perfected in weakness." Most gladly, therefore, I will rather boast about my weaknesses, so that the power of Christ may dwell in me.

GRACE TO GET UP

Laying down, and accepting failure and defeat, is not in your DNA! You're a fighter! You're a winner! God's on your side and despite the unwise choices we've all made, in our past, winning is still a part of our story! So, let's stop using our shortcomings, and our sins, as an excuse as to "why" we can't do better! Holy Spirit reminded me that Jesus paid my ransom, and that all my sins have been covered, and washed by the blood of Jesus! Hallelujah!

Then He told me to, "GET UP!", and I'm led to say the same thing to you today, GET UP! Don't stay down! Don't let the devil convince you that you're depressed, and that you're defeated, he's a liar! The devil is a professional liar, and you cannot afford to give another minute of your attention, to what he's saying to you! GET UP! Get up and go find God again! Get up and go find yourself again!

This is your moment to do better, to be better, and to get better, so don't miss it, thinking about something that cannot be changed! Find God in your bible! Find God in your soul! Find God in your story! And tell Him to be glorified in your life today. It's in Jesus' name I pray, Amen!

JULY 12

1 John 1:9 (NASB): If we confess our sins, He is faithful and righteous, so that He will forgive us our sins and cleanse us from all unrighteousness.

GRACE TO CLEAN UP

You do have a say, in who stays in your life, and in what stays in your life. My prayer is that Holy Spirit would help you to choose better, and that by His spirit, He would wash away the residue of your past. And free you from everything you've done, and from everything that was done to you. I pray for grace to get up, and then clean up!

I pray for courage to rid your house, and your heart, of everything the enemy has used to keep you bound. I pray for a release from the guilt and the shame, and that Holy Spirit would help you to get your groove back! I praise God for freedom! I praise God for wisdom! And I praise God for the desire to please Him with my life! It's in Jesus' name I pray, Amen!

JULY 13

Psalm 23:5 (NASB): You prepare a table before me in the presence of my enemies; You have anointed my head with oil; My cup overflows.

GRACE TO OIL UP

The only reason God's allowed the enemy to attack you, is because He's already given you the victory! This means you cannot lose if you do not quit! So today, we're going to do what we need to do, to get our oil up! We're going to do as David did, and anoint ourselves, even though what we did, we know was wrong! We confess our sins, we plead the blood over our lives, we accept the sacrifice of Jesus, and we believe that the price that Jesus paid, was more than enough to cover us.

This attack is not punishment, it's provision. The devil attacked you, but he wasn't counting on you having the presence of mind, and the courage, to use what he did to hurt you, to get your oil up! What was done to you, and what you did to yourself, crushed you, but at the same time, it produced the oil you needed, to move on to your next place in life. You're still anointed! Yes, you were wrong, and I know it's "your fault", but the blood can fix it! I plead the blood! And I decree and declare, "you shall live and not die!"

Everything that's happened to you, has got to work for you! Even the stuff that wasn't good, it's got to work together for your good! In Jesus' Name! So, take today to get your oil up! Get up, clean up and anoint yourself again if you have to! You're God's child! You're God's favorite! You're anointed for today! And nothing, by any means, will be able to hurt you. It's in the mighty name of Jesus I pray, Amen!

JULY 14

2 Corinthians 5:7 (NASB): or we walk by faith, not by sight

GRACE TO CHANGE UP

You already know that you cannot keep doing what you've been doing, so change! Yeah, it's easier said than done, but Holy Spirit, according to Romans chapter 8, will help us to deal with our proclivities, and with our weaknesses, but we have to ask! So, pray this prayer with me: Father, I pray for Grace to "Change Up", and I ask for wisdom to maintain it. Father help me be better. Help me to change.

Holy Spirit give me the strength I need, to get yesterday off my back, and off my name. Grace me to change my mind, and my approach. Give me a clearly defined strategy to flip the script on the devil, on my haters, and every one of my enemies. Grace me to change, and to defy the odds. Grace me to change things up, and to make up for lost time! Give me the wisdom, and the strength I need, to overcome the huge mistakes I've made, and then Father take the sting out of the stupid stuff I did, that the devil is trying to use, to make you out to be a liar. Grace me to recover from what I did and give me grace to overcome what the devil did. I need you! I trust you! I love you! And I'm completely committed to serve you. It's in Jesus' name I pray, Amen!

JULY 15

Colossians 3:12 (NASB): So, as those who have been chosen of God, holy and beloved, put on a heart of compassion, kindness, humility, gentleness, and patience;

COMPASSION

Father I thank you for everything good that happened to me today. I thank you for the things that happened that I didn't quite understand, and for the things that you allowed, knowing that they were necessary for my growth.

Truth is, I am getting better! I am changing, for good! I am growing, and I'm learning from everything, and from everybody! Even from the people that tried to play me, and for the ones who thought they took advantage of me.

I'm better because of how they treated me, and Father I just want to thank you, for not stopping it, so I could learn. Thank you for using the messenger of Satan to buffet me, because now I've got my head on straight! Now I know how not to treat people, and how to love people unconditionally.

Thank you, Father, for using the enemy to birth compassion in me and I'll never mistreat people again. I'll never do to people, what was done to me, but instead I'll be a walking manifestation of grace and mercy. It's in Jesus' name I pray, AMEN.

JULY 16

Psalm 27:4 (NASB): Delight yourself in the Lord; And He will give you the desires of your heart.

GRACE TO SWITCH UP

I have an ear to hear, what the spirit of the Lord is saying to the church! I can hear God's voice clearly! The distractions are still present, but they no longer affect me like they used to. Jezebel's messenger is still on the job, and the devil is constantly saying things, to try to get me to get in fear, but I shall not be moved! I can hear God clearly, and I know this is my season to do all that's in my heart to do.

I have the grace to hear, and properly perceive, and interpret divine messages, in Jesus' name! I hear God clearly, and I'll never be so distracted, and afraid again, that I miss my moment. I hear the sound, of the abundance of rain, and I'll never come up short, or not have what I need, ever again! It's time for my dreams to become my reality, and with God on my side, nothing shall be impossible!

It's my time to shine! It's my time to live! It's my time to be, all that God needs me to be, and I'm going to be me, unapologetically! Thank you, Holy Spirit, for making me free! Thank you for helping me see who I really am in God, and for setting me on a course for overflow, in Jesus' name! I'm in the best days of my life, and I'll never go back to being, who I was never supposed to be in the first place! It's in Jesus' name I pray, Amen.

JULY 17

Proverbs 14:27 (NASB): The fear of the Lord is a fountain of life, By which one may avoid the snares of death.

BUT I'M NOT DEAD

Life can be a trip sometimes, but I'm not going to lose my joy, or change who I've always been; because something didn't go the way I wanted it to, the devil is a lie! I'm going to keep being and doing, and I'm going to keep dReaming. I'm not going to stop living, and I'm not going to allow the disappointment to keep me from believing.

Father, I pray for peace this morning. I pray that you'll settle my spirit, and give me proper perspective, your perspective, regarding my situation. Give me revelation of the truth, and allow me to see what's really going on, so that the disappointment, doesn't become discouragement. Cause me to discern your will, so that I can embrace the truth, and the lies of the devil won't affect me like they have in the past. Increase my ability to hear your voice, and make me super sensitive to your spirit, in Jesus' name!

Father, I pray that this let down, won't break me down, but cause it to be the thing that builds me up, and draws me closer to you! Let this moment of disappointment mature me, and make me better, and stronger, and wiser, in Jesus' name. Cause it to give me the boldness I need to move forward. I'm disappointed, but I'm not dead. I declare, "I shall live"! It's in Jesus' name I pray, Amen!

JULY 18

1 Thessalonians 5:12 (NASB): But we ask you, brothers and sisters, to recognize those who diligently labor among you and are in leadership over you in the Lord, and give you instruction,

HELP US TO DISCERN

Today we're praying for grace to deal with every direct message, that Jezebel has sent to distract us. And Father I thank you for increasing our ability to discern. Thank you, Father, for causing us to be extremely sensitive to truth, and to be able to know when we're being deceived, in Jesus' Name! I praise you for clarity of thought, and focus, and that no matter what the enemy says, or does, that we will not be distracted! We will not get off our A game! We will not be off emotionally, spiritually, or physically! Our hearts, our souls, and our bodies, will never be affected again, by the hopes and dreams of our enemies, concerning us!

Truth is, if they could kill us, they would've killed us! But the blood blocked every attack, and every attempt to take us out, bless your name! The blood covered us, even though some of the drama, and much of the stress, was created by some of the dumb stuff we did! Thank you, Father, for covering us, and loving us unconditionally! Thank you, Lord, for helping us to change, and for showing us how to be better. We give you praise today, because now that we're free, we can be who you created us to be.

Thank you, for removing every distraction, and for giving us the grace to properly filter every message that Jezebel sends! Purpose, and destiny, have both become the filters, that every distracting message must go through. And we call today, a focused day! It's in Jesus' name I pray, Amen!

JULY 19

Psalm 91:11 (NASB): For He will give His angels charge concerning you, To guard you in all your ways.

GOD'S SENDING ANGELS

You are not alone! You are not fighting by yourself! As a matter of fact, the fight you're in, isn't even you're fight, it's The Lord's! And because it's God's fight, God, is sending angels! God's sending reinforcements, and support staff, to keep you encouraged, and in the fight!

My prayer is that you overcome the temptation to quit. I pray that you maintain your desire to fight, and that you not grow weary in doing well. I pray that your faith won't fail, and that ministering angels would release the strength, and the grace, and the courage, and the patience you need, to win! God's sending angels and I pray that you'd be in the right place, at the right time, to receive what God has prepared for you.

I pray that the help assigned to your life, would find you quickly, and that their ministry would shift you into a better place, in Jesus' name! I pray for fresh favor, restored hope, and renewed faith, and that you would find peace in God's presence. It's in Jesus' name I pray, Amen.

JULY 20

Romans 9:37 (NASB): But in all these things we overwhelmingly conquer through Him who loved us.

I HAVE ALREADY WON

Father I thank you for giving me my fight back! Thank you for restoring my joy, and reassuring me, that I'm not fighting for nothing. I praise you in advance for the victory, and I declare that because Jehovah Shammah is with me, I've already won. I cannot lose, because the Lord is fighting for me, and fighting thru me! When I speak the word over my life, and when I say in time, what God has said in eternity, it's just as if God is speaking Himself.

I am an ambassador for Christ, I'm here in the earth to represent His interest, and to accomplish His will, therefore losing is impossible for me! All I do is win, and I feel my second wind kicking in! I feel my desire to succeed coming back! I feel my strength rising up, and the spirit of fatigue being broken off my life!

To God be the glory! I cannot lose! To God be the glory! I cannot be defeated! So, everything that's happened to me, had to be training, and preparation for what's ahead of me. And I confess, I want it all! In Jesus' name I pray, AMEN!

JULY 21

2 Timothy 1:7 (NASB): For God has not given us a spirit of timidity, but of power and love and discipline.

GRACE TO SAY NO

Father I thank you, for the desire, and the strength of will, to please you with my life. And I give you praise today, for giving me the grace I need, to tell you "YES", and to tell my flesh, "NO!" Thank you, Holy Spirit, for renewing my strength, and for giving me everything I need to overcome the weakness of my flesh. Thank you, for changing my desires, and for giving me the will, and the wisdom to retrain my flesh.

I have authority over my body, and over my mind, and I have the right to dictate, what I do, what I desire, what I say, what I eat, how much I eat, when I eat, and who I eat with! I will no longer live my life, as a person who's got no future! I will no longer be reckless with my relationships, and I will not allow anyone to come into my life, who has not been sent by God! I'm on a mission to please God's Heart with the way I live my life, and I cannot afford another casual, meaningless, dead end connection with anybody! Thank you, Holy Spirit, for teaching me to discern the difference, and for helping me to know who to say "NO" to! I pray for the grace to say "NO!"

No guilt! No shame! And no more torment, because of our past failures. We take our rightful place today, and we declare, "what God has for me, is for me!" We will not live in fear, and we will not allow anyone, or anything, to run us away from the place that God has assigned us to! We're here to stay, and we will not be tricked, manipulated, or convinced to leave our sweet spot, ever again! We're going to occupy, until He comes! It's in Jesus' name I pray, Amen.

JULY 22

Philippians 4:19 (NASB): And my God will supply all your needs according to His riches in glory in Christ Jesus.

BETTER!

Better begins again, for me, today! So, I position myself, and I prepare myself for what God is doing. I set myself in agreement with God's will, and I align myself to move with God, and in God's time. I will no longer be the cause of my setback. I refuse to continue to be the reason why God's will, and God's plan for my life, remains on hold. I set myself in agreement with God, I choose your will Father, and I say 'YES', all over again! I want what you want for my life, so I'm praying for wisdom to live better, and to make better choices. I choose better! Better chooses me, and my life will never be "under" again! I pray for courage to choose what's best, and what's right, over what's comfortable and convenient! And I thank you Father, for the wisdom, and the discernment, to know the difference between them. Better begins for me, today!

I choose to move forward, praying for the strength to never go back, or desire anything ever again, that's beneath me, in Jesus' name! I pray for friends who want to live right. I pray that you'll bring me into the close company with people who are committed to living for God. And that you'll separate me from everything, and everybody that jeopardizes my relationship with You. Better begins again, for me today. It's in Jesus' name I pray, Amen!

JULY 23

Proverbs 16:9 (NASB): The mind of a person plans his way, But the Lord directs his steps.

GRACE TO GET IN PLACE

The devil tricked you into getting out of place, and you let life run you out of your place of grace, but that's all turning around, as we pray this prayer! Father, in the name of Jesus, I thank you for the grace, to get back in place. Thank you, Father, for the courage and the strength to care again. You have not given us the spirit of fear, so today we choose to live a fear free life! We do have a choice, and our choice today, is to confess our sins, acknowledge where we were wrong, and operate in new mercy.

No guilt! No shame! And no more torment, because of our past failures. We take our rightful place today, and we declare, "what God has for me, is for me!" We will not live in fear, and we will not allow anyone, or anything, to run us away from the place that God has assigned us to! We're here to stay, and we will not be tricked, manipulated, or convinced to leave our sweet spot, ever again! We're going to occupy, until He comes! It's in Jesus' name I pray, Amen.

JULY 24

Philippians 4:6 (NASB): Do not be anxious about anything, but in everything by prayer and pleading with thanksgiving let your requests be made known to God.

GRACE TO CUT IT LOOSE

Father help us today and give us the courage and the patience we need, to lay aside every weight, and every sin that holds us back. But don't let us become so desperate, or so zealous, that we get in a hurry, and mislabel the two. Show us the difference and help us to discern what needs to be put to the side, and what needs to be cut off. Don't let us get in a rush, and start making bad choices, and cuts! Show us what to do, and how to do it. And don't let us mistreat anyone, in the process of breaking the yokes, and purifying our souls.

Help us to treat everybody right, especially the ones who've done us wrong. Help us to make defined, precise cuts, so we don't destroy the relationships, and the points of connection, that are still relevant to our future. Grace us, to once and for all, have the strength, not to hold on, but the strength to let go! Father give us the grace to cut it loose! Give us the courage needed, to finally sever the tie! And then Holy Spirit, I pray that you would help us to heal, fully! Don't let us rush you, or the process! Don't let us out, until we're ready to be exposed to people again. Hide us, until there's no remaining evidence of what we've been through! Keep us! Cover us! Then Father, bless us for submitting our lives to your will and to your plan. It's in Jesus' name I pray, Amen.

JULY 25

Ephesians 4:23 (NASB): and that you are to be renewed in the spirit of your minds,

GRACE TO CUT IT OUT

Some stuff, we just have to stop doing! So, we pray for God's help tonight, and we ask that you give us the wherewithal to change! Holy Spirit touch our minds and teach us to think differently. Touch our hearts, and teach us to lean towards our spirits, and away from our feelings. We're tired of the same drama, and the same setbacks, and we need your help to breakout of this prison, that the enemy has us living in. Release your presence again, and release your power, until staying the same, is no longer an option.

Set the captive free, and help us to choose freedom, in Jesus' name! The price we've paid, is way too high, so Father give us the wisdom, and the strength to "CUT IT!" Being free is a lot harder than we thought it was but because your yoke is easy, and your burden is light, we know that staying free is possible! With God, all things are possible, so we speak freedom to our future! We speak patience to our present, and we declare that everything that happened in the past, was a part of your plan for our lives. Father get the glory, as we walk in our freedom! Get the glory, as we lay aside the weight, and the sin! Be glorified Father, as we choose to be better, and do better, and decide that some things, we're just not doing, anymore! It's in Jesus' name I pray, Amen.

JULY 26

Ephesians 4:31 (NASB): All bitterness, wrath, anger, clamor, and slander must be removed from you, along with all malice.

GRACE TO CUT IT

My prayer today, is for wisdom. Holy Spirit, show us who and what, must be cut. Show us when, and how, and please Father don't let us get puffed up, or arrogant, or mean, just because we've finally found the courage to do better. Help us to be better, so we can have better. Help us to lay aside the stuff, that's no longer appropriate for a Christian. Help us to maintain the kind of life, and lifestyle, that would become attractive to the sinner, and cause them to ask questions about our relationship with you.

Father don't let us carry anything, or anybody, that's too heavy or burdensome for this season of our lives. Show us the weight, and the sin, help us to discern the difference, and then help us to sever the ties. Give us the grace to cut it! Give us the desire, and the strategy, to stay free. Don't let the people, places, or things that surround us, give us excuse not to change.

Father we need your help today. So, we pray for wisdom, and for the strength of will, to make the necessary cuts that will keep us on pace, for what you have planned. Your will is what we want! To please you, in every facet of our lives, that's our determination! To glorify you, in everything we do, that's what we seek after. Help our infirmities! Help us to think differently, so we can act differently. Make us free! Cause our behavior, and our appetites, to become a reflection of our newfound freedom! Father we give you praise today, for the grace to "CUT IT!" It's in Jesus' name I pray, Amen.

JULY 27

Psalm 119:15 (NASB): I will meditate on Your precepts And regard Your ways.

GRACE TO CUT IT UP

Father, in the Name of Jesus, I thank you for giving me the grace to lay aside every weight, and the sin, that for generations has continuously plagued my family, and altered my life! I understand that you've given me the authority to change my life, with the words of my mouth, so today I confess, "I have the grace to CUT IT UP!" This isn't the first time I've said this, and it won't be the last, as I'm a work in progress, and I'm growing, and getting better every day! I'm changing and the things that used to throw me off, and set me back, no longer have that kind of power in my life, because I choose to walk in the authority that you've given me! I choose to shift my focus upward, and to turn a deaf ear to what the devil is speaking over my life.

I belong to you! Jesus paid the price for my salvation, and there's nothing I could ever do, to make you change your mind about me, so I choose to reset my life! I choose to reset my focus, and to keep my eyes on you! I intentionally drown out every negative voice, and I position my heart to hear from You. Help me Holy Spirit, to cut it up, and to consistently turn up the volume of your voice. Help me Holy Spirit, to continually give You my heart, and my undivided attention. I need your help! And I need you to teach me how to tune out the forces of negativity, and weariness that surround me.

Show me the people you've assigned to my life, to make my life a happy life! Show me the people you've sent to me, to fill my days with joy! And then Father, teach me how to rid my life of the stuff I'm no longer supposed to be carrying, or doing. Don't let my heart, have me carrying people and stuff, that I'm no longer equipped to carry. Don't let my kindness, become my weakness, and end me up in sin! Father I need your help! Show me what to cut up, and what to cut down! Show me who to let in, and who to put out! Show me! Teach me! Lead me! Guide me! And I'll give you glory. It's in Jesus' name I pray, Amen.

JULY 28

Psalm 20:5 (NASB): We will sing for joy over your victory, and in the name of our God we will set up our banners. May the LORD fulfill all your desires.

GRACE TO SIT

Father, today we take our place! We shift our focus away from where we've been, and we set our eyes on Jesus, who is the author, and the finisher, of our faith! We forget those things which are behind, which simply means that we no longer give them energy, or attention, and we do our part, to stretch ourselves into something greater. Today is going to be one of the best days we've had in a while, because we are going to sit down, and not allow the enemy to have us up, running around, and chasing things, or people, that God never intended for us to have!

This is my prayer today, and my confession of faith, all at the same time! I release peace, and provision over my own life, and I declare today to be a day of victory, and authority! Today I find my way back to my place of grace! Today I find my sweet spot again, and rediscover me! No more chasing! No more begging people to understand, truth is, if you don't "get me" by now, you probably represent a season of my life, that's no longer relevant.

So today I take my seat and I settle myself, into my place of authority, and grace. No more chasing. With God's help today, my mind, and my spirit, will be at peace, In the name of Jesus! No more getting out of place! No more getting upset over things that God has already fixed! I'm going to enjoy Jesus! Today, I'm going to enjoy this front row seat, to the devil's defeat, and I'm going to plan for my future, today! It's in Jesus' name I pray, Amen.

JULY 29

Psalms 16:11 (NASB): When my anxious thoughts multiply within me, Your comfort delights my soul.

GRACE TO GET MY JOY BACK

I'm praying that by the time this day ends, that you will be able to boldly declare, "I got my joy back!" And I don't mean some empty, religious statement, that you call faith, but you know isn't your truth! I'm praying that the power of God would hit your life today, and that all things would be made new. I pray for clarity of purpose, and that you'd finally understand that you cannot lose, because you've already won!

The victory really is yours, and Jesus has defeated every one of your enemies! So, I pray for the strength, to step into the Joy of the Lord! I pray for peace to hit your mind, like a flood, and that everything you need, would fall in place, in the name of Jesus! I command you to get up! Pull yourself together, in the name of Jesus!

Today is the beginning of a new era in your life and you will never again lose your joy over people, and material things! Today is the day you finally "get it", and you'll never be the prisoner of depression, ever again! Get your swag back! Do it! Be it! Overcome it! Beat it! Take it! Grow it! Love it! In Jesus' name!

Love your life today and stop wishing you were somebody else! Love your life today and stop wishing you had somebody else! Love yourself today and stop wishing you were somebody else! Your life isn't perfect, but your life is good, and it's going to get better, as you get better! So be at peace today, be free today, be you today! It's in Jesus' name I pray, Amen.

JULY 30

Deuteronomy 31:6 (NASB): Be strong and courageous, do not be afraid or in dread of them, for the Lord your God is the One who is going with you. He will not desert you or abandon you."

GRACE TO CHANGE

I pray that Holy Spirit gives us strength to stay free, and that God would bless us so good, that the thought of going back, would make us nauseous! I pray for change to hit us in the belly, and that this new place we're in, would resonate in the very core of our being. I pray for permanent changes, and elevated mindsets. I pray for new circles, and connections, that would reflect our freedom.

I pray for courage to go places, do things, that we've always been afraid to do! I pray for friends that'll stretch us beyond our places of comfort and push us into purpose and destiny! I pray for lifelong freedom, from every generation curse and habit, that's plagued our family, and hovered over our heads, like a dark cloud! I pray that the glory of the Lord would rise among us, and upon us, and that the light of God would be so strong, that it blinds your enemies, but illuminates your gifts, so the people who are assigned to bless you, can't miss you! Let's be free today! Let's forget about what happened, and what we did, and take some time to enjoy being His! Let's be free today and vow to never give it up again. It's in Jesus' name I pray, Amen.

JULY 31

Psalm 75:6 (NASB): For not from the east, nor from the west, Nor from the desert comes exaltation;

IT WON'T BE LONG

God's about to bring our process to a close. Everything that we were supposed to learn, and everything that we were supposed to get out of this season of testing and trial, has been accomplished. And now the time has come for us to move on to a better life. Friends, I am convinced that what is in front of us, is way better than what's behind us, and all we have to do to get it, is stay in faith, and keep moving forward. Father help us to stay focused forward, and make us free from everything, and from everybody, that would try to keep us bound to our past.

Thank you, Holy Spirit, for settling our hearts, and our minds. and for giving us the strength to press, and the courage to keep reaching and stretching, even though this is taking a lot longer than we thought it would! Thank you for using what we've gone through to teach us how to wait. Now that patience has had her perfect work, we praise you for this season of breakthrough and promotion! Thank you, Father, for lifting our heads, and for elevating our status! Thank you for walking us through the process, and for assuring us that you'd never leave us, even after people did! We hear you, and we agree, "IT WON'T BE LONG!!!" We decree and declare, that before this year is over, we'll be living in it, renting it to somebody, driving it, working it, doing it, being it, and free from it. It's in Jesus' name, Amen.

AUGUST

AUGUST 1

Galatians 5: 1(NASB): It was for freedom that Christ set us free; therefore, keep standing firm and do not be subject again to a yoke of slavery.

IT IS FINISHED

Father I'm praying for the grace of Galatians chapter 5, verse 1, to come on our lives, and that we choose to, "Stand fast therefore in the liberty by which Christ has made us free, and do not be entangled again with a yoke of bondage." Now that we're free, I pray that we stay free, in Jesus' name! I pray for divine roadblocks, and that you'd make it literally impossible for us to go back to it, or to them!

I pray for permanent cuts, and the severing of every unproductive, negative, debilitating soul tie. I thank you Father for making us free, and for giving us the grace to walk in our truth, without guilt, and without shame! Thank you for the blood and for covering us when we should've been exposed! Thank you for keeping us, and for not giving us what we deserved, but then giving us what you destined for us to have! Thank you! Thank you for closing the door! Thank you for shutting down the attack of the enemy, after it changed me, but before it destroyed me! Thank you for finishing what You started and for honoring your word, even after I didn't, and couldn't honor mine!

I give you praise today, for your goodness, and your mercy! I bless you today, because your thoughts of me are good, and not evil, and because you've given me a future, and a hope!

Thank you for completing the good work that you started in me. Thank you for holding me down, when I thought it was too late, and too bad to ever be something good! I'm looking for a miracle! I expect the impossible. It's in Jesus' name I pray, Amen.

AUGUST 2

Job 22:28 (NASB): You will also decide something, and it will be established for you; And light will shine on your ways.

IT'S NOT WHAT IT LOOKS LIKE

What it looks like, is not what it is like! There is more going on, in the spirit, than your natural eye can see, so don't let how you feel, or what you've been told, change what you believe, and what you confess out of your own mouth! It doesn't matter if what you need to happen, has never happened before, that doesn't mean that God can't or won't do it! I believe we're going to be the first! The first to receive this kind of miracle! The first to see this kind of breakthrough! The first to have this type of testimony, and the first to live, to tell the story! There is NOTHING our God cannot do!

So, we place a demand on the power of God today, and we decree and declare, we have grace to defy the odds! Grace to overcome any and every challenge, sickness, disease, diagnosis, prognosis, medical opinion, and/or symptoms and side effects! This is the day that the Lord has made, and we refuse to be depressed, and bedridden! We refuse to believe the report of the enemy, his messengers, and we choose to believe, the report of the Lord! Our confession of faith is, "I expect a miracle! TODAY!" It's in Jesus' name we pray, Amen!

AUGUST 3

Job 33:4 (NASB): The Spirit of God has made me, And the breath of the Almighty gives me life.

GET IN THE MIDDLE

Father I thank you for blessing me to see another day, and for finishing my day, and fixing my day, so that no matter what happens, I would come out on top!

Thank you, Holy Spirit, for setting things in order, and for blowing in, over, and thru my life in such a way, that everything dead, that wasn't supposed to die, must come back to life!

I prophesy to every dry bone, (Ezekiel37) and I command you to live! I prophesy to everything in my space, that's become lifeless, and command you to agree with, and respond to the word of the Lord, spoken over my life! I speak to my dReams, to my debts, and to my days, and I command you to align yourself with God's will.

I take authority in my situation, and I prophesy, dReams become my reality! Debt will supernaturally disappear! Days produce and extend. In Jesus' name, this is my prayer.

AUGUST 4

Psalm 27:13-14 (NASB): I would have despaired unless I had believed that I would see the goodness of the Lord In the land of the living. Wait for the Lord; Be strong and let your heart take courage; Yes, wait for the Lord.

YOU WILL NOT BREAK

"You are not going to break! You are not going to fail! You are not going to lose it! You're going to stand your ground, and wait on the Lord, and you are going to be of good courage." That's my confession of faith over my own life today, and I pray that you'll take the same stand with me. And that you will keep your eyes on Jesus, the author, and the finisher of our faith. I pray for a stress-free day today and even though God's stretching us and pulling the best of who we are out of us, I pray that the stretching won't stress us!

I pray that we'll keep everything in proper perspective, and that the truth will regulate and justify by faith how we feel about our situation. His thoughts of us are good! His thoughts of us are beautiful! God has not set us up to fail! This is the best season and strongest season of our lives where His strength is being made perfect by our weakness.

Thank you, Father, for stretching me! Thank you for wanting more for me than I could ever want for myself and making complacency a non-option in my life. The stretching will not stress me. I have wisdom, truth, revelation, patience, and God's viewpoint. Therefore, stress is unnecessary, and not allowed on this level. I've been justified by faith, and I choose to live by faith! I'm not stressing over anybody or anything. Everything has got to work for my good. In Jesus' name, Amen.

AUGUST 5

2 Timothy 1:7 (NASB): For God has not given us a spirit of timidity, but of power and love and discipline.

YOU CAN, YOU WILL

Father, in the name of Jesus I come before you today, still in faith for miracles signs and wonders. I thank you Father, that today my faith will produce. Today, my faith will produce your will, and manifest supernatural results on my behalf.

I choose to believe, even in the midst of consistent calamity, and days and days of disappointments. My faith says you can. My faith says, You will.

So even though my Lazarus is already dead, I believe your presence makes all things possible! So, I pray for the same grace to come on my life and that on this day, you would make me a miracle!

I speak to every dead, stinking situation, and I say, "Lazarus, come forth!" I declare, "God's not finished! And I am about to see the hand of God, like I've never seen Him before"! It's in Jesus' name I pray, Amen!

AUGUST 6

Psalm 23:4 (NASB): Even though I walk through the [a]valley of the shadow of death, I fear no [b]evil, for You are with me; Your rod and Your staff, they comfort me.

IT'S NOT THAT BAD

Why get yourself all upset, over something that you know God has already worked out? It just doesn't make any sense, so get somewhere where you can settle your spirit and allow Holy Spirit to give you peace, in Jesus' name! Listen to me, "it's not going to be as bad as you think!" And whatever does happen, is going to work in your favor!

So, enjoy your down time, and let God give you the instructions, and the strategy, for your next move. Do not get in a hurry! Do not put yourself in harm's way! Do not expose yourself to something that you're not built to withstand. Be still! Be still and see the salvation of the Lord. You'll be better after the storm! I promise you, you will! It's in Jesus' name I pray, Amen.

AUGUST 7

Psalm 107:29 (NASB): He caused the storm to be still, So that the waves of the sea were hushed.

THANK YOU FOR THE STORM

Father I thank you, for caring enough about me, not to leave me, or let the devil have his way in my life. I thank you for everything I've gone thru, and overcome, and I give you praise for what's on the other side of what I'm going thru right now! Thank you for this storm! And for how you're going to use it to show me who's really with me.

Thank you, Lord, for using this storm to show me what's important, and who's important, and what I really can do without! I give you praise, for using every single thing that I'm going thru, and for reassuring me, that even my mess ups, were included in your plan for my life! Thank you for the storm, and for using the wind, and the water to move the stuff I thought I'd never be able to break away from. Thank you, Father, for using the rain to cleanse my surroundings, and for using the wind to displace the stuff that didn't want to let me go! I give you praise today, for this storm, and for how you've used it, to get me to move.

Thank you for pushing me out of my comfort zone, even if it is just long enough to get me to re-evaluate and reassess every relationship, and every desire. Everything is working together, for my good! And when this storm is over, I'll be free from yesterday! When this storm is finished rearranging my circle of friends, I'll be free from who I used to be! When this storm has run its course, I'll have everything I need to start a fresh, or to start over, if I want to! When this storm is over, I'll have everything, and everybody I need. It's in Jesus' name I pray! Amen!

.

AUGUST 8

Genesis 50:20 (NASB): As for you, you meant evil against me, but God meant it for good in order to bring about [a]this present result, to keep many people alive.

GODLY CONNECTED

It's time for you to move forward! So, I pray that Holy Spirit would grant you the grace to let it go, to let them go, and to move on with your life. I pray for peace, and confirmation, as you open your heart to new relationships and connections.

I pray against fear, and that one eye opened/one eye closed spirit, that would prevent you from pursuing new doors and new circles. I praise that Holy Spirit would reveal every snake, but that you do not waste too much time focusing on them. I pray that you walk in the grace to focus on the positive, and properly process and discard the negative. I pray against that loner spirit, and that spirit that would keep you isolated, and disconnected from the people, places, and things that God has sent to help you in this season.

I praise God for a discerning spirit, and for a loving spirit, that causes you to love your enemies, and pray for those who've tried to play you! You're better because of what they did! You're bigger because of what they did! And you'll never again fit into that small space you used to occupy. In Jesus' name, it is so! Amen!

AUGUST 9

Isaiah 26:3 (NASB): The steadfast of mind You will keep in perfect peace, Because he trusts in You.

I GOT MY PEACE BACK

My prayer for you today, is that before you close your eyes, you'll be able to claim this as your truth! Say it, "I got my peace back!" And I refuse to let anybody, or anything, take it from me, ever again! This is the peace that Jesus gave to me, and can't nobody take it away! that's right, I said, "can't nobody!" this peace is internal! This peace I have, is eternal, and it's everlasting! This peace I have is situation-proof, people-proof, drama-proof, and idiot-proof! I can't mess this up, even if I wanted to! It's God's gift to His children, and I've finally learned how to accept it, without letting the devil talk me out of it!

I pray this same grace comes on your life today, and that you choose to walk in His peace all day, and for the rest of your days. It's in Jesus' name I pray, Amen.

AUGUST 10

Psalm 16:8 (NASB): I have set the LORD continually before me; Because He is at my right hand, I will not be shaken.

UNDEFEATED

Father I thank you for another day, and another chance to gather in the name of Jesus. Something happens when the saints go to worship, and when we raise the name of Jesus! So, I thank you Father that today is going to be the day, that we corporately, and individually experience the power of God like we've never experienced Him before.

I praise you now, that when this season is over, the record will reflect that in every fight I involved you in, that you were undefeated! You've never lost a fight! You're the doctor who's never lost a patient! The lawyer who's never lost a case! So, I give you praise today, and I thank you in advance for giving me the victory, and for always causing me to triumph!

I cannot lose because you are with me! I cannot lose because the Lord of hosts is fighting in my place! I win every fight I involve you in, so today, I'm getting out of your way, and I say, "have your way Holy Spirit", fix it how you want to! Do whatever you need to, and for this I give you praise! I overcome every challenge today. In Jesus' name, AMEN!

AUGUST 11

Psalm 90:17(NASB): May the kindness of the Lord our God be upon us; And confirm for us the work of our hands; Yes, confirm the work of our hands.

I HAVE GRACE AND FAVOR

Father I thank you for this season of miracles signs and wonders! I praise you for the days of unprecedented access, and I bless your name God, for opening doors for me that no man can close! This is my season, for grace and favor. Things are about to start happening for me that have never happened for anybody in my family. Thank you, Father, for the grace to be the first one! Thank you for giving me the strength, and the courage to keep going, even when people tried to hold me back, and when they tried to block my elevation. I praise you for breaking me through, and for thwarting every plan of the enemy to get me out of place and disqualified!

Glory to God for the grace to breakthrough. Glory to God for the grace to succeed anyhow. I prophesy over my own self, and I declare, the next thing God does for me, is going to be big! It's going to make me one of a kind, and it's going to be so big, that my entire industry will see my good works, and have no other choice, but to glorify my Father in Heaven! God's doing something supernatural, and even the non-believer will have to give Him the credit, and the praise. It's in Jesus' name I pray!

AUGUST 12

2 Corinthians 10:5 (NASB): We are destroying arguments and all arrogance raised against the knowledge of God, and we are taking every thought captive to the obedience of Christ,

I WILL BE OPTIMISTIC

My prayer today, is that we learn to look at our lives, thru the lens of faith, and thru the eyes of God. Even on your worst day, God is still good, He's still faithful, and He can yet be trusted! So Holy Spirit, help us to see. Help us to discern the truth, and don't allow the facts to cause our faith to fail. Give us a sneak peek into your plan, and give us something to hold on to, other than just a gut feeling. Open our eyes and cause us to see what you see. Show us what it really is, and give us the courage to hold on, until things change for the better.

Cast down, cast out, and cause us to stay free from every depressing, pessimistic spirit and don't let anybody else into our personal space who'll try to talk us out of walking by faith. Help us to see the good, as well as the not so good, and help us to keep it all in proper perspective in Jesus' name! My glass is half full! My glass is not half empty and whatever isn't in my glass, isn't supposed to be! I have everything I need to be happy. I have everything I need to live a full life! Nothing about my life is empty, except for my jealous jar! I'm happy for me, and for everybody else too, and from today forward, I'm going to enjoy what I do have, and continue to pray for wisdom, and for strength, to work for what God wants me to have! It's in Jesus' name I pray, Amen.

AUGUST 13

Hebrews 11:6 (NASB): And without faith it is impossible to please Him, for the one who comes to God must believe that He exists, and that He proves to be One who rewards those who seek Him.

FINISH STRONG

The spirit of the quitter is broken off your life, in the name of Jesus! Father I thank you for a good day today. I give you praise for setting my day in order, and for structuring things in such a way that I cannot be distracted, and I cannot be detoured! Thank you for refreshing my focus, and for increasing my ability to pay attention. Thank you for the grace to finish strong.

I am not a quitter, and everything you've given me to do, I'm going to finish, without frustration! I declare the peace of God over my day, over my house, over my job, and over every interaction I have today, with people. No cussing today! No displays of anger today! No acting out of character today! No settling for less today! And no following the crowd today! I'm going to run my own race at my own pace. And the entire time, I'm going to stay in your face, so I don't get off course or off target. I'm going to finish strong, and I'm not going to finish last! I'm going to finish strong, and I'm not going to finish mad! I'm going to enjoy every minute of my journey and I'm going to keep my joy, and stay in my happy place, the entire time. The spirit of fainting, and the spirit of heaviness, have been overtaken by the garment of praise, and today is going to be good! It's in Jesus' name I pray, Amen.

AUGUST 14

Deuteronomy 20:4 (NASB): for the Lord your God is the One who is going with you, to fight for you against your enemies, to save you.'

I WILL NOT LOSE

I pray for every person, including myself, who's in a fight, and fighting for their life! I pray that you give them peace, and patience to endure the process. I pray that they don't faint, before they reap!

I pray for strength, and for joy, to flood their minds, and their space. I thank you now Father, for sending help, and for sending reinforcements to help us fight this fight of faith. I praise you for organizing my enemies, in such a way, that winning becomes impossible for them!

We cannot lose because the fights are fixed! Thank you for dealing with the devil, and for putting all things, under our feet! This is a fixed fight, and there's no way we can lose! I said there's no way we can lose! In Jesus' name!

So, I will lift up mine eyes, to the hills, from whence cometh my help! My help comes from the Lord! I cannot, and I will not lose, it's in Jesus' name I pray!

AUGUST 15

Isaiah 41:10 (NASB): Do not fear, for I am with you; Do not be afraid, for I am your God. I will strengthen you, I will also help you, I will also uphold you with My righteous right hand.'

GOD'S HAND IS ON IT

STOP tripping! God has not left you! God has not abandoned you! He is right there, in the middle of your fiery furnace with you. So, keep your eyes on Jesus, and do not allow the threats, and the heat, to become a distraction. He will never leave you, nor forsake you. Despite how it looks and how it feels, the truth is, God's got His hands on your circumstance!

God's will for your life is dictating what can and cannot happen! Your enemy can't do anything to you, that is not going to elevate you in the long run. So, stay the course! Stay with God! Stick to the plan God gave you, and do not allow your faith to waver! You're stronger than you think you are! You're more important than you think you are! And God cannot afford to let you fail or die! So, hold on. Something good is about to happen to you. It's in Jesus' name I pray, Amen.

AUGUST 16

2 Corinthians 9:8 (NASB): And God is able to make all grace overflow to you, so that, always having all sufficiency in everything, you may have an abundance for every good deed;

IF GOD BE FOR ME

This is my season to make history. This is my season to do something for you God. This is my season to do something that's never been done. This is my season to do something that no one in my family has ever done. So today my heart cries for your glory God, I will do anything for you. I will not be afraid of their faces. I will not be intimidated by anybody, or anything!

I have the peace of God, guarding my heart, and my mind, and I rest in the truth, not the facts. So, if God be for me, who can stand against me!

Today I wait on the Lord, and I choose, because I do have a choice, I choose to be of good courage! I choose to only be strong, and very courageous! In Jesus' name, Amen

AUGUST 17

Isaiah 25:1 (NASB): Lord, You are my God; I will exalt You, I will give thanks to Your name; For You have worked wonders, Plans formed long ago, with perfect faithfulness.

I WILL BLESS HIM

Father I thank you for your word, and I thank you for the word you've released over my life. I'm encouraged today, even in the middle of the biggest fight I've ever been in, because I know that the word over my life, must come to pass! I give you praise today, and I bless your name. Because I'm certain that what you began in me, you're God enough to finish! I am sure, that my end is so much better than my beginning, and that when this fight is over, victory shall be mine!

So, although I choose to hold my peace, and let you oh Lord, fight my battles, I refuse to hold my praise! I will bless the Lord at all times! Your praise will continually be in my mouth. My soul shall make its boast, not in me, or in anything that I've done, but my boast is in The Lord!

I choose to take a praise break, in the middle of my fight, and in the middle of my day, believing that this prayer will stop it, and then this praise will break it! It's in Jesus' name I pray, AMEN!

AUGUST 18

James 5:16 (NASB): Therefore, confess your sins to one another, and pray for one another so that you may be healed. A prayer of a righteous person, when it is brought about, can accomplish much.

I BELIEVE YOUR WORD

Father your word says, "If my people who are called by my name will humble themselves, and pray and seek my face, and turn from their wicked ways, then I will hear from heaven, and will forgive their sin and heal their land."

So, Father we declare these prayers stopped it! That our willingness, and our desire to have fresh dialogue with you, has put an end to this season of attack.

This prayer, broke it, and stirred up the anointing, that has destroyed every yoke, in Jesus' name!

My life will never be the same! My life will never as hard as it's been, again! So, I declare it's already getting better! It's already getting easier! God's already moving on my behalf. In Jesus' name I pray, AMEN!

AUGUST 19

Psalm 46:7-8 (NASB): The Lord of armies is with us; The God of Jacob is our stronghold. Come, behold the works of the Lord, Who has inflicted horrific events on the earth.

LOOSE MY STUFF

Father I thank you for divine intervention! I intentionally stop to pray, believing that as I declare "Thy Kingdom come, Thy will be done, on earth, as it is in Heaven", that my prayers release divine providence. And that by the end of business, today, I will be the recipient of miracles signs and wonders!

I stop to pray for daily bread, and I speak to every spirit that would fight against the manifestation of the finished works of Christ in my life, and I command them to lose my stuff! I pray for suddenlies, and immediatelies, and I decree and declare breakthrough for the believer! The just shall live!

And I prophesy quick moves, speedy manifestations, and supernatural turnarounds in the name of Jesus! These prayers have provoked your hand. By this time tomorrow, my enemies will know, that the Lord of Hosts is with me! Amen! Amen! Amen!

AUGUST 20

Mark 16:17 (NASB): These signs will accompany those who have believed: in My name they will cast out demons, they will speak with new tongues;

MIRACLES ARE COMING

Father I thank you for a good day so far! Thank you for giving me access to your presence, on a consistent basis, via my Pastor, and I thank you for speaking directly to me today!

I stop to pray, knowing that this prayer is going to stop something, that's been trying to stop me! I've intentionally pressed the pause button on my day, to give you praise. Knowing that this prayer, is going to break the thing, that's been trying to break me!

Father I give you glory, for consistently giving me access to your presence, via the community of faith, and for planting people in my life, that encourage my relationship with you! Thank you, Holy Spirit, for purging my circle of those people, places, and things, that drained my faith! I bless your name for adding good people, good places, and good things in my life, that encourage me to grow, and to get better. In Jesus' name I pray, Amen!

AUGUST 21

Psalm 25:4-5 (NASB): Make me know Your ways, Lord, Teach me Your paths. Lead me in Your truth and teach me, For You are the God of my salvation; For You I wait all the day.

I SUBMIT TO YOUR WILL

Father! Thank you for saving my soul, and for filling me with your precious Holy Spirit. I give you praise this morning, and I thank you that my mind, my will, and my emotions, are all under the influence of the Holy Ghost.

My thoughts are subject to and submitted to the Holy Ghost! My cognitive abilities are determined by your will for my life, and every thought has now become captive to the obedience of Christ.

Father I thank you for the Holy Ghost, who helps me to choose what's best for me, and what you desire for me, even when I'm craving something that's the complete opposite!

Thank you, Lord, for helping me to make righteous choices, and to deny my flesh daily! In Jesus' name I pray, Amen!

AUGUST 22

Proverbs 3:5-6 (NASB): Trust in the LORD with all your heart And do not lean on your own understanding. In all your ways acknowledge Him, And He will make your paths straight.

JUST FINISH IT

I know your story's unheard of, I know you don't personally know anyone else who's gone thru what you're going through, and then gone on to do something that changed the world, but you have to trust God, and stick to the original plan that He gave you!

You're not switching gears, so you can try to save face, you going to finish it. God's made you able, and you have the grace to finish strong! You will not walk away from the thing you've invested your life in, you will not. You are going to stay the course. So, I pray for another yes in your spirit, and that you will hear what the spirit of the Lord is saying.

I pray that you'll go back to the original plan God gave you, and that you'll stop feeling sorry for yourself, and start seeing your situation as God sees it. Truth is, you're carrying something that's going to change the world, and save your family. So, you're not abandoning it, just because it looks like it might not work out.

AUGUST 23

Proverbs 18:21 (NASB): Death and life are in the power of the tongue, And those who love it will eat its fruit.

BECAUSE I SAID SO

Good morning Holy Spirit, today's going to be a good day for us! The reason I know, is because I said so! I decree and declare, I've entered a season of rest, and things are already getting easier for me.

I declare my mind will be free of clutter today and my thoughts will be clear! My thoughts will be fresh, and free of stress, and today, Holy Spirit's going to give me answers, strategy, structure, innovative ideas, new business models, and something catchy, that will open the door for more, in Jesus' name!

This is my season for increase, and I declare the second half of the year, will produce three times what the first half produced! I'll never be broke another day in my life! God's making me a blessing. He's establishing His covenant in my life, fulfilling His promise to me, and making a fool out of every one of my enemies! To God be the glory! It's in the mighty name of Jesus I pray, AMEN!

AUGUST 24

Revelation 12:11(NASB): And they overcame him because of the blood of the Lamb and because of the word of their testimony, and they did not love their life even when faced with death.

I'VE ALREADY WON

Father I thank you today. I thank you that the blood of Jesus has already facilitated a victory for me. I thank you that no matter what I face, I cannot lose, because I've already won! Before the world was framed, before Adam ever fell, and before I did what I did, Jesus had already eternally secured my victory!

So today I choose the joy of the Lord! Today I choose to bless your name! With tears pouring, and my heart broken, I choose to praise your name. Believing that as I worship, the Host of Heaven is responding, and bringing closure, and giving directions for my next place in life. I will see Jesus! It's in His name I pray, AMEN!

AUGUST 25

Deuteronomy 1:11 (NASB): May the Lord, the God of your fathers increase you a thousand times more than you are, and bless you, just as He has [a]promised you!

JESUS DID IT

Father in Jesus' name, I ask for a special release of your Spirit in my life. I pray that Holy Spirit will overflow, and that every area of my life will be overwhelmed with grace and power.

I pray for the anointing on my life to continue to be fresh, and that Holy Spirit would keep me relevant, and cutting edge, in everything I put my hands to. Cause me to increase!

Cause me to rise to the top! And I promise, I'll tell everybody that JESUS DID IT! It's in Jesus' name I pray, amen!

AUGUST 26

2 Corinthians 9:10 (NASB): Now He who supplies seed to the sower and bread for food will supply and multiply your seed for sowing and increase the harvest of your righteousness;

IT'S REAPING SEASON

I declare that in this season, I will reap the harvest of the seeds that I've sewn. I've worked hard sacrificed and this is my time, to reap the reward.

There have been times throughout this journey that I've grown tired and weary. There have been times when I felt like giving up. I am so glad I didn't. I am so glad that your grace gave me strength.

I declare today that everything that I lost and every time that I may have felt overlooked, that this is the season where I'll win. This is the season that I will see the manifestations of your promises. I will no longer be weary in well doing. I will not allow my emotions to distract me from my assignment. I will stay faithful and wait on you.

I pray that Holy Spirit changes your perspective, immediately, and that He proves your negative predictions to be wrong! In Jesus' name, it is so! In Jesus' name I pray, Amen!

AUGUST 27

Psalm 41:11 (NASB): By this I know that You are pleased with me, Because my enemy does not shout in triumph over me.

I WILL OBEY GOD

Good morning Holy Spirit, today's going to be a "walking on the water" kind of day for us today! I'm praying for the grace to discern the difference between, my divine assignment, and a demonic attack. And I thank you Father that I will no longer live my life in fear, but every day and in every situation, I will walk by faith.

I sense you calling me out of the boat and calling me to demonstrate your power in my generation, and my soul says "yes"! I will not get in fear! I will not allow the storm to take my focus away from you! I declare I'm full of faith, and supernaturally focused, in Jesus' name! I called to do something no one in my position has ever done before, and I declare, "I will not drown, obeying God"!

Peter's example in Matthew chapter 14, verses 22 thru 33, is all the example I need, and I'm ready now to be used by you Father, to walk supernaturally in the earth. It's in Jesus' name I pray, AMEN!

AUGUST 28

Zephaniah 3:17 (NASB): The Lord your God is in your midst, A victorious warrior. He will rejoice over you with joy, He will be quiet in His love, He will rejoice over you with shouts of joy.

I CELEBRATE ME

You've been good to everybody else, and you've done everything you could do for them! You've gone out of your way and even bent over backwards, trying to make sure everybody else was happy and that everyone else had what they needed. But, for the rest of this year, you're going to be good to yourself. I pray for the desire, and for the strength of will to forgive yourself. I pray that you hold your own self accountable, not letting yourself off the hook. I pray that you'll be gracious and merciful to yourself, just as you have been to everybody else. Especially to those who abused your kindness and took advantage of your big heart.

I pray that Holy Spirit reminds you just how valuable you are, and how important your success is to God's plan for mankind's redemption. Don't get it twisted, your success matters to God! Your abundant life, your ability to overcome and succeed, are a huge part of what God is doing. So, get over it! You messed up, more than once, more than twice, but you're still God's child. You're still God's choice. So, you better be careful how you treat God's child. Be good to yourself today. Do something for you! Take yourself to dinner! Whatever you do today, be good to yourself. It's in Jesus' name I pray, Amen!

AUGUST 29

Zephaniah 3:15 (NASB): The Lord has taken away His judgments against you, He has cleared away your enemies. The King of Israel, the Lord, is in your midst; You will no longer fear disaster.

WHEN PRAISES GO UP

Father, I just want to thank you, because I made it! If the enemy would've had his way, I would've died days ago!

If the enemy's wish had come true, I wouldn't have survived last night, but I'm still here! So, Father I stop to pray, believing that this is just what I need to stop the unrelenting attack of the enemy!

Father, I take a praise break, believing that my faith is just what you need, to justify your involvement in my fight. I'm praying that while I'm praising, that you'll get in the middle of my situation! In Jesus' name I pray, AMEN!

AUGUST 30

Psalm 23:4 (NASB): Even though I walk through the valley of the shadow of death, I fear no evil, for You are with me; Your rod and Your staff, they comfort me.

I AM FREE FROM FEAR

Father, I thank you for making me free from the spirit of fear. I thank you that I am no longer the puppet of "well what if", and that I will never again be controlled, and manipulated by the fear of failing.

Thank you, Holy Spirit, for leading me, and guiding me, into all truth! And because I have the truth, I no longer have to live my life afraid. I declare I'm free to dReam! I'm free to live the life that Jesus paid for me to live! The truth has made me free, and today I'm getting out of the boat!

I'm going to do something today! Something that Jesus has called me to do! Something that everybody else with me is too afraid to do! And I'm going to do it, knowing that I will not drown! The grace to walk on water is on me, so today I walk supernaturally, with NO MORE FEAR! It's in Jesus' name I pray, AMEN!

AUGUST 31

Isaiah 43:19 (NASB): Behold, I am going to do something new, Now it will spring up; Will you not be aware of it? I will even make a roadway in the wilderness, Rivers in the desert.

RESET

Good morning Holy Spirit, thank you for another day. For another chance, and for another fresh set of days, that I can use to do something good with my life.

Thank you, Father, that this fresh set of days represent a time of refreshing, an opportunity for me to reset, and a window for me to start over. Thank you, Holy Spirit, for giving me to strength, and the courage, and the desire to want to try again.

Thank you for breaking the spirit of frustration off my life. And for gently nudging me and sometimes pushing me, into my purpose and destiny. I declare this week is a destiny week, and I will not waste another set of days, chasing something that's got nothing to do with my purpose!

Today, I press toward the mark, without distraction, and without delay. It's in Jesus' name I pray, AMEN!

SEPTEMBER

SEPTEMBER 1

James 1:4 (NASB): And let endurance have its perfect result, so that you may be [c]perfect and complete, lacking in nothing.

DON'T LET IT GET TO YOUR HEAD

I pray that the peace of God that surpasses all understanding, would literally stand guard to protect and cover your heart, and your mind. I pray that you walk in the grace to properly process your problems, and that you won't allow the formation of the weapons, to mess with your faith nor your mental stability. I pray for your mind and your thoughts. I call every one of them subject to God's will. Our fight is not against flesh and blood, so I pray that what people say and do to you, doesn't move you! I plead the blood over your mind, and I rebuke every suicidal thought, and inclination. I break the hold of depression and release the joy of the Lord over your life. You will not break! You will not lose it! You're going to stand on the word, and rest in His promise over your life!

Patience will have her perfect work in your life. You will not faint or grow weary! I speak another wind is about to blow through you, and more grace is about to come upon you. You will not lose your mind! I speak to every spirit that would cause any kind of chemical imbalance, and/or mental breakdown, and I say, "GO! Loose your hold, in the name of Jesus! I call you free today, never to be bound again, in Jesus name, Amen!

SEPTEMBER 2

John 1:26 (NASB): But the Helper, the Holy Spirit, whom the Father will send in My name, He will teach you all things, and bring to your remembrance all that I said to you.

THANK YOU, HOLY SPIRIT

Good morning Holy Spirit, I'm excited about today, and all that you're going to say, and reveal to me today. I thank you in advance, that nothing will slip up on me, that nothing will surprise me today, and that from today forward, I'll have a heads up on any and everything!

Thank you, Holy Spirit, for speaking to me clearly, and consistently. Thank you for giving me wisdom, and strategy to navigate my day, without fear, or frustration. Thank you, Lord, for showing me what to do, and what to say and how to say it!

Thank you, Holy Spirit, for hindsight, for the mental upgrade, for the mental makeover, and for mentally preparing me for greater! It's in Jesus' name I pray, AMEN!

SEPTEMBER 3

Psalms 37:11 (NASB): But the humble will inherit the land And will delight themselves in abundant prosperity.

IT'S GOING TO BE BIG

Good morning Holy Spirit, today's going to be a super day for us! So, I thank you in advance for the favor, for the breakthroughs, and for the miracles that I will walk in today!

You kept me alive for a divine purpose, and so I place a demand on purpose and destiny, and I declare that this is my season, to operate in the supernatural! I may be struggling with my flesh, and dealing with my humanity, but it's only to increase my divinity.

I may be grieving the loss of a loved one, or the loss of a relationship, or something or someone important to me; but it's all a part of your plan to increase this anointing that's on my life!

I'm anointed, not abandoned! And this storm cannot kill me! Because the purpose of this storm, is to provide me with an opportunity to operate in the supernatural! So today I'm getting out of the boat, and I'm walking on the water! In Jesus' name, AMEN!

SEPTEMBER 4

Ephesians 4:3 (NASB): being diligent to preserve the unity of the Spirit in the bond of peace.

KEEPING MY PEACE

Father, I thank you for life, for health, and for strength! I thank you for keeping me all week long, and for not allowing the trials of life to consume me. Thank you, Holy Spirit, for giving me peace, and for correcting my posture, and my perspective.

I give you praise today, for not allowing my thoughts to get away from me, and for stopping me, before I started to panic. I thank you Lord, for peace, for your peace, the peace that surpasses all understanding! That God kind of peace that guards my heart, and my mind!

So, I go into the day in peace, and I declare this will be a peaceful day, no matter what happens! No matter who does what! I will not relinquish my peace! It's in Jesus' name I pray, AMEN!

SEPTEMBER 5

Psalms 31:3 (NASB): For You are my rock and my fortress; For Your name's sake You will lead me and guide me.

A PRAYER FOR ME

I am believing God for the best day you've had in a long while. I'm praying you find strength in everything you do today. That everything you deal with today, fuels your fire. I pray for a refreshing in your spirit and that God supernaturally restores your desire to live and to live for Him!

I pray for your house and that every spirit there that is not assigned by God would have to leave now. I pray for peace, patience, faith, and forgiveness to flood your house again. I rebuke offense and cast out every spirit that would help you to hold a grudge.

I declare you have the strength to let it go in Jesus' name! That for the rest of the year, you will have the joy of the Lord, in your head space, living space, workspace and in every place the soles of your feet trod! It's in the mighty name of Jesus I pray, amen!

SEPTEMBER 6

Psalms 102:13 (NASB): You will arise and have compassion on Zion; For it is time to be gracious to her, For the appointed time has come.

THIS IS MY SET TIME

The just shall live by faith! So, I make a conscious decision to walk by faith, and not by sight! I choose to believe God, and His word! Despite my surroundings, and the things that are visible, I choose to put my trust in the Lord. And I pray for a shifting in my situation!

I pray that the hand of God takes hold of my circumstance and turn it in my favor! I pray for a move of God, that will make the doctors go back, and reevaluate, reassess, and rethink their medical opinions! I pray for a move of God, that'll turn the hearts of bankers, mortgage brokers, lenders, judges, prosecutors, and attorneys, in my favor! I make this prayer, and believing that this is the divinely inspired strategy, that'll provoke the hand of God, and trigger the power of God to work on my behalf!

I decree and declare, according to Psalms102:13, that you will arise, and have mercy on me, for the time to favor me, yes, the set time has come! I don't need anybody to say it for me, because the strength of God has come upon me, and I can say it for myself! THIS IS MY SET TIME! This is my time. It's in Jesus' name I pray, Amen!

SEPTEMBER 7

Colossians 3:23 (NASB): Whatever you do, do your work heartily, as for the Lord rather than for men,

GET READY

Good morning Holy Spirit today is going to be a really productive day for us. So, I thank you for focus, for renewed faith, and for freedom from fear! I begin my day today declaring that I will not, be afraid! I will not be controlled or manipulated by the spirit of fear. Truth is, God heard my prayers! God answered my prayers. Although this process is taking way longer than what I had hoped, I'm committed to waiting on the Lord. I'm going to wait, until my change comes!

I will not change my prayers! I will not reduce my vision! I will not lower my expectations! But what I am going to do, is wait on Jesus! What I am going to do, is praise my way through! What I am going to do, is keep saying what God has already said, about my future!

It's taking longer than what I'd hoped for, but it's getting ready to happen. I'm just a few moments away, from the best breakthrough I've ever had. It's getting ready to happen. For me, and for my family. It's getting ready to happen in my business, and in my career! I cannot see it, but glory be to God, I can, hear it. It's getting ready to happen! In Jesus' name I pray, AMEN!

SEPTEMBER 8

Philippians 1:6 (NASB) being confident of this, that he who began a good work in you will carry it on to completion until the day of Christ Jesus.

NOT TODAY

I'm not dying, not today! I'm not quitting, and I'm not about to give up, not today. So, Father I pray for strength to endure, and the wisdom to make the necessary adjustments, to sustain my peace. I pray for patience to stay the course, and for the mental toughness, to honor my righteous choice.

I've made mistakes in the past, and done some things, simply because they felt good, and I wanted to, but I've changed, and I'm still changing. I'm not who I once was, and do I possess the wherewithal to say to everything I once fell to, "not today!" I'm free because the Son has made me free. So, I won't be falling today. I won't be walking in fear today. I won't be losing my faith today, and I for sure won't be giving up on God, not today. It's in Jesus' name I pray, Amen!

SEPTEMBER 9

Genesis 22:18 (NASB): and through your offspring all nations on earth will be blessed because you have obeyed me."

I'M PRAYING FOR YOU

I'm praying for you, that you stay focused on God and that you refuse to give your attention to people, and to things that have become distractions. I'm praying that your purpose becomes your determination, and the thing that motivates you. I pray that the eyes of your understanding would be enlightened, and that the vision blockers would be removed. I'm praying that you finally see it. I'm praying that you finally get it, and that you realize that everything you've gone through was necessary and a part of God's plan to make you relevant, and your gift in demand.

Everything is working together. It's all coming together. The pieces are falling in place. The people, and the resources, that you need to complete your process, and to solidify your strategy, it's all falling in place. I decree and declare, you're ready to have the best day ever, the best week ever, the best month ever, the best year, ever! It's in Jesus' name I pray, Amen!

SEPTEMBER 10

Galatians 5:1 (NASB): It was for freedom that Christ set us free; therefore keep standing firm and do not be subject again to a yoke of slavery.

GOD'S GOING TO MOVE

I'm praying for you today, and my prayer is that Holy Spirit would immediately make you free and grant you freedom from everything that wants to keep you bound by what you did!

I pray for an immediate severing of every soul tie, and that Holy Spirit would break the chains, and remove the residue, from every bad relationship, and every connection that was not of God! I pray for your mind, I pray for your spirit man, and I declare strength to break free is yours, today!

I pray for an immediately, and that in a matter of seconds, Holy Spirit would change the way you see it, the way you see them, and the block out every memory that would cause you to go back to them, or to it. In Jesus' name I pray! Amen!

SEPTEMBER 11

Lamentations 3:22-23 (NASB): Because of the Lord's great love we are not consumed, for his compassions never fail They are renewed every morning, great is your faithfulness.

THEY'RE NOT STRONGER

I keep hearing the Lord say, "the demons that are warring against you, are not stronger than the angels that are warring for you!" So, get out of your feelings, and get in faith for a comeback like you've never seen. That's my prayer today, that we'd stop looking at the opposition and adversity, and that we'd turn our attention to opportunity to do something that's never been done before.

They are strong, but they are not strong enough to defeat you. They are strong, but they are not strong enough to change what God has predestined and ordained to be so. Victory was given to us from the foundation of the world, and the outcome cannot be reversed. So, hold on because something good is about to happen for you. I pray for strength to hold on, because something life changing and better is just a few days away. They're strong, but you're stronger. So only be strong, and very courageous. In Jesus' name I pray, amen, amen, and amen!

SEPTEMBER 12

Matthew 7:6 (NASB): Do not give dogs what is sacred; do not throw your pearls to pigs. If you do, they may trample them under their feet, and turn and tear you to pieces.

GOD'S CHANGING YOUR ENEMY'S PLANS

I know you're in a fight, but please don't lose sight of the truth. The battle is not yours. I know that's difficult to resolve, but you cannot get tricked into fighting the wrong fight. Your fight is mental, and spiritual. It's not against flesh and blood, so let's pray for clarity of direction, and thought. Let's pray for patience, and for peace, so we don't get in fear, and start doing stuff, trying to get ourselves out of trouble. The Lord of war is on our side, and He's already won the victory for us.

So, let's stay focused, let's stay on task, and let's stay in faith, knowing that God has already dealt with every one of our enemies. I'm praying that God shows us what the enemy is up to. That He gives us peace to properly process the insight. I pray that what Holy Spirit reveals, gives us an indication of just how loved, and how valuable we are. I pray that frustration of the enemy's plan would sharpen and increase our plan and create opportunities to for us to move forward. And to finish what we started. Holy Spirit encourage our hearts, and keep us strong, and keep us together, it's in Jesus' name I pray, Amen!

SEPTEMBER 13

Philippians 4:4 (NASB): Rejoice in the Lord always. I will say it again; Rejoice!

I'M NOT CRAZY

Sometimes you just have to say this to your own self. I may have done some crazy stuff, and yes, I have acted out, but I'm not crazy! I'm still working through some things, and God is definitely still working on me, but I'm not crazy. I have been born again, the spirit of the living God lives in me, and I have the mind of Christ. I'm not what I did, I'm not who they said I was, and God is still for me. God is still for me and His plans for my future are good.

I have not lost my mind! And what I see for my future has everything to do with the power of the blood winning over the consequences of my past. To God be the glory! I got my right mind. I'm thinking straight, and I'm sure that God is on my side. In Jesus' name, Amen!

SEPTEMBER 14

Psalms 10:6 (NASB): He says to himself, "I will not be moved; Throughout all generations I will not be in adversity."

I'M NOT MOVED

Good morning Holy Spirit today is already a good day! And I thank You in advance, for everything that will happen, and for everything that won't. I give You praise, for teaching me how to look beyond my current conditions, and how to stay focused on the bigger picture.

Thank you, Holy Spirit, for helping me to look through the obstacles, and to see past every hindrance. Thank you for teaching me how not to allow what I see, to affect what I saw. Thank you, Holy Spirit, for training me to stick to the vision, and teaching me how not to allow what I see with my natural eye, to alter what I've seen with my spirit's eye. I will not be moved by what I see! What I believe, dictates what I do and what I say. Everything I need is falling in place, and it will not be late. What I need is going to be in my hand when I need it! Every dollar, every person, every professional and personal relationship, everything I need, I'll have, at the time it's required of me, in Jesus' name!

So, it doesn't matter how things look because I know how things really are! It doesn't matter what people say, or how they try to make me feel, because I know the truth, and the truth has made me free, so I'm going to be free today. It's in Jesus' name I pray, Amen!

SEPTEMBER 15

2 Corinthians 12:9 (NASB): "My grace is sufficient for you, for power is perfected in weakness

YOU'RE BEING PREPARED

Don't let the devil play you and don't let him tell you, that God has abandoned you, because of what you did. The blood took care of your sin, so the price for what you did, for what you've done, and for what you will do, has already been paid. Selah. What you're going thru now, is God allowing life, and the devil to test you, but only to prove you and to qualify you for what He's promised. So, I pray for revelation of the truth, and that Holy Spirit will allow you to see His intention.

I pray for boldness, for courage, and for patience to endure hardness as a good soldier. I pray for a disciplined mouth, and a made-up mind, so the devil doesn't trick you into saying something, that negatively affects your future. I pray that you ignore Job's wife's advice, and that you choose to trust God, live for God, and praise God, while you're waiting on your miracle. I pray for renewed strength, to withstand and to hold out. I pray that Holy Spirit will cause you to see beyond where you are now and give you a glimpse of what's to come. In Jesus' name, AMEN!

SEPTEMBER 16

Romans 8:28 (NASB): And we know that God causes all things to work together for good to those who love God, to those who are called according to His purpose.

IT'S FOR MY GOOD

Good morning Holy Spirit, today's going to be a super day for us! Today, I am going to worship you! Today, I'm going to worship, in spirit, and in truth! Today, I'm going to hear from you, and my life will never be the same!

Today, time and purpose collide. And what I'm called, gifted, and graced to do becomes my focus. I will never again live a distracted life!

What the devil meant for evil, God meant it, and God's using it for my good! And everybody who laughed at me, and talked about me, is going to have to eat their words!

God's going to have the last laugh because God's going to have the last word! In the name of Jesus I pray, AMEN!

SEPTEMBER 17

John 16:33 (NASB): These things I have spoken to you, so that in Me you may have peace. In the world you have tribulation, but take courage; I have overcome the world."

WHILE I REST

Father before I go to sleep tonight, I want to thank you for this day, and for keeping me this day. Thank you for keeping your word, and for sustaining my life.

Thank you, Father, for cutting off every attack, and for keeping the enemy in check! I praise you tonight, for a good night's sleep, and for real rest, thank you!

Thank you in advance, for protecting me, and my family, all night tonight, and for restoring our strength, and our joy, while we sleep. I declare peace over the night, no nightmares, no bad dreams, no panic attacks, no sickness in the middle of the night, no overnight emergencies of any kind, and no disruption whatsoever in our sleep. In Jesus' name, AMEN!

SEPTEMBER 18

1 John 1:9 (NASB): If we confess our sins, He is faithful and righteous to forgive us our sins and to cleanse us from all unrighteousness.

HE IS FAITHFUL

Father I thank you for speaking to me today, whether it was at church, or in prayer, or at my job, or at the house!

I'm glad that you keep talking to me, and to know that every word you've spoken, is coming to pass!

Father I thank you for your promise, and for your faithfulness to watch over it, and to bring it to pass. Not one jot or title of your word can fail!

Not one word that you've released over my life will fall to the ground! Everything you've spoken, has secured my future, organized my past, and it's presently preparing me for something BIG! BIG is here and God's going to do it this week!

God's going to do it big. He's going to do exceedingly, abundantly, above all that I could ever ask or think! And this time I'm ready. In Jesus' name I pray, AMEN!

SEPTEMBER 19

Psalms 9:9-10 (NASB): The Lord also will be a stronghold for the oppressed, A stronghold in times of trouble; And those who know Your name will put their trust in You,

HE WORKED IT OUT

Today was a good day, and Father I want to thank you for arranging things today, so that no matter happened, I'd still have the advantage over my enemy. I'm going to enjoy my space, and my family and friends. I'm going to sleep tonight, knowing that I've got angels watching over me. And that no hurt, harm, or danger can come near me.

I'm going to sleep like a baby tonight! I'm going to rest tonight, and I'm not going to lose sleep over anything! Tomorrow will take care of itself, so I'm going to sleep tonight, casting all my cares upon the Lord, because He cares for me! I choose the peace of Jesus, and I refuse to stress over anything that God's already fixed. Truth is, while I'm sitting up here, trying to figure it out, Father you've already worked it out! So tonight, and for the rest of this week, I put my trust in You!

Make this week a week full of miracles, signs, and wonders, and I'll give all glory, all honor, and all praise to you. In Jesus' name I pray, AMEN!

SEPTEMBER 20

Proverbs 18:10 (NASB): The name of the Lord is a strong tower, the righteous run to it and are safe

GET SOME SLEEP

Don't let the devil keep you up all night, worrying about things that are out of your control. Put it in God's hands and know that it has to work together for your good. Go to sleep and let your soul rest from the pressure of trying to fix stuff that only God can.

You need wisdom! You need divine intervention! You need a miracle, and the good news is that your God is a miracle worker. The God that you serve is a way maker. He keeps His promises, and He can be trusted. Now get some sleep and let your soul be at rest. In Jesus' name, Amen!

SEPTEMBER 21

1 Corinthians 10:13 (NASB): No temptation has overtaken you that is not common to man. God is faithful, and he will not let you be tempted beyond your ability, but with the temptation he will also provide the way of escape, that you may be able to endure it.

I HAVE OPTIONS

Prayer is still a viable option. I rebuke the spirit of fear, and frustration and I command the church to take her place. Father in the name of Jesus, I pray for wisdom and for courage. I pray for our officials and I'm asking that you show us how to turn things around. Holy Spirit shine your light on the truth. Expose every demonic strategy that's been put in place to keep us divided and in fear. Help us, for the sake of our children, and for the sake of the generations that are coming behind us. Don't let us grow weary, don't let us become overwhelmed by the drama and the ignorance. Give us grace to endure and to do the right thing.

Give us the strength to stay the course, and to be consistent in love. Don't let the way we've been treated change our character or cause us to act out. Father we need your help. We need a miracle! We need immediate, divine intervention. So, we call on your name, and we plead the blood. We plead the blood over our government and law enforcement, and we pray that you would constrain every demonic power, in Jesus' name. We expect a turn-around. We expect a miracle. In Jesus' name we pray, Amen.

SEPTEMBER 22

Ezekiel 36:26 (NASB): Moreover, I will give you a new heart and put a new spirit within you; and I will remove the heart of stone from your flesh and give you a heart of flesh.

HE CHANGED ME

Father I thank you for changing me! I thank you for using everything, and everybody in my life, to mature me, and to grow me up. Thank you, Jesus, that life and circumstance, is making me better and not bitter!

And I praise you today for the process of sanctification. Thank you for taking the stuff away, that I just wasn't strong enough to walk away from. So, I decree and declare that from today forward, I'll be changing every day. I'll be getting stronger, every day. I'll be getting wiser, every day. And what the devil meant for evil, Father I praise you, that you're going to use it for my good! It only gets better from here! So, I declare, the worst is over!

And the best, glory to God, is yet to come! I prophesy "the best", on everyday that's in front of me! And I declare unusual favor. In Jesus' name I pray, AMEN!

SEPTEMBER 23

Psalms 5:12 (NASB): For thou, LORD, wilt bless the righteous; with favor wilt thou compass him as a shield.

UOENO!

Despise not the day of small beginnings. You may be the least of these now. Your life may feel like it's untied, but I promise you if you hold on and stay faithful to who and what God's assigned you to sooner or later, you're going to walk into something that bigger than you could've ever imagined.

So, be encouraged today and let patience have her perfect work. Your season to lead is closer than you think. Stay focused and don't let your "feelings" get the best of you. That's my prayer today, that everybody's who's next, won't faint or grow weary. You're next and you don't even know it. God's about to call your name, and that's why the devil wants you to quit, without your reward. I'm praying that your faith won't fail and that you'll find grace to stay the course. It's in the name of Jesus I pray, Amen!

SEPTEMBER 24

John 8:44 (NASB): You are of your father the devil, and you want to do the desires of your father. He was a murderer from the beginning and does not stand in the truth because there is no truth in him. Whenever he speaks a lie, he speaks from his own nature, for he is a liar and the father of lies.

BREAKTHROUGH

Breakthrough is happening today, in the name of Jesus! I pray now, that Holy Spirit would strengthen and comfort those, who've been under attack. And those whom the enemy has threatened, and tried to force into idol worship, with the fear of losing everything they've worked for.

The devil is a liar! Our God whom we serve is able to deliver us, and He will. But even if He doesn't, we will not take our focus off of the almighty God. We will not worship our jobs, our relationships, our money, our children, nor any of our material possessions, we worship Jesus! And we worship, free from fear!

We cannot lose because we've already won! And even though things look crazy, and uncertain, the truth of the matter is, that eyes have not seen, nor ear heard, the things that God has prepared for me. Thank you, God. Amen.

SEPTEMBER 25

Jeremiah 33:3 (NASB): Call unto me and I will answer thee and show thee great and mighty things, which you know not.

GOD SAW ME

Your labor was not in vain, and even though people may act like what you've done wasn't about anything, Holy Spirit told me to tell you, "God saw you!" The devil is a liar, you did not go unnoticed. What you did, meant something, to somebody. Despite what the devil is trying to put on you and trying to get you to start feeling worthless, as if you don't matter, the truth is, God saw you. He saw every sacrifice you made this year. He saw everything you did to serve and to bless other people, even when your personal life felt like it was falling apart. God 's about to reward you for being faithful. You don't even know this, because you're all up in your feelings, but you've been chosen. God just called your number, and somebody who has what you've been praying for, is about to call your name.

God told me to tell you to wake up every day, expecting a miracle. Holy Spirit was clear with me, and He told me that many of you are about to become miracles, signs, and wonders. I'm telling you; God saw you, and He's about to give you something to shout about, soon. I pray you don't get weary in doing well and for endurance. You will not quit, give up, or change your mind. You're going to stay the course, and keep believing God, until your prayers, become your portion. It's in Jesus' name I pray, Amen!

SEPTEMBER 26

Exodus 33:14 (NASB): And He said, "My presence shall go with you, and I will give you rest."

I DECLARE REST

What a day, but God! Father I want to thank you, that as I lay my head down to rest tonight, that I do so knowing the truth! I praise you, because despite everything that happened today, and in spite of all the facts that I was confronted with today, I go to sleep knowing that better is on the way!

I know the truth, and the truth has made me free! Free from my past, and even free from my present manifestation. I know, that's what's coming, is better than what's been! So, I choose to be at peace tonight! I choose to take your yoke upon me, and allow Holy Spirit to teach me your ways, and show me to stay focused and on task. Things have got to get better! So, I choose to keep my mind stayed on thee, knowing that the promise is that you'll keep me in perfect peace!

The peace of God is my portion, it's been freely given to me, it's my right as a believer, and so I refuse to give it away. I refuse to lose one minute of sleep, stressing over something that you have already handled!

I declare sweet rest tonight! Rest for the weary! Rest for the faithful! Rest for the worshipper! Rest for the intercessor! Rest for the believer! It's in Jesus' name I pray, AMEN!

SEPTEMBER 27

Luke 10:19 (NASB): Behold, I give unto you power to tread on serpents and scorpions, and over all the power of the enemy: and nothing shall by any means hurt you.

DETAILED INSTRUCTIONS

Stop tripping, God's about to show you what to do, how to do it, when to do it, who to do it with, and then He's going to make it crystal clear why He told you to do it, in Jesus' name. You have nothing to fear because God's already releasing the master plan to you. He's already made it impossible for you to fail, and He's set people in your path, who are already prepared to use their power, their influence, and their resources, to help you do everything God's given you to do.

I pray for humility to rise up in you, so the devil can't use pride, to get you to reject the help. There's something big on your life and God's about to do something thru you that's going to make history! Expect to be first! And don't be afraid because you have no one else to compare yourself to, you're the first one. The grace on your life, is to be the first, to be the example, to be the standard, to be the one that people look at, when attempting to define what it means to be successful. So, stand up, take your place, and obey God. Just do it! It's in Jesus' name I pray, Amen!

SEPTEMBER 28

Habakkuk 2:4 (NASB): "Behold, as for the proud one, His soul is not right within him; But the righteous will live by his faith.

THE JUST SHALL LIVE

The just shall live by faith. So, Father I give you praise today, that I have the right, and the authority to choose, and I choose life. I choose to live by faith. I refuse to allow situations and circumstances, to influence my choice. I have the wisdom, the vision, and the strength of will, to choose correctly and the desire to choose God.

I do have my right mind and no matter what happens, I will not die! I pray for the grace to overcome every attack of the enemy. I decree and declare, that no weapon formed against me, will work against me, and that everything the devil meant for evil, has worked for my good!

I prophesy favor and elevation in my life, and for every believer who's been attacked by a snake. I pray for your mind, and for your emotions, and I speak strength to you, in Jesus' name! I pray that you shift your focus away from the snakebite, away from the pain, and away from the attack, and that you respond like a believer!

I command you to shake it off! Whatever happened, cannot, and will not kill you! This isn't the season for you to die, because the just shall live by faith! So, live! Thrive! Do better! Be better! Be healed! Be free! It's in the name of Jesus I pray, AMEN!

SEPTEMBER 29

Psalms 103:12 (NASB): As far as the east is from the west, So far has He removed our transgressions from us.

MY FLESH WON'T WIN

Father, I thank you, for the blood of Jesus, that washes and cleanses me from all unrighteousness. Thank you, Lord, for privilege, and for the right of the believer to repent. I lay everything I've done, and everything I've thought about doing, on the altar, and I praise you that according to 103rd Psalms, verse 12, "As far as the east is from the west, so far has He removed our transgressions from us." Thank you, Holy Spirit, for giving me the victory over my mind and my fleshly desires.

Thank you for perfecting me, confirming me, strengthening me, and establishing me! Thank you, Father, for taking the taste out of my mouth, and for giving me the strength to tell my flesh "NO!" Thank you, for setting me up for my future! Thank you, for picking me up, turning me around, and planting my feet on solid ground! Hallelujah!

I declare this is my season! My set time! The proper time, a day of promotion and elevation! My time! In Jesus' name, it is so! Amen, Amen, and AMEN!

SEPTEMBER 30

Romans 8:28 (NASB): we know that God causes all things to work together for good to those who love God, to those who are called according to His purpose.

I'M GOOD

Father, I thank you for letting me see another day! Thank you, for holding me down, and for not allowing life to get the best of me. I give you praise today, because everything that's happened, everything that's happening, and everything that's going to happen, has to work together, for my good!

Thank you, Father, for exposing the lie of the enemy, and for reassuring me that my life is not out of control! My life is in your hands! My future is already planned out, and it's already secured. The blood of Jesus locked the plan for my life in place, for eternity. And there's nothing the devil can do to stop your will from coming to pass in my life.

Glory to God. So, come what may, I'm good. I'm good, because of Calvary. I'm good because I belong to the creator, the maker, and the sustainer of the universe! I'm good because I want to be good! I'm good because I choose to be good! And today I decide that I'm going to stay good. In Jesus' name I pray, Amen!

OCTOBER

OCTOBER 1

John 14:27 (NASB): Peace I leave with you; my peace I give to you. Not as the world gives do I give to you. Let not your hearts be troubled, neither let them be afraid.

CLEAR DIRECTIVES

Holy Spirit help us not to miss it. Please Lord, show us what to do next. And don't let our flesh govern or determine when or with who that next will look like. Show us the fallout first and don't let us do anything with anyone that will jeopardize, or put at risk, what you've got planned ahead. Free us from the pressures of people's opinions. And don't let our righteous convictions be swayed in any way. Don't let our faith waver. Speak to us so clearly, that even the deaf and dull of hearing will hear. We pray for clear directives. And we speak clarity of thought, vision, and speech in this season. We will not be double minded or double-tongued in our thinking or speaking, saying one thing today and thinking and saying something else tomorrow.

In Jesus' mighty name, we call every thought subject and obedient to Your will. We decree and declare that we have clear directives. We know what to do, when to do it, with whom to do it with, and we know our why. We are coming out of the dark, as the spirit of the living God is shining His light on every situation that's perplexed us and kept us outside of His will. Today is the day we come out of darkness and into the light. Today is the day we get wisdom and peace with our divinely inspired choices. It's in Jesus' name I pray, Amen!

OCTOBER 2

Proverbs 23:7 (NASB): For as he thinks within himself, so he is..

AS A MAN THINKETH

Good morning Holy Spirit, today's going to be a big day for us! I declare things will work in my favor today. I won't be frustrated. I won't be disappointed. I won't be sidetracked. I will not surrender my ability to think to anything or anyone!

I am a thinker! I am not a reactor. I decree that the days of reacting, instead of responding intelligently are behind me. I am a thinker! I have the grace to think under pressure. I possess the divine ability to conceive, to judge correctly, to properly process information and the patience to consider the consequence before I act.

I am a thinker, not a reactor and from today forward, I commit to myself to think better! I free my mind to imagine and my spirit to dReam. My life is already getting better! For as a person thinks within themself, so they already are. In Jesus' name I pray Amen!

OCTOBER 3

I Kings 11:38 (NASB): If, then, you heed all that I command you, walking in my ways, and do what is right in my eyes by keeping my statutes and my commandments like David my servant, I will be with you.

LORD HELP ME TO WALK RIGHT

Father I need your help! My mind, my body, and my soul are yours, but yet I still feel myself struggling with my flesh. So today I stretch my hands to you because you really are the only help, I know. So, help me to walk right and to live right. Help me to master my flesh and call every one of my desires, subject to your spirit.

Holy Spirit, I yield to you. I'm praying that you will help me to get my walk together. Don't let me live another day, outside of your will. Don't let me waste another second of my life, pursuing something that takes me outside of your will. Help me to walk right and grant me the grace to leap over, what I've always tripped over.

Change me! Cleanse me! Cover me! Help me to walk upright before you. My soul says yes, again! I give permission, for the constraining power of the Holy Ghost to take full control of my life. It's in Jesus' name I pray, Amen!

OCTOBER 4

Ephesians 2:4 (NASB): But God, being rich in mercy, because of His great love with which He loved us,

THANK YOU FOR MERCY

Good morning Holy Spirit, I'm so glad that you're still with me, and most importantly that you're alive within me. Thank you for still talking to me, especially on the days when I wouldn't talk to you.

Thank you for your mercies that are new every morning and for your truth that endures. I praise you because what you've said about me is still true! And I thank you Lord, that while my enemies were planning my funeral, your mercy was producing what you've planned for my future!

I praise you for the furnace that I'm about to walk into, and that although my situation may not change, that everything else around me will! Jesus is getting in the furnace with me! So, I give you praise today, for the next thing! I give you praise today, because even though I fell. Even though I was tied up, Jesus is with me now, and He's walking me through it. Thank you for not leaving me! Thank you for showing up, and for making me free!

Thank you, Jesus, for walking me out, and for walking me into the greatest season on my life! It begins today! It's in the name of Jesus I declare these things to be so! Amen, amen, and AMEN!

OCTOBER 5

Malachi 4:3 (NASB): You will tread down the wicked, for they will be ashes under the soles of your feet on the day which I am preparing," says the LORD of hosts.

IT WON'T BE LONG

God is preparing a table for you, in the presence of your enemies, so stop tripping about the trouble. It's a sign that you're getting to eat! Trust me, God's got way too much of Himself invested in you, and your family, to allow the devil to mess it all up! Whatever you're going thru, and whatever happened to you, is nothing more than God preparing you for what's ahead.

So, you need to start living your life like what's in front of you is better than what's behind you. Don't fight the process! Let God do what He needs to do, because in just a few days, you are going to be walking in your blessing! Your enemies were necessary, but once they've served their purpose, God's going to wipe them out of your life! Get ready because God told me to tell you, "IT WILL NOT BE LONG!" God's going to do it! And it's going to happen so fast, you won't have time to get ready. Get ready now! Set your spirit in order now. Set your house in order now and make ready for the biggest blessing you've ever had! It's in Jesus' name I pray, Amen!

OCTOBER 6

Joshua 1:9 (NASB): Have I not commanded you? Be strong and courageous! Do not be terrified nor dismayed, for the Lord your God is with you wherever you go."

I AM STRONG

Good morning Holy Spirit, thank you for giving me the strength I need to make this the best day I've had this year! Thank you for the courage to face my fears. And to confront everything, and everybody that's kept me locked down, and stuck in my past.

I'm declaring today "Freedom Day"! I thank you Lord that I'm closing out this day, this month, and this year, strong! Your strength is made perfect in my weakness, so I declare, "I AM STRONG! I'm strong in my mind! I'm strong in my soul! I'm strong in my faith! I'm strong in my spirit! And today I will only be strong in the Lord, and in the power of His might!

Being weak is no longer an option for me! I will only be strong and very courageous, in Jesus' name! Today I'm going to follow the leading of Holy Spirit and do something I've been too bound by fear to do!

Today is the beginning of my journey to break records, raise the bar, reset the standard, and do the impossible! It's in Jesus' name I pray, AMEN!

OCTOBER 7

Ephesians 3:20 (NASB): Now to Him who is able to do far more abundantly beyond all that we ask or think, according to the power that works within us,

STUPID RICH

What God is about to do for us, will not make sense to us, or to anybody who knows us. It's going to be big! As we set ourselves in agreement with God and follow His instructions, we are about to walk into the greatest spiritual and financial season that we have ever known. So, Father, give us the courage to obey. Give us the mental strength to follow through on what we've committed to do. Don't let us fall short, or find an excuse, and don't let us off the hook. Holy Spirit give us the wisdom to work around life's challenges and setbacks. Show us how to navigate the emotional roller coaster, and don't let the devil play tricks with our minds.

Filter every thought through your word and the truth. Free us from the opinions of people, who have no revelation, and no relationship with you. Build us up and make us strong where we're weak. Break every chain, and every stronghold that kept us thinking, and acting like orphans, with no inheritance. Open our eyes to the enemy's plan, and show us everything, and everybody, he's used to keep us broke, busted, and disgusted. Give us the will to walk away. Release the blessing. Bring us into our wealthy place and cause us to find joy and peace in your presence, and not in material things. In Jesus' name, Amen!

OCTOBER 8

Romans 8:37 (NASB): But in all these things we overwhelmingly conquer through Him who loved us.

NEVER GOING BACK

Good morning Holy Spirit! Thank you for waking me up and keeping me in my right mind. I love you this morning and I give you praise for every promise you have spoken over my life. Thank you for never leaving me, even when I walked away from you. Thank you for staying with me, and not allowing my back and forth, to make you change your mind.

I praise you for your love today and I thank you again, for being here. Your love has changed me! Your love is changing me, and I will NEVER be the same again!

So today I declare strength to sustain this change. I speak strength to my mind, and my will, and I decree and declare, "I'm NEVER going back!" I'm never going back, and yet I'm under no pressure to keep myself from going back. It's in Jesus' name I pray, AMEN!!

OCTOBER 9

*Jeremiah 29:11 (NASB): For I know the plans that I have for you,'
declares the Lord, 'plans for prosperity and not for disaster, to
give you a future and a hope.*

GOD HAS A PLAN

Maybe your plans couldn't work because they weren't His
plans. I pray for renewed strength today, and that God would
restore your joy, so that you don't miss your window, do to
spiritual, mental, and physical fatigue. I pray that Holy Spirit
reveals to us the truth, so we don't waste another week chasing
a lie. I pray that God opens our eyes again and gives us insight
for this new place we're in, in Jesus' name.

Holy Spirit don't let the enemy deceive us in this season. Don't
let us get played or taken advantage of by anybody. And
break the spirit of bitterness off our lives, in the name of Jesus.
Set us free from everything that didn't work. Set us free from
every relationship that wasn't in your will and cause us to know
and to discern the will of God, for this season. We trust you and
we believe that your plans are good. We trust you and we're
leaning and depending on you; and we know that all things
are working together for our good. So, glorify yourself in our lives
today. In Jesus' name we pray, Amen!

OCTOBER 10

Isaiah 48:17 (NASB): This is what the Lord says, He who is your Redeemer, the Holy One of Israel: "I am the Lord your God, who teaches you to benefit, Who leads you in the way you should go.

HE'S STILL SPEAKING

I know that sometimes it may not seem like it, and I know you may feel far away from victorious, but God is still speaking. He is still leading and guiding your every step, and every thought.

I pray that as you go about your business today, that you will hear God's voice clearly. I pray that the guiding Holy Spirit will guide you and surround you with love and peace. I pray that you feel the warmth of His love and the comfort of his embrace throughout your day today.

I pray that the decisions that you need to make, that you will do so boldly, knowing that you have heard from God. I speak clarity in your thoughts, and I command that the spirit of confusion leave your mind this day. Because you have the grace to overcome anything, now we celebrate the continuous hand of God over all our affairs. It is in Jesus' name I pray, Amen.

OCTOBER 11

Ecclesiastes 3:11 (NASB): He has made everything appropriate in its time. He has also set eternity in their heart, without the possibility that mankind will find out the work which God has done from the beginning even to the end.

DON'T FORGET BRICKS

Anybody can tear something up, but it takes courage, faith, and integrity, to build something. I'm praying that you rediscover all three of these critical virtues. And that you purpose in your heart, that when you die, it will have mattered that you lived. I pray for laser focus, and increased discernment, so that every distraction, becomes a definite steppingstone. Father help us to keep our eyes on you, and not on what's gone wrong. Help us to see You in everything we go through, so that we don't lose sight of our purpose and our life's assignment.

Thank you, for every setback and every heartbreak, because now I have my own testimony. Thank you for every failed attempt and for every negative voice, because now you can get the glory out of my win. I'm not done, I'm just getting started, and I'm building something that matters. What I'm building is going to bless my family, and everybody connected to me. I'm walking in the grace to build because the spirit of the Lord is upon me. For every negative word that was spoken against me, and for every person that counted me out, I'm going to use those as bricks to build. I'm going to use fear to fuel my future. God will be glorified! In Jesus' name, AMEN!

OCTOBER 12

2 Kings 2:9 (NASB): When they had crossed over, Elijah said to Elisha, "Ask me what I should do for you before I am taken from you." And Elisha said, "Please let a double portion of your spirit be upon me."

ASK FOR IT

Show me in the bible, where being broke, and barely getting by, honors God! The devil is a liar. I pray that the truth be revealed, and that God shows you His better plan for your life. Then I pray for the power of God to break you free from the spirit of poverty, in Jesus' name. I pray for wisdom, and for courage, and that you would come into the saving knowledge of the Lord Jesus Christ.

I know you've made mistakes, God knows I have, but I pray that you'd accept the truth concerning God's will for your life. That you would know that what He's planned for you has nothing to do with what you've done. But everything to do with what Jesus did. God told me to tell you, "you got to ask for it!" And not for what you think you deserve, but for everything the blood of Jesus already paid for. Ask for what you want and don't let the enemy convince you to dumb down your desires, because your desires are God given. According to the 37th Psalms, verse 4, ask for what you want, and don't let your past restrict or limit your future, in any way. God's already provided it, but you got to ask for it! In Jesus' name, Amen!

OCTOBER 13

Proverbs 18:20 (NASB): With the fruit of a person's mouth his stomach will be satisfied; He will be satisfied with the product of his lips.

GET IN THE MIDDLE

I can do all things through Christ who strengthens me! So, in the name of Jesus, I declare that today is the day that I put on my strength. Today is the day that I accept the truth about who I am. And I've decided to be who God has already made me, and said that I am. I'm not sick, I'm healed! So even though I'm still being treated for what they say I have, I understand I'm only going thru the process for the development of my testimony. I can do this! I'm not broke, I'm living in overflow. Overflow is my new norm. I have more than what I need, and the blessing of the Lord makes me rich, in the name of Jesus!

So even though I'm presently walking out of a season of lack, and not enough, I decree and declare that all my needs are met. That the grace on my life attracts money, the wisdom to manage it, and increase it, for the glory of God! I CAN DO THIS! I speak strength to every area in my life where there's weakness, and confidently declare that I can do all things through Christ who strengthens me!

I'm strong in my mind! I'm strong in my body! and I'm strong in my spirit! I CAN do, whatever I have to do to, and whatever I must do to participate in the fulfillment of God's will in my life. It's in Jesus' name I pray, AMEN!

OCTOBER 14

Jeremiah 32:25 (NASB): Yet You have said to me, Lord God, "Buy for yourself the field with money and call in witnesses"— although the city has been handed over to the Chaldeans.'"

CATCH YOUR BREATH

I know life has a way of taking your breath, and things will happen that knock the wind out of us. But today, I'm praying that Holy Spirit teaches us how to settle our spirits, collect our thoughts, and start breathing again. His yoke is easy, and His burden is light. So, whatever the weight is, we can lift it, but we have got to breathe.

Holy Spirit teach us. Holy Spirit show us how, and don't let life overwhelm us. Give us peace, in the midst of the pain, and grace us to keep pushing back, against the pressure. I speak to the wind, and I command everything dead to breathe, in the name of Jesus. I speak wind to your dreams, wind to your vision, wind to your body, wind to your finances and wind to your ministry. In Jesus' name, I command you to catch your breath, and breathe. And it is so, Amen, amen and amen!

OCTOBER 15

Isaiah 26:3 (NASB): The steadfast of mind You will keep in perfect peace, Because he trusts in You.

I'M MOVING FORWARD

Good morning Holy Spirit, I'm grateful for another day, that I get to live, and enjoy the blessings of the Lord that are on my life. I praise you early, knowing that although things are not perfect, they could've been way worse! Thank you, Holy Spirit, for keeping me focused, and for helping me to keep moving forward. Things aren't perfect, but things are getting better! Glory to God. My life isn't exactly where I want it to be, but this go around, I can see where I'm going. I can see my way. Hallelujah!

I can see that you are with me, and I feel you helping me! Thank you, Holy Spirit, for the grace to look ahead, and yet be laser focused, and present. Thank you that I'm not so forward focused, that I fail to enjoy where I am now, and forget to celebrate the victories that I have now! I choose the joy of the Lord, and I declare that I'm going to enjoy my life and not just endure my life! I prophesy better things. I'm confident that what you started you're going to finish God!

So today, all throughout the day, I'll be praying and talking to you, talking with you, and giving you glory for what you've done. For what you're doing and for what you're going to do! In Jesus' name, Amen!

OCTOBER 16

Genesis 26:12 (NASB): Now Isaac sowed in that land and reaped in the same year a hundred times as much. And the Lord blessed him,

DISEASE AND DEBT FREE

As you sow, you gain access to the grace that's in the ground where you sowed. So please don't take this lightly or view it as another casual opportunity to give. I believe God has opened a huge door here, and it's for all of us to access the grace to live disease free, and debt free. So, Father I pray that as we sow, that the spirit of infirmity would lose its hold on our lives. I pray that you would give us the courage, the strength, and the wisdom, to change the way we eat, and the way that we look at food. I pray that the power of God would touch our minds, our bodies, and our souls, and that sickness and disease would become a thing of the past.

I pray for wisdom to monetize our experiences. For the wisdom to create fluid revenue streams from the things that we love to do, and we're gifted to do! I pray for favor with banks, with debt collectors, and with the people who control the licenses, and who determine who the franchises are awarded to. Father lean in our direction again and cause money to flow to our houses like water. Wash away every unnecessary debt. And give us the wisdom and the relationships we need, that will teach us how to manage wealth, and riches, in Jesus' name. We declare that this is the season of the wide door. This is the season that we live disease free and debt free. It's in Jesus' name we pray, Amen.

OCTOBER 17

James 1:4 (NASB): And let endurance have its perfect result, so that you may be perfect and complete, lacking in nothing.

YOU'RE BEING PREPARED

Don't let the devil play you and don't let him tell you, that God has abandoned you, because of what you did. The blood took care of your sin; so, the price for what you did, for what you've done, and for what you will do, has already been paid. Selah. What you're going thru now is God allowing life and the devil to test you. But it's only to prove to you and to qualify you for what He's promised. So, I pray for revelation of the truth, and that Holy Spirit will allow you to see His intention.

I pray for boldness, courage, and for patience to endure hardness as a good soldier. I pray for a disciplined mouth, and a made-up mind, so the devil doesn't trick you into saying something, that negatively affects your future. I pray that you ignore Job's wife's advice, and that you choose to trust God, and live for God, and praise God, while you're waiting on your miracle. I pray for renewed strength, to withstand and to hold out. I pray that Holy Spirit will cause you to see beyond where you are now and give you a glimpse of what's to come. In Jesus' name, AMEN!

OCTOBER 18

Ephesians 3:20 (NASB): Now to Him who is able to do far more abundantly beyond all that we ask or think, according to the power that works within us,

THINK BIGGER

Good morning Holy Spirit, I welcome your presence into my space today, and give you authority to do whatever it is you want to do. Have your way in my life today Holy Spirit and change me for the better, forever. Change my mind and cause my thoughts to align with your will for my life. Cause my thoughts to reflect my faith, what I believe, and not a regurgitation of what I've gone through. Hallelujah! Change the way I think! Change the way I process information and cause me to live by faith.

Holy Spirit cause my creative genius to flow like a river! Increase my mental capacity! Expand the borders of my mind, and cause me to think better, to think bigger, and to think like a child of God! I declare my mind has changed, about me, about my family, about my future, and about my finances! I have been divinely enabled to think! I am, a thinker, not a reactor, and God's bringing me into a season of overflow. In Jesus' name, Amen, Amen, and AMEN!

OCTOBER 19

Proverbs 19:21 (NASB): Many plans are in a person's heart, But the advice of the Lord will stand.

GOD WANTS MORE

This will not be another wasted day. We are not going to continue to chase pipe dreams, or anything else, that belongs to somebody else. This week, we're going to rediscover God's will for our lives, and we're going to be at peace with what He's planned for our future. I pray that Holy Spirit teaches us how to be content, and how to know when we're in God's will. I pray for elevated discernment, and that we'd know when we're off, without anybody having to tell us, and before we make a mess of things.

I pray for grace to correct our behavior, and courage to change our direction. Holy Spirit show us what your will is and teach us how to pursue it without distraction, in Jesus' name! Give us what you want us to have. We want it. We desire it. And once you reveal it, we will submit to it, and pursue it, with all our strength. Help us to course correct today, and we will give you praise for it, in Jesus' name we pray, Amen!

OCTOBER 20

Exodus 34:10 (NASB): Then God said, "Behold, I am going to make a covenant. Before all your people I will perform miracles which have not been produced in all the earth nor among any of the nations; and all the people among whom you live will see the working of the Lord, for it is a fearful thing that I am going to perform with you.

I EXPECT A MIRACLE

Father, I thank you for another safe day. I praise you for keeping me from dangers seen, and unseen. I praise you for keeping the enemy off me, and off my family, and for rebuking the devourer for my sake!

Everything the enemy planned and plotted, was a waste of his time, and every person he thought was working for him, was actually working for God, and for my good! It was all for my good!

Today I am looking for miracles, any moment now, I'm going to see God intervene. The hand of God moving miraculously in my life!

I'm expecting something supernatural to show up in my house TODAY! In Jesus' name, Amen!

OCTOBER 21

Lamentations 3:25 (NASB): The Lord is good to those who await Him, To the person who seeks Him.

KEEP LOOKING

My prayer for all of us today, is that patience would have her perfect work! I pray that we don't get in a rush, and that we take the time needed, to thoroughly vet our options. I'm praying for peace, as we walk through and endure the process of elimination.

I pray that the eyes of your understanding would once again be enlightened, and that Holy Spirit would exponentially increase your ability to see the truth, even when we are surrounded by good looking lies. I pray that we be able to discern God's will, and that we have the courage to choose it. I pray for the strength to keep looking, and not be deceived or drawn in by counterfeits. I pray for your spirit's eye, that it would be sharp, and unbothered by the present options, that look good, but do not represent God's best.

I pray that Holy Spirit gives you the courage to keep looking, and to manage the process of elimination like a Believer! I pray for the patience of Adam, and that you would be constrained from choosing anything, or anybody, until it's exactly what God wants you to have. Wait I say, on the Lord. And be drama free today. Be stress free today. Be worry free today. It's in Jesus' name I pray, Amen!

OCTOBER 22

Colossians 3:12 (NASB): So, as those who have been chosen of God, holy and beloved, put on a heart of compassion, kindness, humility, gentleness, and patience;

HELP ME NOT TO JUDGE

Today, I declare that my prayers are not based on my opinion, but on my assignment, Selah

Everybody, even those who are dead wrong, needs somebody to pray for them. Today, help me to keep my "opinion" to myself, until the whole truth comes out. And then help me to share my feelings without judgment or condemnation because that's what Jesus would do.

Father guard my tongue today. Help me to not be judgmental even in my thoughts. Help me approach everyone with love and compassion. Help my light look like Christ today. It's in Jesus' name I pray, Amen!

OCTOBER 23

2 Corinthians 5:17 (NASB): Therefore if anyone is in Christ, this person is a new creation; the old things passed away; behold, new things have come.

BEGINNING TODAY

Better begins again for me today. I position myself, and I prepare myself for what God is doing. I set myself in agreement with God's will, and I align myself to move with God, and in God's time. I will no longer be the cause of my setback. I refuse to continue to be the reason why God's will, and God's plan for my life, remains on hold. I set myself in agreement with God, I choose your will Father, and I say yes all over again! I want what you want for my life.

So, I'm praying for wisdom to live better, and to make better choices. I choose better. Better chooses me, and my life will never be under again. I pray for courage to choose what's right, over what's comfortable and convenient. I thank you Father, for the wisdom and discernment, to know the difference between them. I choose to move forward, praying for the strength to never go back, or desire anything ever again, that's beneath me.

I pray for friends who want to live right. I pray that you'll bring me into the close company with people who are committed to living for God. Separate me from everything and everybody that jeopardizes my relationship with You. Better begins again, for me today. It's in Jesus' name, Amen!

OCTOBER 24

Galatians 6:9 (NASB): Let's not become discouraged in doing good, for in due time we will reap, if we do not become weary.

I WON'T BE WEARY

I'm praying for patience to endure the process. I pray that you do not grow weary in doing well. That you refuse to settle for something that is beneath you, but available.

I pray for courage to carry on, and to be consistent in "waiting on the Lord". I pray for fresh perspective, and that Holy Spirit would give you another sneak peek at your future. I pray for quitting to leave your life, and that fainting, and losing heart becomes impossible.

I pray for a mind to keep working at it! I pray for renewed strength, to go hard at it, and to keep grinding, until your dReam becomes your reality. I pray for a restored praise, and that my future would immediately begin responding to my faith. I praise you Father, by faith! I give you glory, by faith! I worship your name, by faith! Because the just shall live, by faith! It's in Jesus' name I pray, AMEN!

OCTOBER 25

Hebrews 10:36 (NASB): For you have need of endurance, so that when you have done the will of God, you may receive what was promised.

RISE ABOVE IT

Father I thank you for strength today, and I thank you that the words of Isaiah chapter 40, verses 29-31 are still true concerning my life. That my waiting has not been in vain. That I have not wasted my time serving and obeying you, and that the days ahead of me will prove, to me, and to everyone who knows me, and my situation, that God is Good! I speak the words of verse 29 over my life today, "He gives strength to the weary, and to him who lacks might He increases power." And I declare the next 42 days to be strong days in Jesus' name! I pray the words of verse 31 over my life, and I declare, "those who wait for the Lord will gain new strength; They will mount up with wings like eagles, they will run and not get tired, They will walk and not become weary."

Father, in the name of Jesus, I speak endurance, and patience, and elevated perspectives over my life. Whatever happens, I will rise above it! Whatever happens, will lift me up, and make me the better person in Jesus' name! I'll never be who or what I was again! I'll never see things the way I used to see them again! I'm better now! I didn't just survive what happened, I'm better because of what happened! No matter what happens, I have the strength to rise above it. In Jesus' name I pray, Amen!

OCTOBER 26

Psalms 143:10 (NASB): Teach me to do Your will, For You are my God; Let Your good Spirit lead me on level ground.

YES TO YOUR WILL

Good morning Holy Spirit! Thank you for keeping me last night, and for preparing this day, to be one of the best days of the year, so far. I've made up my mind, that I will not defile myself with the king's choices. I'm siding with the bible, and from today forward I'm going to yield to Holy Spirit and allow Him to lead me and guide me into all truth.

I know what I feel, and I know what I like. I can see what everybody else is doing, but I will not defile myself! I say, "Yes to your will, yes to your way". I choose the truth over what I crave. Help me Holy Spirit to maintain this conviction and to trigger the release of favor, and compassion in my life.

I declare "double for my trouble". God's leaning in my direction, favor! And He's sending people into my life, who can feel me, and who will help me, compassion! In the name of Jesus, I decree and declare "I WILL NEVER BE THE SAME AGAIN!" In Jesus' name I pray, Amen!

OCTOBER 27

Hebrews 12:1 (NASB): Therefore, since we also have such a great cloud of witnesses surrounding us, let's rid ourselves of every obstacle and the sin which so easily entangles us, and let's run with endurance the race that is set before us,

GET OUT

Today is the last day that we're going to allow people, our proclivities, and our past, to hold us hostage. The word to the believer today is, "get out!" The guilt, and the shame, and the fear, no longer have a hold on you, and now is the time to make a move. I heard the spirit say, "Get out!

Get out of that relationship. Get out of debt. Get out of fear. Get out of sin. Get out of that box. Get out of that shell. Get out of that bondage. Get out of that self-inflicted prison of pain and shame. God said to tell you to, "Get out!" Don't let the enemy trick you into going back to anything, that the blood has already made you free from, in Jesus' name, Amen! Now get up, get over it and get out.

OCTOBER 28

Proverbs 8:35 (NASB): For one who finds me finds life, And obtains favor from the Lord.

I HAVE FAVOR

Good morning Holy Spirit today is going to be a life lifting day for us! So, I thank you kind Spirit, that because you are with me, and because you will never leave me, that my life is as low as it will ever be.

I thank you Lord, that today begins a new season for me. That from today forward, I will never be without peace, patience, provision, and people to help me. Thank you, Lord, for favor, and for turning the hearts of kings in my direction. I give you praise for sending people for my life, into my life to help me. I won't have to beg, I won't have to ask them for help, and I won't have to make anybody do anything. I declare you're sending people into my life with exactly what I need, and because I've asked you for it, I will not have to ask them for it!

This is my season of help and rescue, and for everyone who left, You're sending three to help me! In Jesus' name I pray, AMEN!

OCTOBER 29

Genesis 41:51-52 (NASB): Joseph named the firstborn Manasseh "For," he said, "God has made me forget all my trouble and all of my father's household." 52 And he named the second Ephraim; "For," he said, "God has made me fruitful in the land of my affliction."

I'M LETTING IT ALL GO

I am praying for you today, that Holy Spirit would give you the grace to forgive, and the grace to live. I pray that Holy Spirit gives you the grace to focus on you, and the grace to forget what's behind.

I pray Holy Spirit would give you wisdom to move on. The strength and desire to let everything and everybody go, who keeps you chained to your past and to what happened back there. I declare you have the grace to let it go!

You have the grace to overcome, and you are, already better! What happened helped you! What they did pushed you, promoted you, and positioned you, for this season of breakthrough and overflow that you are about to walk into. You didn't just survive, YOU'RE BETTER! It's in the name of Jesus I pray, AMEN!

OCTOBER 30

Psalms 121:42 (NASB): I will raise my eyes to the mountains; From where will my help come? My help comes from the Lord, Who made heaven and earth

GOD, OPEN MY EYES

Good morning Holy Spirit, thank you for staying with me, for giving me wisdom, for always showing me what to do, and how to do it. I'm excited about another day and about another set of days to do something productive with my life! I declare this is going to be the best week I've had all year, because I said so! This week, the company I keep and the people I do business with is going to change.

God's going to send people into my life who can help me. People who will willingly add to me. God is opening my eyes to those things and people who drain me. He's opening my eyes to anything that causes me to remain comfortable with who I used to be. My eyes are open now and my spirit is sharp. I can identify and restructure my relationships with every person who's sent to hold me back. I have the mental strength to embrace the people God's sent to move me forward.

God is doing a new thing, and I refuse to keep fighting it, my soul says "YES", and I'm focused! It's in Jesus' name I pray, Amen!

OCTOBER 31

Lamentations 3:22 (NASB): The Lord's acts of mercy indeed do not end, For His compassions do not fail.

BLESSINGS BEYOND MY FAULTS

Father I thank you for your grace to finish. I thank you for proving to me, that I can finish something. Thank you, Father, for maturing me. For growing me up. And for helping me to overcome my feelings and my flesh. I'm so glad I've got the Holy Ghost and that you speak to me and through me, using me to help people have these encounters in your presence.

Thank you! Thank you for looking beyond my faults and seeing my needs! Thank you! Thank you for fresh grace, for new mercies and for delivering me from me! Thank you, Lord! For saving me from myself!

Thank you for changing my mind about me and about my place in culture and in the kingdom. My life means something! My life is a gift to somebody! I thank you, for saving my life, and for cleansing my soul in Jesus' name! These prayers and declarations are setting my life on a good course. I'll never go back to being small and thinking small again! It's in Jesus' name I pray!

NOVEMBER

NOVEMBER 1

II Corinthians 1:20 (NASB): For as many as the promises of God are, in Him they are yes; therefore through Him also is our Amen to the glory of God through us.

I'VE GOT A PROMISE

Life's pressures are real and there is no way to escape them, but we do have a choice. In First Corinthians chapter 16, verse 9, Paul says this, "for a wide door for effective service has opened to me, and there are many adversaries." I am feeling the same way, as I'm sure you are too. So, my prayer today is that we stay focused on the right thing. I pray that we overcome the temptation to make the adversity the focus and that we choose to focus on the wide door. I pray against the spirit of anxiety and fear. I pray that we'll find the faith to set our affections on what God has promised. Yes, we're in a fight, but the battle is the Lord's, not ours! His name is on the line, not ours. His character is at question, not ours. All we have to do is obey His commands and do what He has instructed us to do, and all things will have to work together for our good.

I pray for the strength of will, to make the hard decisions. I pray for the mental fortitude to stick to what we've committed to do. I pray that the promise will become our focus and not the pressure. I pray that we will position ourselves to leap and let everything against us, push us. I pray that the pressure pushes us, and that the opposition will become the thing that guarantees the victory! In Jesus' name I pray, Amen!

NOVEMBER 2

John 8:32 (NASB): and you will know the truth, and the truth will set you free."

NOW THAT'S THE TRUTH

Give me the strength to believe God for a miracle. Not only after I've done the right thing, but even after I've done the wrong thing; knowing that you chose me, fully aware of who I was, what I liked, and what I'd do!

Thank you, Lord, that even after I've made a mess of things, I'm still the one you choose, and that's what I know to be true.

I'm forgiven, and that's the truth. You do have good things planned for my close future, and that's the truth. I'm better now, than I was then, and that's the truth!

So, I commit to meditate on the truth, and to let the truth, make me free, TODAY! It's in Jesus' name I pray, Amen!

NOVEMBER 3

Deuteronomy 31:6 (NASB): Be strong and courageous, do not be afraid or in dread of them, for the Lord your God is the One who is going with you. He will not desert you or abandon you."

PROTECTION

Stop tripping, and stop making what you did, and who you did it with, bigger than God. It's time to let it go. It's time for you to move on to something divine. Something that God's chosen and prepared for you. But you will never do that, as long as you're afraid of what might happen if you leave.

Father, in the name of Jesus, I pray for the courage to obey you. I pray that we'll realize, once and for all, that there is nobody greater than you. And that whenever you give instructions, they're always accompanied by divine protection. We do not have to be afraid of what we know we have to walk away from, it cannot hurt us. We do not have to fear satanic retaliation, because whatever the enemy tries to do, in response to our obedience, will not work!

The promise of Isaiah chapter 54, verse 17 is this, no weapon that is formed against you will prosper; And every tongue that accuses you in judgment you will condemn." So, Father I claim that promise for my life, and I praise you for protecting me from my past. I give you praise for covering me, and for helping me to stop tripping over what did not work. Greater is coming, and I have nothing to fear. I have nothing, and nobody to be afraid of, because you are with me. Psalms 3 says, "But You, O Lord, are a shield about me, my glory, and the one who lifts my head". And I claim that promise for my life, that whatever the enemy tries to do to me, that you've already blocked it, and that you're causing everything to work together for my good. It's in the name of Jesus I pray, Amen!

NOVEMBER 4

Psalms 22:5 (NASB): To You they cried out and they fled to safety; In You they trusted and were not disappointed.

IT'S WORKING TOGETHER

Father, I need you! So, I lift up my head, even though I don't feel like it! I choose the joy of the Lord, even though my flesh wants me to break down in a fit of disappointment and depression. I choose to trust you, even though I'm fighting my flesh and struggling to hold on to what I believe.

I choose to wait on you Father, and while I'm waiting, your peace is fixing my mind. It's calling every thought subject to your word, and your will for my life.

I know now that no matter what happens and no matter how things turn out it's a win-win for me. Because all things are working together for my good! Even the bad, and the ugly, the stuff the devil did, and especially the stuff I did. All of it, is working, together, for my good! Father, I thank you, AMEN!

NOVEMBER 5

Deuteronomy 28:2 (NASB): And all these blessings will come to you and reach you if you obey the Lord your God:

UNUSUAL FAVOR

I pray for unusual favor today. I pray that the Holy Spirit would touch the hearts of people you barely know and lead them to bless you. I pray that the blessing of the Lord manifest in your life today, in unusual ways, thru and from unusual people, in Jesus' name!

I pray for help to come to you from outside of your circle. And from people who won't fully understand why they're helping you! I pray that by the end of the day, you have 3 or 4 testimonies of how unusual things, good things, and undeniably God things happened for you, unexpectedly and thru unusual people.

I pray that by the time you get home from work, that you'll be fully convinced, that God still loves you, and that God is still with you! It's in Jesus' name I pray, Amen!

NOVEMBER 6

Exodus 33:17-18 (NASB): The Lord said to Moses, "I will also do this thing of which you have spoken; for you have found favor in My sight and I have known you by name." 18 Then Moses said, "Please, show me Your glory!"

BE GLORIFIED

Father I thank you for watching over your word to perform it! I choose your peace today, knowing that what you started in me, you will finish. Father I set myself in agreement with what you've spoken over my life, and my soul says "yes" again! I praise you for making me your choice forever. And for not allowing the accuser of the brethren, nor my dumb days to persuade you to change your mind! Thank you, Father, for securing my future! Thank you for forgiving my past! And then Father I thank you for walking me thru my present. I can confidently declare that God is with me!

This I'm sure of, so I stop, in the middle of my day, to pray, and to purposely take a praise break. To God be the glory, for the things you've done! Be glorified for healing my body! Be praised for healing my family! Get the glory for rebuking the devourer, for my sake! Be glorified in the heavens, and in the earth! The name of Jesus be lifted high for saving me from myself! Your name be exalted for making a way out of no way! Today Father, I command my soul to make her boast in the Lord, the humble, the cast down, the cast out, the broken, the hurting, and the hopeless, will hear, and be glad! I declare 24-hour turnarounds, for the believers. It's in Jesus' name I pray!

NOVEMBER 7

Hebrews 10:22-23 (NASB): lets approach God with a sincere heart in full assurance of faith, having our hearts sprinkled clean from an evil conscience and our bodies washed with pure water. 23 Let's hold firmly to the confession of our hope without wavering, for He who promised is faithful;

DON'T LOSE FOCUS

Do not lose your focus! Keep your eyes on Jesus, who is still the author and the finisher of your faith. Knowing that if He put it in your heart, He will do His part to bring it to pass. Keep your eyes on the prize and stay out of your feelings because your feelings cannot be trusted to tell you the whole truth. Stay focused on what you heard God say and guard your ears, so that the enemy and the fearful people around you don't talk you out of your promise.

Listen to me, you're just a few days away from everything about your whole life is going to be better. So, hold on to your faith. Fight for your focus, and don't quit until you have the prize in your possession. Better is coming. Better is here. So, you better be present and accounted for. I love you! It's in Jesus' name I pray, Amen!

NOVEMBER 8

Psalms 5:12 (NASB): For You bless the righteous person, LORD, You surround him with favor as with a shield.

EXPECTING A SHIFT

I'm praying that God gives you a miracle today! I pray that the power of God shows up on your behalf, and that God puts an end to this attack of the enemy, today! I pray for your mind, that the peace of God would guard and protect it, and that Holy Spirit would free you from every negative seed, and every negative thought that's been planted in your heart.

I'm declaring today to be a type of resurrection day for you. That by morning, you'd be on your way back and totally free from every dead situation and relationship in your life.

I speak grace, mercy, favor, and compassion over your life, and prophesy a shifting of seasons in the name of Jesus! I prophesy that by morning, you will have undeniable proof that God has leaned in your direction! I declare that by, or before morning, you'll know for sure that God has thrown His weight around for you. That He has put pressure on your enemies and shifted the way they perceive you.

This day you get your mind back! This day you get your energy back! This day you reclaim your vision, and your passion for life! It's in Jesus' name I pray, Amen, Amen!

NOVEMBER 9

1 Peter 2:17: (NASB): Honor all people, love the brotherhood, fear God, honor the king

PRAYER WILL CHANGE THE COUNTRY

I pray that the frequency of the trauma doesn't paralyze us and prevent us from praying. I pray that the constant attacks, and displays of anger, and evil, doesn't stop us from loving one another, in Jesus' name. Holy Spirit help us. Don't let the attacks, the storms and the difficulty that remains, cause us to get weary.

Give us the courage, and the patience to pray without ceasing and to love without strings and conditions. Help us to pray through how we feel, and to love one another, until hate, racism and rejection are all defeated. In Jesus' name, Amen!

NOVEMBER 10

2 Peter 3:9 (NASB): The Lord is not slow about His promise, as some count slowness, but is patient toward you, not willing for any to perish, but for all to come to repentance.

IT'S IN YOUR BLOOD

Father I thank you for my spiritual inheritance. I thank you, that you picked the right father, you picked the right mother, and despite how I've felt at times, you picked the perfect family for me to be born into. I praise you for every test and for every trial. I bless you for every obstacle and for every hurdle, they were all necessary. Everything I've gone thru has produced a champion. Everything that's happened to me, brought the best me to the forefront. I thank you Father for making sure that everything I needed to overcome and to succeed was in my blood. Thank you for choosing the right parents, both biologically and spiritually. Everything I need, to be who you called me to be, is already in me.

I am the living manifestation of your answer to my grandparent's prayers. I am the living proof that you still hear and respond to the believer, and there's nothing that can hold me back. Every mistake, disappointment, and all the heartache and pain, under the blood. I make a conscious decision today, to stop tripping. I'm set up for greatness. I'm on a path to wealth and significance. I'm a mastermind, clever and gifted and I belong to God. I declare today is the day that the manifestation of the blessing begins, and curse ends. It's in Jesus' name I pray, Amen!

NOVEMBER 11

Lamentations 3:58 (NASB): Lord, You have pleaded my soul's cause; You have redeemed my life.

ENJOY EVERY MOMENT

Father I thank you for another day. I praise you for every moment today that I'll have to reflect on your goodness. Yes, I'm still in faith for a bunch of stuff! Yes, I'm still waiting on some things to change, and for a bunch of stuff to get better. But I commit to you and to myself today not to waste another moment waiting to enjoy what I already have! I vow to praise you, through the good and the bad! And I'll praise you, for what I already have. I vow to enjoy the moments, the small, but daily consistent victories that you give me. I will not, allow another moment to get away from me, without acknowledging your grace, goodness, and your mercy towards me.

Truth is that things should've been way worse. Things could've turned out completely different, but your plan for my life, recycled my mistakes, covered my sins, and redeemed my soul! So, to God be the glory! For every moment! For every mountain! For every miracle in the making, I give you praise! I say, " blessed be the name of the Lord! You are worthy to be praised and adored". I lift up holy hands, for every moment, and for every breath, I give You praise! I give you praise for this moment, that's changing my life and setting me on course to enjoy the ride and to enjoy every moment! It's in Jesus' name I pray, Amen, Amen, and Amen!

NOVEMBER 12

2 Timothy 1:7 (NASB): For God has not given us a spirit of timidity, but of power and love and discipline.

I REBUKE CONFUSION AND OFFENSE

The devil would love for us to end the year feeling misunderstood, and rejected, and discouraged! He would love for us to waste an entire month, focused on what "they" said, and on how "they" are treating us. But I stood up tonight to take authority over every distractive, lying spirit. I rebuke the spirit of confusion and offense in the name of Jesus! I cast down every image, that the enemy would use to discourage your soul, and to make you discount who you are, and what God is doing in your life. I take authority over the spirit of fear and rejection. I call you out of that so-called safe place, and back into your set place!

I pray for undistracted devotion, in Jesus' name, and I declare, "You will not fall for the trick of the enemy!" You are peculiar! You are God's! You are special! You are in the right place! At, the right time! You are loved! You are appreciated! You are valuable! You are necessary! You are enough! You are the one! You are smart! You are important! You are who God says you are! You are favored! You are not quitting! You are not backing up! You are not going to lose! You ARE! It's in Jesus' name I pray, Amen!

NOVEMBER 13

1 Peter 5:7 (NASB): having cast all your anxiety on Him, because He cares about you.

I PUT IT ALL IN HIS HANDS

"I put it ALL in His hands! He can handle it, that's a fact!" My suggestion to you, is that you do the same! I pray that you commit to yourself to take your hands off of that situation and trust God to handle it and to handle them. I pray that today would be drama fRee, stress fRee, and full of joy and peace, in Jesus' name. I pray for help to come from everywhere. That strangers would look favorably upon you and be moved with compassion to help you. I pray for divine hook ups and deals, that the things you need that you couldn't quite afford, would be reduced in price, in Jesus' name.

I pray that favor wouldn't just find you, but that favor would run you down and overtake you until you have so much, that you have to share, in Jesus' name. I pray for peace to take your hands off that unbearable situation. Grace to get through it and get you out of it with no hurt, harm, or damage to anything or anybody you love and need, in Jesus' name. I pray that things would start happening for you SUPERNATURALLY, today! It's in the mighty and matchless name of Jesus I pray, Amen, Amen, and Amen!

NOVEMBER 14

Hebrews 13:8 (NASB): Jesus Christ is the same yesterday and today and forever.

WHAT REALLY MATTERS HASN'T CHANGED

Stop falling for the same foolishness and the same tricks! It's nothing more than a distraction tactic to try to get you off your game. What's happening to you, does not change, what's about to happen for you. How you "feel", does not change what God said in any way! So, then we must deduce that what really matters, has not changed. Now let's go. Let's go get this joy, and this peace, and this money for these last few weeks of this year, and let's go do it now!

What really matters has not changed, so what are you sitting around waiting for? Who are you wasting your precious time on, sitting around waiting to get their approval? Let's go get this destiny stuff and let that dumb stuff go. Let's go get this generational wealth stuff and leave those generational weaknesses in the past. What really matters hasn't changed but you have. Now get up and act like it! Hold your head up, like you have hope and a future. Smile like God's got beautiful thoughts of you and plans to prosper you. Get your game face on and leave those tears in yesterday. We got people to help, a city to touch and wealth to accumulate! The time is now! Amen!

NOVEMBER 15

Isaiah 54:17 (NASB): "No weapon that is formed against you will prosper; And every tongue that accuses you in judgment you will condemn. This is the heritage of the servants of the Lord, And their vindication is from Me," declares the Lord

GOD'S GOT YOU

God's going to walk you out of it! God's going to give you the wisdom you need to circumvent the plans of the enemy. God's about to lead you into something better, and into something bigger, but you are going to have to obey God! So, I pray for your inner ear, that Holy Spirit would increase your ability to hear and to discern His voice. I break the hold of confusion and fear, and I declare, "We have ears to hear what the spirit of the Lord is saying to His church!" We can hear! We can obey!

We will obey! And our obedience is going to set in motion a series of events that will release the power of God in our lives, in a way that our generation has never seen! I decree and declare, that things are about to start happening for us supernaturally and we are going to see a demonstration of God's power on our behalf before the end of the year! It's in Jesus' name we pray, Amen!

NOVEMBER 16

Ephesians 3:20 (NASB): Now to Him who is able to do far more abundantly beyond all that we ask or think, according to the power that works within us,

IT CANNOT BREAK YOU

However, it comes at you, or whoever comes for you, the word of the Lord still stands, "It cannot break you!" So, don't misread where you are, and let the devil convince you that's you're dead, and it's over. You are NOT dead, and you are NOT defeated! It took this attack from the side to produce this anointing and to develop your testimony.

So now you have enough to win. Now you have everything you need to overcome, and they overcame him, by the blood of the Lamb, and because of the word of their testimony." So, to God be the glory, for the things He has done! You say it, "Now, thanks be unto God, who gives me the victory in my mind, in my will, and in how I feel". No more relenting my faith to my feelings. I'm going to stand my ground and believe God. I'm going to stand firm on the word and put a demand on what God has spoken over my life. I decree and declare, that the word will not return void, but it will accomplish everything it was sent to do. I have the mind of Christ, so whatever weapon the enemy forms, cannot and will not break my mind! I'm not crazy, I'm not losing it and I know in whom I can trust. This trouble and this trial will not break me! In Jesus' name I pray, Amen!"

NOVEMBER 17

Psalms 110:1 (NASB): The LORD says to my Lord: "Sit at My right hand Until I make Your enemies a footstool for Your feet."

YOU WILL NOT BE OFFENDED

Your life has way more significance than the devil wants you to realize, that's why the attack on your life has been so deep, destructive, and discouraging. It's because the enemy wanted you to stay in the shallow water. His plan is to keep using people who are close to you. Or people who are further ahead than you, to convince you that you're better off being in the shallow water. The truth is that you were never supposed to be that person you used to be. You were never supposed to try swimming in something that you can stand up in. I heard the Lord say, "just stand up, because the water you're in now isn't deep enough to drown you!" It's time to stand up and make an intentional move. Something deeper, something significant, and signature, is calling your name! It's time for you to stop dealing with things on the surface, and with shallow/surface type people.

I heard the Lord say, "work ethic was never your issue. Your issue is that you didn't allow Jesus to use your boat (Luke5:1), your gift, nor your passion". The devil had you feeling like a failure because of what happened, but the devil is a liar. Do something divine today. OBEY GOD! You're about see the blessings of the Lord like never before! In Jesus' name, Amen!

NOVEMBER 18

2 Corinthians 4:16 (NASB): Therefore we do not lose heart, but though our outer man is decaying, yet our inner man is being renewed day by day.

YOU ARE NOT CRAZY

You're not crazy! This is not an ordinary fight you're in! You're in the fight of your life, but please remember that you've already been given the victory! You're under this extreme pressure because of this extraordinary power that's about to come forth from your life. So, don't be distracted by the pain, nor the pressure, because both are necessary to produce the oil of the anointing.

So, Father we thank you for fresh oil. And for taking the trials of our lives and using them to make us ready. Thank you, Lord, for repurposing every test and for using them to demonstrate your power, on our behalf. This fresh anointing destroys every yoke! This fresh grace enables us to do what we were once unable to do. In Jesus' name! So, we celebrate the crushing! And we anticipate the breakthrough! It's in Jesus' name I pray, AMEN!

NOVEMBER 19

2 Corinthians 12:9 (NASB): And He has said to me, "My grace is sufficient for you, for power is perfected in weakness." Most gladly, therefore, I will rather boast [c]about my weaknesses, so that the power of Christ may dwell in me.

—

KEEP GOING

However, you're being challenged in this season, please know that it is not without divine constraints and oversight! The devil cannot just do whatever! He can only do what God allows. And God's only going to allow what you can bare, and what's necessary to push you through to your next place in life. So, my prayer today is that the peace of God would guard your heart and mind. That Holy Spirit would be your comforter and your guide. And that you see with your own eyes God's hand of protection working for you and not against you.

I pray courage to keep going, even though you're hurting, and wounded. I pray that you don't get out of character, because of what's happened to you. I pray that you find the strength of will to keep your eyes on the prize, and on the things that really matter. I pray that those feelings of being overwhelmed and in above your head, would be defeated by the truth. That you would quickly realize that you're in a fixed fight, and you cannot lose. Holy Spirit have your way, and don't let my feelings cancel out my faith. It's in Jesus' name I pray, Amen!

NOVEMBER 20

Galatians 6:9 (NASB): Let's not become discouraged in doing good, for in due time we will reap, if we do not become weary.

YOU ARE NOT CRAZY

Your present condition is not your destiny! James chapter 1, verse 4 says this: "And let endurance have its perfect result, so that you may be perfect and complete, lacking in nothing." So, I want us to get in faith for perfect results, and for the best outcome possible.

Father we set our faith in agreement with one another and we decree and declare that our faith will not fail. Holy Spirit we ask now, that you would give us your peace to endure. We pray that the pain and the unanswered questions will not shake us, nor cause us to question our faith. We're hurting, we're confused and some of us are angry, but we declare, "Our faith will not fail!" Patience is at work and we're learning how to endure hardness as a good soldier.

You're building our story and giving us our own testimony, so that we know you outside of who our parents, and our pastors told us you were! Glory to God! We can, and we will endure this season of pain, because it's a part of our process. And once endurance has had its perfect work, and the pressure of this season has produced the perfect results, we will be perfect, complete, and lacking in nothing! It's in Jesus' name we pray, Amen, Amen, and Amen!

NOVEMBER 21

Psalms 150:6 (NASB): Let everything that has breath praise the Lord!

I WILL ALWAYS WORSHIP

Father in the name of Jesus, I speak peace and joy over my life and over my family. I break the chains of confusion and fear, and I receive the peace of God that surpasses all understanding. I declare and decree that angels are standing guard over my spirit and over my thoughts. And that while I should be anxious and stressed, my response and reaction, is that of faith! I will not allow what I see with my natural eye, make me discount nor disbelieve, what I know I saw with my spirit's eye.

I choose to walk by faith and not by sight! I choose to trust in the Lord, with all of my heart, and to stop leaning on what I've come to "understand", in my flesh. I choose to acknowledge you Father, in all of my ways, knowing that come what may, you will always direct my path.

So, I give you glory! I give you praise! I bless your name! I rest upon your promise today, declaring, "this, is going to be, one of the BEST years, of my life!" It's in Jesus' name I pray. Amen!

NOVEMBER 22

1 Timothy 5:8 (NASB): Be of sober spirit, be on the alert. Your adversary, the devil, prowls around like a roaring lion, seeking someone to devour.

MAN UP!

Holy Spirit open our ears, but don't allow any negative words or voices to get past our faith filter. Don't allow anything, or anybody who doesn't represent you, or speak for you, to maintain or acquire our ear. Cut off every negative influence and every doubting voice. Give us grace to shut down the conversations that take us back and the circles that keep us tied to yesterday. Mute the voices of the naysayers, so that even though we'll know they're talking, we won't be able to hear what they're saying, in Jesus' name!

Holy Spirit grant us grace to not only pay attention, but to be sober and vigilant. Grant us the grace to "Listen Up" selah. Elevate our ears! And only allow what's fresh to pass through our ear gates! In the name of Jesus, I decree and declare, "We have an ear to hear, what the spirit of the Lord is saying to the church!" Our ears are elevated. Our ears are pure! Our ears are ready, and nothing old or untrue, will ever again be able to reduce our vision. Faith comes by hearing, and hearing by the word of God. Our faith will make us well today. It's in Jesus' mighty name we pray, Amen!

NOVEMBER 23

Luke 17:5 (NASB): The apostles said to the Lord, "Increase our faith!"

I AM NOT SMALL

Staying small, is no longer an option for you! So, you have to make it up in your mind, right now and declare this with me today, "I am ok with outgrowing people, who were a part of my past, but are not a part of my future". I decree and declare today that I refuse to shrink to accommodate anybody! It's above me now. So Holy Spirit, give us the courage to break away. Give us the strength of will to obey you, and to trust you, and not to be bound by "them" or their opinions, or their lack of faith. The place we've been in, is too small, and we've been here for too long.

So today we say, yes. As we can sense your hand pulling us out and pulling us up. Our souls say yes to your will. Our souls say yes to your way! Do what you want to do today, and don't let our past, hold our future hostage! Let your power fall. Prove the doubters wrong, and don't let what they've said, delay what you have spoken over our lives. Have your way today. Blow our minds. Blow us up. Make our names great! Make our hands strong, and help us to align our character, our behavior, our regimens, and our routines with your will. It's in Jesus' name we pray, Amen!

NOVEMBER 24

Isaiah 50:4 (NASB): The Lord God has given Me The tongue of the learned, That I should know how to speak A word in season to him who is weary. He awakens Me morning by morning, He awakens My ear To hear as the learned.

YOU SPEAK!

Isaiah Chapter 50, verse 4, says this, "The Lord God has given me the tongue of the learned, That I should know how to speak A word in season to him who is weary. He awakens me morning by morning; He awakens my ear to hear as the learned." This is our prayer today that God would help us think with our minds, speak with our mouths, create with our hands, and love with our hearts. I pray that Holy Spirit gives us the words and the wisdom to go along with them, so we don't misspeak or speak out of season.

I pray for wisdom to hit our mouths, so not only will we know what to say, but we'll know when to say it. I pray not only for holy boldness, but for holy constraint, in the name of Jesus. I pray that we will speak the word in its season, knowing that "the truth spoken out of season, is just as powerful and painful, as a lie". Holy Spirit, give us, "the tongue of the learned", and don't let us speak out of turn. You speak and cause us to be earthen echoes of Heaven's decree. You speak, and let the word do the work. You speak, and break every generational curse and chain, in Jesus' name. Holy Spirit, you speak to us, in us, through us, and for us. Set us free from every setback, hold back, and clap back. Let the words of our mouths and the meditation of our hearts be acceptable in your sight and useful in our salvation. It's in Jesus' mighty name we pray, Amen!

NOVEMBER 25

James 1:4 (NASB): And let endurance have its perfect result, so that you may be [c]perfect and complete, lacking in nothing.

HELP US TO HOLD ON

Holy Spirit help us to hold on, while you put us on! Help us to wait while you add weight to our testimony. Teach us to trust you when we can't really track you. Let the word over our lives ring louder and louder, until our faith gets stronger and stronger, in Jesus' name!

Show us how to take the focus off us, and how to put the focus back on God. Teach us how to lean not to our own understanding, but how to acknowledge you in all our ways. Let today be a turning point. Let today be the day we see what we heard, and we will give you all the glory, and all the honor, and all the praise. It's in Jesus' mighty name we pray. Amen.

NOVEMBER 26

Luke 17:5 (NASB): The apostles said to the Lord, "Increase our faith!"

HELP MY UNBELIEF

Holy Spirit help our unbelief! Help us to start walking with God, like He is God. Don't allow us to continue to mishandle His word and His promise. Forgive us for our lack of faith and honor. Forgive us for treating you like a man, who can't be trusted. Holy Spirit teach us how to walk by faith, and how to live by faith! Teach us your ways, and we will follow. Lead us, guide us, push us in everything we do and everything we get, we'll give the glory to you!

Whatever you do, just don't do it without us! Whatever you do, please Father, don't let the disrespect and the doubt, disqualify us from the destiny that you've already determined for our lives. Our hearts cry out for you. Our souls say yes, and now that we've obtained mercy, we come boldly before the throne of grace. That we might get the help we need, to heal, to mature, to prosper and to glorify you, in everything we do! It's in Jesus' name we pray. Amen.

NOVEMBER 27

John 1:50 (NASB): Jesus answered and said to him, "Because I said to you that I saw you under the fig tree, do you believe? You will see greater things than these."

BELIEVE! BECOME!

Believe! Become! These two simple words are going to change the very course of our lives today! I pray that we find strength to believe God over our circumstances. I pray that not only the blessing of Abraham, but the grace of Abraham rises up within us today, and that we choose to hope against hope, again. I pray that we do not waste any more time in fear, in doubt or in disbelief, but that we emerge from this day, becoming! I pray for grace to put the focus back on God, and that all the pressure to perform falls back on Him. I pray for a fully persuaded kind of day, and that for the next 24 hours, God would send signs and wonders to confirm the coming miracle. I pray that today is full of confirmation, and that our faith increases exponentially.

Holy Spirit raise up somebody, somewhere, with a same-like situation, and faith, who will confirm what we believe. Let today be the day that it all starts coming together. Let the next 24 hours awaken something within us spiritually, emotionally, physically, and financially. Send the perfect people into our personal space, with the proper processes, to align with our passion, to produce something supernatural, in the name of Jesus. All things are working together for our good. It's in Jesus' name, we call these things to be so. Amen!

NOVEMBER 28

Psalms 115:14 (NASB): May the Lord increase you, You and your children.

GRACE FOR BIGGER

It's above me now, and what God has planned for me, is going to blow my mind! My prayer is, that I will take the focus off me and put the focus back on God. I pray that I find grace to answer the upward call. And that settling for anything beneath me would no longer be an acceptable option. I pray for grace to push myself and grace to go beyond the limits of what I've already done. I pray that my desire would align with God's desire, and that God's will, will dictate my will, and my actions.

I pray for grace to do something bigger. For grace to do something better. For an extraordinary, legendary grace to hit my life, in the name of Jesus! Holy Spirit, I pray for clarity of thought and purpose. I pray for outside help, unexpected help, consistent help, and grace to manage every helpful partnership and relationship in Jesus' name. Expand my life and legacy. Increase my influence and broaden the scope of my gift. Don't let me stay regular. Don't let me remain common. Cause everything about my life, business, and ministry, to grow exponentially. And all the glory, honor, and praise, belongs to you! It's in Jesus' mighty name we pray, Amen.

NOVEMBER 29

1 Corinthians 2:9 (NASB): but just as it is written: "Things which eye has not seen and ear has not heard, And which have not entered the human heart, All that God has prepared for those who love Him."

THE PREPARED PLACE

Father, in the name of Jesus, I lay ever dRem and every vision, back at your feet. Every desire that you've given us, we give it back to you. In the name of Jesus, we call time into divine alignment with purpose and we step out of that old fearful place and into our "Prepared Place." No fear, no envy, no strife, no jealousy, no hating, and no settling for less just to relieve the pressure, or to try to save face. We believe that what you've prepared for us, no one can possess, but us. We decree and declare, that time and destiny are about to collide, that opportunity and preparation are about to mesh, and produce something supernatural. We call it done! We are ready!"

We're ready for the next move to occupy the next place. We're ready to take possession of what you've prepared, and we have no fear as relates to the future. We will not blow it. We will not mess it up and we will not lose what you set in our hands. You've not only blessed us, but you've given us grace to steward the blessing. So, we approach today boldly, and free from anxiety and stress. We approach today with joy and peace. We have the confidence that what you started you will finish. We call today, a winning kind of day. No L's today. W's ONLY! It's in Jesus' name we pray, Amen, Amen, and Amen!

NOVEMBER 30

Job 8:7 (NASB): Though your beginning was insignificant, Yet your end will increase greatly.

GRACE TO STRETCH

Holy Spirit give us the courage and the strength of character, to answer the call. Grant us grace to obey, and the grace to shift everything in our lives that keep us tied to what was. In the name of Jesus, we pray for grace to establish a living legacy. We pray for wisdom, patience, and truth to reset everything that needs resetting. And for the wherewithal to re-evaluate where we are and why we're still there.

Help us Holy Spirit to see the bigger, and to see the greater, and to have prophetic perspective on our life and legacy. Help us to step out of every situation and every circumstance that keeps us comfortable. Stretch us, so that what's on our lives doesn't die when we die! Do something bigger in us and cause the grace we carry to positively affect generations, for the glory of God. It's in Jesus' mighty name we pray. Amen.

DECEMBER

DECEMBER 1

Psalms 46:1 (NASB): God is our refuge and strength, A very ready help in trouble.

THE PREPARED PLACE

Father, my prayer is that you will not allow the enemy to use people and their character flaws, to turn you away from your set place. I pray for mercy, for grace, and for patience to manage and to work through other people's character flaws, the same way other people had to work thru mine. I pray that ministry remains your burden. And at the same time, your biggest blessing. I pray that as you love people unconditionally, just as Jesus loves you, that He would reward your faithfulness, and restore the joy of serving in church.

I break the hold of offense and I expose the lie of the enemy. Your season is not up! You don't have another new daddy! God didn't tell you to leave your church! It's not "time to move on", that's a lie! So, I pray for discernment when I'm weary. When I'm spiritually and mentally exhausted and for every son and daughter in ministry who's about to be elevated when they pass the test. Holy Spirit, open our eyes, open our ears, open our hearts. Show us what to do and how to move past this hard place. Make us one. Help us to hear. Teach us forgiveness and walk us thru this season of adjustments, so we don't get out of position and miss our season of harvest. It's in Jesus' mighty name I pray, Amen!

DECEMBER 2

Hebrews 11:8 (NASB): By faith Abraham, when he was called, obeyed by going out to a place which he was to receive for an inheritance; and he went out, not knowing where he was going

GLORY TO JESUS

Father, in the name of Jesus, we give You praise for a stress free, drama free week! And we set our faith in agreement with one another, for something supernatural to pop off today! We decree and declare that we will not lose our joy, dealing with people who have lost theirs! We will not lose our peace, fooling with people who don't even realize the never had any!

Thank you, Holy Spirit for teaching us how, when and for showing us "who", and for never letting us lose sight of why we say, "Glory to Jesus". We go into the week declaring, that all of the glory, all of the honour, all of the praise, belongs to you!" We go into the week declaring, "take your seat, with you we can't be beat! So, we lay our burdens at your feet". Our prayer is, that you would Settle Here. It's in Jesus' mighty name we pray, Amen.

DECEMBER 3

John 14:26 (NASB): But the Helper, the Holy Spirit whom the Father will send in My name, He will teach you all things, and remind you of all that I said to you.

WE CHOOSE THE HOLY SPIRIT

We pray that Holy Spirit gives us His peace again today! In the name of Jesus, we break the hold of weariness and frustration. We decree and declare we have everything we need to wait on the Lord. We have the ability to keep waiting, to endure hardness and the grace to stay in faith for things to get better. The just shall live by faith, and we choose life today! We choose to follow the leading of Holy Spirit and move into the things He has planned for us. We choose life, this abundant life, that Jesus promised us in the 10th chapter of the book of John.

We choose to leave mediocrity behind and walk by faith, into the realm of the extraordinary. Knowing that there's a grace on our lives to do something that's never been done before. The grace of God on our lives has prepared us, positioned us, and now it's pushing us into destiny and purpose. Into a place that only legends can occupy. When God gets done showing us who we really are, we'll be living in a place where the legends live. It's in Jesus' name we pray, Amen

DECEMBER 4

Hebrews 11:8 (NASB): By faith Abraham, when he was called, obeyed by going out to a place which he was to receive for an inheritance; and he went out, not knowing where he was going

DOUBLE GRACE

DOUBLE GRACE! That's our confession of faith today. We decree and declare that we have ears to hear what the spirit of the Lord is saying. We have the courage and the boldness to do what we heard, in Jesus' name!

We will not be hearers only, but we have grace to hear and to do. We are no longer bound be fear, nor by the "what ifs" of life. We choose now to walk by faith, and not by sight. If we heard it, we can do it! If we heard it, we can have it. So, we're expecting to see the supernatural today and tomorrow, and the next day, and the day after that, and for the rest of our lives. In Jesus' name, Amen!

DECEMBER 5

Matthew 2:12 (NASB): And after being warned by God in a dream not to return to Herod, the magi left for their own country by another way.

LOOK UP

So be encouraged, knowing that whatever the devil did, and whatever else happened in your life that you considered to be a negative; it is yet working together for your good! I pray that you find grace to "look up" and elevate your perspective. I pray that your spirit will see beyond the places your natural eyes can look. I pray for revelation of the truth, so you can go into the weekend, free!

I pray for insight, and that you will get an "understanding", that you are where you're supposed to be, and that you can win from where you are. Nothing about your situation has to change for you to get the victory, because the issue has already been decided.

So, then we pray for endurance! We pray for patience! We pray for strength! We pray for wisdom! We decree grace and peace over your life and over your mind!

You will not stop, you will not quit, you will not give up, not until you're finished, not until you've done everything God's put in your heart to do. It's in Jesus' mighty name we declare these things to be so, Amen!

DECEMBER 6

Proverbs 17:17 (NASB): A friend loves at all times And a brother is born for adversity

MY RELATIONSHIPS

God's cleansing your relationships and purging your connections. So, I pray for discernment, and for the courage to stop and start over. I pray that pride, ego, or the fear of losing people won't prevent you from doing what you know you have to do. I pray for a renewed desire, to want to please God with your life, and in every relationship, whether it be with your family, your friends, or your foes. I pray that Holy Spirit would sever every soul tie, that God hasn't arranged, and that you would come into the knowledge of who's been sent by God, and who was sent by the devil! I pray that your ability to discern spirits, motives, and intentions, would increase exponentially, and overnight, and that every undercover demon be exposed, and eliminated from your life in Jesus' name!

I decree and declare, that we've come into a new dispensation of the grace of God, and that God is sending people into your space, who'll make the thing in you, that God gave you, leap for joy. I decree and declare, that we're coming into a season of life, into a season of movement, and that everything God's given you, is about to come forth. This is our season to produce. This is our season to bring it forth. I speak to every gift, every talent, every dReam, every prophetic vision, and strategy, and I command it to break through! It's in Jesus' name, Amen!

DECEMBER 7

Romans 8:37 (NASB): But in all these things we overwhelmingly conquer through Him who loved us.

IT'S WINNING SEASON

It's your winning season! It's my prayer for you that you'll show up! I pray that you'll be present and that you'll actually be there physically, mentally, and emotionally! I pray that you find peace and grace, to actually enjoy the fruits of your labor. I pray that your hard work produces and that it produces again and again, and over and over!

I pray that losing remains in your past, and only a part of your testimony, not your present reality. I command you to believe for a win! I command your soul to expect the best, and let God handle the rest. In the name of Jesus, I decree and declare, "Everything attached to you, WINS!" We call it finished! We call it done! In Jesus' name, Amen!

DECEMBER 8

2 Peter 1:3 (NASB): Seeing that his divine power has granted to us everything pertaining to life and godliness, through the true knowledge of Him who called us by His own glory and excellence.

I CAN HANDLE IT

You are not going to mishandle what God has given you. You are not going back. You have the grace to steward every gift and blessing that God has entrusted to you. You will not lose what God gave to you. Fear will not make you mistreat it. Anxiety will not get the best of you, but it will bring out the best in you. You have been given more grace and life is going to get easier and extremely fulfilling for you, your family, and your circle of friends. In Jesus' name!

The best is yet to come. This is going to be one of the best years of your life, spiritually, emotionally, physically, and financially. You can handle it! It's in Jesus' name we pray, Amen!

DECEMBER 9

Exodus 17:15 (NASB): Moses built an altar and named it The Lord is My Banner..

I'M BUILDING MY ALTAR

I pray that as you build God an altar, that every ungodly attachment would burn off because of His presence. I pray that every unfruitful connection would drop off as you continue to pursue God's presence. I pray that any and everything you're vested in and committed to, that God isn't behind or that God didn't ordain, would fall by the wayside, in Jesus' name! I pray that everything, and everybody you're connected to, would be the manifestation of God's plan for your life. No more mistake relationships! No more unproductive exchanges or interactions.

I pray for divine connections, that will connect you to everything God's willed you to have. I pray for people, and for process, and for patience, and I'm asking Holy Spirit to help you sanctify your mind, your mouth, and your motives. In the name of Jesus, I decree and declare the next 48 hours belong to God! The next 2 days belong to the kingdom, and even now, God is repositioning you. He's correcting your posture, purifying your soul, and setting you in place for the release of glory, that's about to elevate your life forever. The charge is, "guard the next 48 hours!" No fear! No foolishness! It's in Jesus' name we pray, Amen.

DECEMBER 10

Isaiah 26:3 (NASB): "The steadfast of mind You will keep in perfect peace, Because he trusts in You.

KEEP LOOKING

My prayer for all of us today, is that patience would have her perfect work! I pray that we don't get in a rush. That we take the time needed to thoroughly vet our options. I'm praying for peace, as we walk through and endure the process of elimination.

I pray that the eyes of your understanding would once again be enlightened. That Holy Spirit would exponentially increase your ability to see the truth, even when surrounded by good looking lies. I pray that we be able to discern God's will and that we have the courage to choose it. I pray for the strength to keep looking, and not be deceived or drawn in by counterfeits. I pray for your spirit's eye, that it would be sharp and unbothered by the present options, that look good, but do not represent God's best.

I pray that Holy Spirit gives you the courage to keep looking and to manage the process of elimination like a believer! I pray for the patience of Adam, and that you would be constrained from choosing anything, or anybody, until it's exactly what God wants you to have. Wait I say on the Lord. And be drama free today. Be stress free today. Be worry free today. It's in Jesus' name I pray, Amen!

DECEMBER 11

Proverbs 3:4 (NASB): So you will find favor and good repute in the sight of God and man

I HAVE FAVOR

God's about to do something! He's leaning in your direction! Tipping the scales in your favor and turning the hearts of the decision makers to you. No's are becoming yeses, supernaturally! People who were against you, are about to be for you! And what used to be dreadfully difficult, is about to get supernaturally easy in Jesus' mighty name! So, Father, help our unbelief, and use the resistance to strengthen our faith. Show us how to have bold faith, even in crisis, and grant us grace to stay strong, to stay steady, and to stay ready, knowing that "things are about to start happening for us, SUPERNATURALLY!"

Holy Spirit keep our eyes on the prize, and help us to keep pressing and reaching, in Jesus' name! Show us what's ahead, and don't let anything, or anybody, catch us off guard, or unprepared. Lean in our direction! Turn the tables in our favor and put us in a better place by tomorrow Let today be full of miracles, signs and wonders and unexpected blessings! Let today be the turning point so that by next week, we have something completely different, and brand new to thank You for! It's in the mighty name of Jesus we pray, Amen!

DECEMBER 12

Acts 25:26 (NASB): Yet, I have nothing definite about him to write to my lord. Therefore, I have brought him before you all and especially before you, King Agrippa, so that after the investigation has taken place, I may have something to write.

YOU'RE BEING VETTED

You are being vetted for high office. So, don't misinterpret your trouble. Please don't misread your circumstances. God only allowed it to prove you who He is and who you are. God only allowed the pressure so He could justify the promotion. So Holy Spirit, help us. Help us to properly discern the times, and the season.

Don't let us fail the people test. Don't let us fail the patience test. Don't let us miss our moment. Don't let us miss our window. Don't let us waste our time seeking revenge. Don't let us waste our energy on restricted and constrained enemies.

Let the truth be our guide! Let the truth make us free and cause us to be fully present and enjoy every minute of our elevation! It's in Jesus' mighty name we pray, Amen!

DECEMBER 13

James 1:22-23 (NASB): But prove yourselves doers of the word, and not merely hearers who delude themselves. [23] *For if anyone is a hearer of the word and not a doer, he is like a man who looks at his natural face in a mirror*

JUST DO IT

What are you waiting for? The enemy will always provide you with a good excuse to keep things on hold. So, you need to decide today, to stop accepting the misery of mediocrity and take a chance on doing something great! There's greatness in you dying to get out of you. But you have to decide to stop being afraid.

My prayer for you, my prayer for "US", is that we overcome the spirit of fear and do all that God has put in our hearts to do. I pray for courage to press past the mistakes and the naysayers. I pray for the strength to get up again, even if you must pick your own self up! I pray for vision to see beyond the present standard and to do something that's never been done before, in Jesus' Name!

I pray that you will keep trying, until you start winning. That winning becomes your standard and your fresh reputation. JUST DO IT! Who cares if you fail? JUST DO IT! It doesn't matter if you must start over. JUST DO IT! God's on your side. The glory is on your life and nothing you do, that God gave you to do can fail. So, DO IT!

DECEMBER 14

Colossians 3:2 (NASB): Set your mind on the things above, not on the things that are on the earth.

HEAR THROUGH PAIN

Don't let the pain become a complete distraction. You're still who you are, and you've still got work to do. So, put your game face on. Holla when you need to but don't lose sight of your assignment and today's agenda. I pray that focus won't become a casualty of war, and that despite what's going on physically, mentally, and emotionally we'll remain the masters of our hearts.

I pray for stability in every area of our lives, and that we'll finally learn how to fight and focus at the same time, in Jesus' name. I command our ears to be open to God's voice and to the voices that He's assigned to help us manage our new seat of authority. I pray for the ability to separate the voices in the wind, from the voice of the wind. And that pain won't cause us to hesitate, after we know we've heard from God. We can still hear, even though we're still hurting because the grace of God is our enabler and our help. It's in Jesus' name I pray, AMEN!

DECEMBER 15

Romans 8:26 (NASB): In the same way the Spirit also helps our weakness; for we do not know how to pray as we should.

I WILL NOT QUIT

I am not a quitter. I know things are crazy and you're disappointed. You feel let down and left to figure this out on your own; but remember, your feelings cannot be trusted. Your feelings are connected to your flesh, and your flesh, according to Romans Chapter 8, is at war with your spirit. What you're going to do is settle yourself, find a place to worship, and wait for Holy Spirit to bring peace to your soul.

I pray now for strength to fight your feelings. I pray for courage to obey what you hear Holy Spirit leading you to do. I pray that you find boldness in the word of God, both written, and spoken. I pray that you finally find you and that you discover just how valuable, and precious, and loved of God you are.

I pray for patience, and endurance, and that you do not grow weary, in Jesus' name! You are not a quitter! So, stop thinking about it! You are not alone, so stop acting like it! God is with you, and He will never leave you, nor will He forsake you. So, pick yourself up, dry your eyes, and let's go be who God has called us to be. It's in Jesus' name I pray!

DECEMBER 16

Ephesians 6:10 (NASB): Finally, be strong in the Lord and in the strength of His might.

PUSH THROUGH

Father, I come before you today, in the name of Jesus, pleading the blood over my life! I thank you Father, that you've given me the strength to move past my failures. I give you praise today, that I no longer have to sit around and wait for permission to go on with my life.

I choose to forget those things which really are behind me and I choose to reach for what's ahead. But all the while trusting you to help me to never repeat what's behind. I choose to move on and today I commit to stretch myself, and push myself, until I do something, I've been afraid to do. Today, I'm going to be great! Today, I'm going to do something greater!

Today is the day, that the Lord has made, so I'm going to get up, dust myself off, forgive myself, pace myself, push myself, and be who God wants me to be. It's in Jesus' name I pray, AMEN!

DECEMBER 17

John 4:24 (NASB): God is spirit, and those who worship Him must worship in spirit and truth."

I WILL WORSHIP

I declare, "this is the day you've turned my mourning into dancing!" So today I'm going to dance like David danced!

The devil is a liar, I am going to worship God today in everything that I do! I will bless the Lord in my home, and on my job, and in my car and with my family. Today, I'm going to praise God like a rich man! Today I'm going to worship like a man with no debt or outstanding bills!

This is the day, that I make an outward show of the enemy's defeat, and praise you like a man with nothing to worry about. For the Lord is good, and your mercy endures forever. I vow to praise you, for the rest of my days! In Jesus name I pray, Amen, Amen, and AMEN!

DECEMBER 18

Genesis 26:22 (NASB): Then he moved away from there and dug another well, and they did not quarrel over it; so he named it Rehoboth, for he said, "At last the Lord has made room for us, and we will be fruitful in the land."

I WILL NOT QUIT!

I will not quit! That declaration has to be your determination, so you don't quit, and so you don't let anybody else make you quit prematurely! You control your own destiny, you plan and prepare for your own future, and you're not going to let anybody or anything, determine how you behave, Amen!

Let's pray together: Holy Spirit help us! Help our weaknesses, as you promised you would and don't let our emotions distract us. Don't let our responses to being mistreated and done wrong by people, who know better, and know they're wrong, forfeit what's ahead!

Help our weaknesses and the tendency to unplug, and to disconnect. Help our weaknesses and teach us how to walk away from the drama, without giving away our destiny. Help us to keep digging until we hit a well of water and resource, that the enemy has no more energy to fight us for. We promise to give you glory, honor, and praise. It's in Jesus' mighty name we pray, Amen!

DECEMBER 19

Mark 4:22 (NASB): For nothing is hidden, except to be revealed; nor has anything been secret, but that it would come to light.

IT WAS ALL LIES

Thank you for exposing the lies of the enemy! I thank you for flushing my ear gates. And for purging my soul of every lie the enemy presented to me as truth. I praise you today, for the grace to know the truth. For the freedom, that this knowing brings into my life.

I will never discount, degrade, or devalue who I am, ever again! I will never settle for something smaller, or lesser than what you promised, ever again! From today forward, I commit to live by faith, to walk by faith, and not by sight and to patiently wait, until my change comes! I commit today to live by revelation, and not by emotionally fueled reality, thank you Jesus!

Thank you for exposing the lies and uncovering the truth! I realize now that everything the devil told me, was all lies! I am the head, and not the tail! I am above, and not beneath! I am blessed, and not cursed!

My sins are covered in the blood. Every negative thing the devil has whispered in my ear, I know now it was all lies! So today I set myself on a course to walk in the truth, and to put every lie under my feet!

I'm NOT losing my children...LIES!
I'm NOT losing my mother...LIES!
I'm NOT losing my inheritance...LIES!
I'm NOT losing my health...LIES!
I'm NOT losing my wealth...LIES!
I'm NOT losing my mind...LIES!

It was ALL LIES! So, I decree and declare truth prevails over my day today. It's in Jesus' name I pray, Amen!

DECEMBER 20

Matthew 11:26 (NASB): So if the Son makes you free, you will be free indeed. Yes, Father, for this way was well-pleasing in Your sight.

I'M IN PLACE

I will never, be out of place again and I will never, be out of grace again. Father I give you praise today, for divine placement. I thank you for showing me "where", I praise you for showing me "when", and I bless you for the courage to obey, even if I don't know "why".

I pray for an obedient spirit, and a consistent yes. I pray for signs, and wonders, that will affirm my obedience and cause me to know that I'm in your will. I pray Holy Spirit, that you'll begin to send people into my life to make my transition easier, and that staying where I was will no longer be a viable option! Make moving easy for me. Take my "yes Lord" and use it against my enemies. Take my "yes Lord" and use it to make the way plain for me, in Jesus' name. My soul says "YES" to your will, and to your way.

I give you praise for divine placement, that I'll not waste another day, trying to figure out where I'm supposed to be. I won't waste another year of my life, trying to work somebody else's grace, and in somebody else's lane. Thank you, Lord, for showing me where I'm supposed to be and when I'm supposed to be there. I'll never be out of place again because the spirit of the living God is with me.

I'll never be on the wrong job again, or pursuing the wrong people, or the wrong things again. Because Jesus walks with me, and He talks with me, and He tells me what to do and when to do it. I'm on my way to something exceedingly and abundantly.

I'm stepping into something big, something above everything I've asked for, and thought about. No devil in hell can hold me down. It's in Jesus' name I pray, Amen!

DECEMBER 21

Philippians 3:13 (NASB): Brothers and sisters, I do not regard myself as having taken hold of it yet; but one thing I do: forgetting what lies behind and reaching forward to what lies ahead,.

OVER IT

Good morning Holy Spirit. I can sense your presence and I know that you are with me; and for this I give you praise! I thank you today, for setting me free in my mind! I thank you, for giving me the mental strength I need to move forward, and to never again consider quitting, ever!

Thank you, Lord, for teaching me how to forgive myself, and for showing me that the only way to stop tripping over my past, is to stop walking backwards! Thank you, for the grace to go!

Thank you, for the will to get over it! I confess, "I'm over it! I'm never going back to it! I'm done with that stinking thinking, and I'll never again suggest to you, that what Jesus did at Calvary was not enough to cover my sins! Truth is that the blood did its job!

I'm covered, I'm saved, I'm forgiven, and I'm next! It's in Jesus' name I pray, AMEN!

DECEMBER 22

Psalms 24:5 (NASB): He will receive a blessing from the Lord And righteousness from the God of his salvation.

TEACH ME PEACE

The biggest threat and fear in this season are other people's hands and breath. So, God says, I'm going to show you my hands, so you can break free from the fear and properly discern His intentions for this unexpected pause from people. My prayer is that you will not be consumed with bills nor fear what tomorrow may bring, that you miss what God is doing for you today!

So Holy Spirit, teach us to trust your presence. Teach us how to discern your presence in the midst of chaos and crisis. Teach us to be at peace and how to let the pressure work for us and not against us. And teach us how to allow the pressure and the pain to push us forward instead of knocking us backwards. Teach us your ways and how to discern your will when our flesh won't cooperate. Teach us to trust your plan and Father we promise to give you praise. It's in Jesus mighty name we pray Amen and Amen.

DECEMBER 23

2 Corinthians 5:7 (NASB): for we walk by faith, not by sight—

HELP ME TO SEE

I don't see it. That's what you've been saying to yourself for the past month or so. But God has not forsaken you and He has not abandoned His plan for your life. My prayer for you is that you will learn to stop limiting God based off what you see. But that you will learn how to walk by faith and not by sight.

I'm praying that your discernment re-ups. That you will walk in the grace that has been given to you for this season. I pray you find the courage to decide today that you won't be moved by what you see, but only by what you believe. I pray the spirit of faith will consume you in such a way and that doubting, quitting, or settling will no longer be viable options for you. It's in Jesus' name we pray AMEN.

DECEMBER 24

Romans 8:28 (NASB): And we know that God causes all things to work together for good to those who love God, to those who are called according to His purpose.

HELP IS ON THE WAY

It has to work for you! That's the word of the Lord concerning your life. So, lift up your head because you have no more time to waste looking down. Lift up your head because God's about to do something that's going to change your life, to better your life for the rest of your life.

Who you are now, is not who you will be! So, hold on because God's using this trouble to transition you. And God's only allowed what happened to you so that He could move you out of an old place into a prepared place. So, I'm praying for your mind today, that the devil doesn't convince you to abandon your faith. I'm praying that your faith won't fail and that you pass this test in Jesus' name.

I'm praying that your Holy Ghost kicks in for real. And that you discern the times and know what the devil meant for evil has to work for your good. That what "they" did to harm you is going to end up helping you. That attack and all of those attacks we're really disguised as tests that are about to become testimonies, in just a few days. Hold on! Help is on the way! It's in Jesus' mighty name we pray, Amen!

DECEMBER 25

1 Chronicles 4:10 (NASB): Now Jabez called on the God of Israel, saying, "Oh that You would greatly bless me and extend my border, and that Your hand might be with me, and that You would keep me from harm so that it would not hurt me!" And God brought about what he requested.

I SEE INCREASE

I pray that today's prayer will push you into a prosperous place. And as you pray, I pray that Holy Spirit will respond to the word of the Lord in such a way that your perspective evolves and elevates. I pray that you find grace to see your situation the way God sees it. Through his eyes you will fully understand why He allowed you to go through what you went through.

I'm praying for every test over the course of the next few hours, days, or weeks to become your testimony. I'm praying that what the enemy meant for evil starts working for your good in Jesus name. This is the season for you to personally see the power of God demonstrated through your life. This is the season for you to see the power of God demonstrated through your hands, gifts, and business. He's about to increase your volume, exposure, platform, significance, and the demand for and of your gift. The grace and favor of God on your life is expanding exponentially. It is increasing supernaturally and in just a few days you're going to be able to look back on what he brought you through and delivered you from.

This is the day that the Lord has made, I will rejoice, for he has made me glad! Shout this out, He has made me glad! He has made me glad! I will rejoice for he has made me glad! It's in Jesus' mighty name we pray Amen.

DECEMBER 26

Galatians 6:9 (NASB): Let's not become discouraged in doing good, for in due time we will reap, if we do not become weary.

I WILL NOT QUIT

You're one chapter away! I'm praying you don't quit, before your crossover. I'm praying you find grace and wisdom to stay the course. And that you will be able to correct the course as needed and outlive your old reputation.

I'm praying for people who are days away from changing, getting better and becoming their true selves. I'm praying you don't quit on you and that you find the mental strength to keep moving forward. That you will know God's about to do something for you that is going to shock and convert everybody who knew the Saul version of yourself.

I call the Paul in you to come out of you and I command you to step into purpose and truth. I call every gift, talent, and skill to the forefront. And I decree and declare you have grace to forget the foolishness and the wherewithal to immediately change the way you walk in Jesus' mighty name.

DECEMBER 27

Proverbs 4:25 (NASB): Let your eyes look directly ahead And let your gaze be fixed straight in front of you.

I WILL NOT FREAK OUT

Not today and not this morning! You will not be distracted nor off emotionally. You will not be angry with people in your past, nor the people who are present in your life. You have grace to control your emotions and grace to manage your mind. Anger is not your portion today. Relinquishing control of your day, to yesterday and yesterday people is not how you flow.

You have grace to focus on your present and your future. Grace to organize your past both mentally and emotionally so that you can learn and grow from it the good, the bad and the ugly. No more Post Traumatic Stress! No more Disorder!

I speak clarity of thought and keen discernment over your mind today. As you prepare to have one of the best weeks you are going to have. It's in Jesus' name we pray, Amen.

DECEMBER 28

Psalms 1:2-3 (NASB): But his delight is in the Law of the Lord, And on His Law he meditates day and night. ³ He will be like a tree planted by streams of water, Which yields its fruit in its season, And its leaf does not wither; And in whatever he does, he prospers.

I WILL ADJUST

Stay the course! Listen to me! The devil knows that God doesn't and hasn't changed His mind. His only option now is to get you to change yours, don't do it. And stop letting people make you think that something is wrong or off because you have to make adjustments. Adjustments are the precursors to increase and overflow so go with it. Let Holy Spirit lead you and trust that when he's done talking you are done doing. That your new path will lead you to something bigger and better.

I am praying now, that you won't grow weary in doing well and that you will allow patience to perfect you and perfect your product. I pray that Holy Spirit opens your eyes and ears again, and that you will be fruitful and productive in Jesus' mighty name I pray Amen.

DECEMBER 29

1 Kings 7:1 (NASB): Now Solomon built his own house over the course of thirteen years, and he finished all of his house.

I WILL FINISH STRONG

What you did for God mattered! So be encouraged. And stay focused and don't allow anybody to tell you that your gift and your life isn't making a difference. What you did for God kept somebody from taking their life! The way you pushed through and kept pressing your way kept somebody from giving up. God told me to tell you, "What you did, what you're doing and what you will do matters!" What you did for God and the sacrifices you made to do it provided a model and a perfect example for people who were trying to find God. For people who were trying to figure out the what, how, when and the why.

So, stay the course! Stay faithful! And whatever you do don't quit! Your life matters! And I'm not just talking about your ministry life I'm talking about your day-to-day life and how you live it. The way you take care of your family, your children, your spouse, and the way you take care of you. Know that it's helping people that you don't even know were watching you. So, I'm praying for the courage to keep going. I'm praying for strength of will to encourage yourself. I'm praying for desire to stay on your grind until you reach your goals. I'm also praying for another release of grace to establish new ones. Holy Spirit help our weaknesses. And give us the grace we need to finish and to finish strong. It's in Jesus name we pray Amen.

DECEMBER 30

2 Corinthians 3:17 (NASB): Now the Lord is the Spirit, and where the Spirit of the Lord is, there is liberty.

MY HOUSE WILL WIN

God's got a foothold in my house! And because God's in the foundation of my house, my house cannot fail. Because Holy Spirit has established his presence in my house, no other presence can remain in my house. Fear has to go! Anger has to go! Sickness has to go! Grief has to go! Confusion has to go! Depression has to go! Lack has to go! And any other presence or negative spirit has to go in Jesus' mighty name!

We declare our freedom today and decree where the spirit of the Lord is there is liberty. Because we know if the Son makes you free you will be free indeed (John 8:36). So, we commit to walk by fate today and not by sight. We commit to standfast therefore in the liberty by which crisis made us free and never being tangled again with the yoke of bondage in Jesus name. We are free and with the help of Holy Spirit we will be free. It's in Jesus' name we pray Amen.

DECEMBER 31

Matthew 14:29 (NASB): And He said, "Come!" And Peter got out of the boat and walked on the water, and came toward Jesus.

OBEY GOD

I will obey God! I will not be pressured into staying on the boat. I will not be talked down or talked out of my moment. This is my time and my season to do something for God. and with God I will do something that nobody I know has ever done before. So Holy Spirit, help me to overcome the fear and the voices that bombard my mind in my emotions. Help me to push past the what ifs and the negative people around me who want to continue to play it safe. Especially those who think obeying God is an unnecessary risk. Help me to discern the difference between foolishness and faith. Show me the difference between when I'm tripping and when I've really heard from you. And give me the courage, strength of will and the desire to obey you no matter what they might say!

Do something in me, through me and for me. Those things you wanted to do but you've been unable to do because you didn't have anyone willing to walk by faith. My confession of faith is, I will not drown obeying God! And I will learn from Peter's example as recorded in Matthew 14:30. Moving forward I'm walking on water. Moving forward I'm leaving the fear, frustration, and the fake faith behind. I'm getting out of the boat and I'm following the path that leads directly to Jesus.

I have grace to stay on the top of everything that consumed others and took them under. And I decree and declare I see the supernatural manifest in my life and in the faces of everything and everybody I'm connected to. It's in Jesus mighty name I pray Amen.

CONCLUSION

We made it! After all we've had to endure, fight through, and overcome; somehow God gave us the grace to keep going. After the falls, failures, and faith fights; somehow, we managed to keep praying through it.

I want to personally thank you for not fainting, for not giving up and for finding your way back to this place of prayer every day. I want to personally thank you, not just for purchasing the book, but for actually praying through the year with us. Thank you for making this circle of faith a priority in your life. I believe your life and your family will never be the same again. So, thank you, for staying the course and for sticking with the script. Your decision to choose these words to pray daily has impacted your life. Although these prayers didn't initially start off as your words, day by day they quickly became your own.

We have discovered together that our prayers change things. We have seen for ourselves this year, that our prayers, change people, predicaments, relieve pressure, and make managing the birth pangs, and the growing pains of life, possible. We know now that there is nothing we cannot get through if we just make the commitment to pray through. And after these daily, face to face encounters in the presence of God, "Praying Through It", is no longer a list of prayers, but it has become our lifestyle.

I pray that because of these prayers, and this connection, our testimony has become, "Praying is no longer a job, because it's become a joy. I pray that talking to God is no longer scary, but it's become sacred, serious, and special for us. I pray that conversations with Jesus just because, is now our norm. I pray that because of this enlightened relationship, we will never go back into hiding, like Adam. I pray that because of these prayers, consulting Holy Spirit first, becomes our, "modus operandi"; our mode of operation, our new way of living and our elevated approach to all-things life. This assures that we never go back to anybody or anything, that represents who we once were.

There is NOTHING we cannot pray our way through! There is NOTHING we cannot pray our way out of. The completion of 'Volume II' represents the beginning of a new day, another dispensation, and release of grace for every one of us. We will never be, who we used to be ever again! We're different! We're better! We're healed! We're fRee! We're NOT behind! We're ahead! We are THEE head, and NOT the tail. In Jesus' mighty name, Amen!

Until the 3rd Volume...

+William Murphy, III

ABOUT THE AUTHOR

William Murphy, III can always be counted on to bring in the presence of God; because it's just a part of his DNA. The 3rd generation Bishop, Pastor, Producer, Songwriter, and Vocalist, is while best known for his music, has dedicated his life to ministry and has led this generation to worship. Murphy's approach to radical ministry is most recognized by the soul stirring lyrics, and lead vocals on his Platinum Selling song "Praise Is What I Do", and the recent Grammy Nominated "It's Working"

William Murphy faithfully serves as the Lead Pastor of The dReam Center Church of Atlanta, and as the Bishop of Worship, for The Full Gospel Baptist Church Fellowship, International. He blesses people all around the world, with his ministry of music, message of hope and through his ministry of prayer.

Bishop Paul S. Morton, Sr., Founding Bishop of The Full Gospel Baptist Church Fellowship, is quoted as saying, "This 21st Century David, has not only caused me to go to deeper depths in my time of worship, but he has blessed the lives of so many across the world."

Praying Through It, the prayer and daily devotional is just another testament to Murphy's dedication to being a difference maker and changing the culture of the way we do church. Having started the mandate to prayer as a social media movement to get 1000 people praying, Murphy pulled the collection of prayers and heart-felt expressions all together in a book to further spread the message that "prayer changes things".

The ministry of William Murphy captivates the hearts and souls of believers around the world. His hit single "It's Working" climbed the charts to #1, and has become one of the most requested, and most played songs in gospel radio.

Murphy released his latest solo project, "Settle Here" in 2019 which includes the powerful singles "Settle Here", "Bliss", and "Same Grace". With more music on the way, there is no doubt that William Murphy was born to worship. His music, and his ministry of the word, both serve as evidence of the special calling, and anointing, that God has placed on his life.

Made in the USA
Columbia, SC
01 February 2022

55172965R00252